D0992486

DATE DUE

The OPIUM WARS

The OPIUM WARS

The Addiction of One Empire and the Corruption of Another

W. TRAVIS HANES III, PH.D. AND FRANK SANELLO

SOURCEBOOKS, INC.®
NAPERVILLE, ILLINOIS

Map on pg. 308 from *The Opium War, 1840-1842: Barbarians in the Celestial Empire in the Early Part of the Nineteenth Century and the War by which They Forced Her Gates Ajar* by Peter Ward Fay. Copyright © 1975 by The University of North Carolina Press. Used by permission of the publisher.

Published by Sourcebooks, Inc.
P.O. Box 4410, Naperville, Illinois 60567-4410
(630) 961-3900
FAX: (630) 961-2168
www.sourcebooks.com

Library of Congress Cataloging-in-Publication Data

Hanes, William Travis, 1954–
  Opium wars: the addiction of one empire and the corruption of another /
  By W. Travis Hanes III and Frank Sanello.
    p. cm.
    Includes bibliographical references and index.
    1. China—History—Opium War, 1840–1842. 2. China—History—
Foreign intervention, 1857–1861. I. Sanello, Frank. II. Title.

DS757.5 .S26 2002
951'.033—dc21

                                                        2002003136

Printed and bound in the United States of America
MV 10 9 8 7 6 5 4 3 2 1

For Robert Buckley, 1941–1991
—F.S.

For Eddie Glover
—T.H.

ACKNOWLEDGMENTS

———·——·———

Thanks to Daniel Abraham, Jennifer Andersen, Kris Andersson, Michael Anketell, Edith and Martin Barcay, Dan Berrios, Professor Joseph Boone, Dr. Daniel Bowers, A. Scott Berg, Linda and John Branca, André Brooks, Charles Casillo, Louis Chunovic, Dr. Gary Cohan, Ghalib Dhalla, Vic Dinnerstein, Michael Dorr, Anita Edson, Mike Emmerich, Morgan Gendel, Stephanie Goldfarb, Cyrus Godfrey, Lawrence C. Goldstein, Mary and Art Goodale, André Guimond, Cary Harrison, Scott Hill, Dr. Scott Hitt, Chris Hix, Frederick Hjelm, Brad Kane, Steven Kay, Chuck Kim, Gary Kirkland, Lin and John Knorr, Pamela Landsden, Robert Lent, Michael Levine, Will Litchfield, Christina Madej, Charlie Medrano, Paul Manchester, David Marlow, Kevin Moreton, Jim Murphy, Tom Packard, James Robert Parish, Sia Prospero, Lee Ray, Linda Reinle, Ray Richmond, Doris Romeo, Marjorie Rothstein, Dr. Maria Santos, Sarkis, Catherine Seipp, Guy Shalem, Professor Benjamin Sifutentes-Jauregui, Dorie Simmonds, Bryan Smith, Monica Trascendes, Christopher Villa, Denise Wallace, Professor Jack Wills, Dan Wise, Dean Wong, and Jeff Yarbrough.

I especially want to thank the editors of this project, Hillel Black and Peter Lynch; my agent, Mike Hamilburg, for all his hard work on my behalf over the years; and Gene Balk of the *Orange County Register* for his invaluable research guidance.

—Frank Sanello

It is always a pleasure to acknowledge those without whose help and advice a book would not otherwise see the light of day and, hopefully, reach an interested public. I would like to simply say "thank you" to all those who have contributed to this project along the way (you know who you are!), and especially to Hillel Black, in the New York office of Sourcebooks, who understood the vision, and Peter Lynch, in the Naperville office, who understood not only the vision but also the mechanics and artfulness necessary to achieve it.

—W. Travis Hanes III

TABLE OF CONTENTS

———•+•———

CHEMICAL
WARFARE

—·—

I magine this scenario: the Medellin cocaine cartel of Colombia mounts a successful military offensive against the United States, then forces the U.S. to legalize cocaine and allow the cartel to import the drug into five major American cities, unsupervised and untaxed by the U.S. The American government also agrees to let the drug lords govern all Colombian citizens who operate in these cities, plus the U.S. has to pay war reparations of $100 billion—the Colombians' cost of waging the war to import cocaine into America. That scenario is of course preposterous and beyond the feverish imagination of the most out-there writers of science fiction. However, a similar situation occurred not once, but twice in China during the nineteenth century. In both cases, however, instead of thuggish Colombian drug dealers, it was the most technologically advanced nation on Earth, Great Britain, that forced similar conditions on China.

Carl von Clausewitz wrote, "War is diplomacy by other means." If the Prussian military theoretrician had studied China's Opium Wars with Britain, he might have added that substance abuse is another alternative to diplomacy, and in some cases, more effective than war. The two wars of 1839–1842 and 1856–1860, collectively known as the Opium Wars, which pitted the British and later the French Empires against the Qing empire are conveniently forgotten or largely ignored in the West today. Yet for the Chinese and others, the conflicts remain embarrassing symbols of

Western imperial domination, with repercussions that have lingered to the present day. The conflicts remain embarrassing symbols of how shabbily the West treated the East for centuries. Some might argue that this cavalier behavior and colonial mind-set continue to this day with the American embargo of Cuba and the presence of British troops in Northern Ireland. Previous books on the conflicts published in the West tend to be filtered through the eyes of Eurocentric historians who downplay or ignore critical issues about the two wars, which ended up legalizing a devastating narcotic and allowing Western powers to colonize an advanced civilization.

Yet while the Opium Wars were fought more than a century and a half ago, the issues they involved seem remarkably contemporary. The Opium Wars are also a dramatic narrative of power and corruption, of human frailty, greed, and stupidity. While the international drug trade lies at the heart of the tale, it is ultimately a narrative of cultural confrontation—the clash of two worlds, each convinced of its own superiority. The stakes were high and involved fundamental moral, ethical, political, and social questions.

The roots of the conflict lay in three interlocking problems. First, China's conviction, sustained by nearly four thousand years of historical memory, that it represented the pinnacle of civilization on the planet and that all other nations were barbarians, to be dealt with no as equals but as "tribute bearers." Second, China's monopoly of the production of tea (and to a lesser extent other luxury items such as silk and porcelain), combined with its insistence on being paid for such goods only with silver bullion. Third, the emergence of Britain as the premier industrial power of the world, with an equally overweening conviction of its own Christian civilization's moral, ethical, and material superiority, and a determination to be treated by other peoples and nations not as a subordinate, but as an equal (if not a superior)—even if this meant supplying millions of fellow human beings with a devastating drug.

Opium entered China on the back of a camel, one historian wrote, and it ended up breaking the back of an entire nation.

METHODS
AND MEASURES

———·—·———

A ccording to the Consumer Price Index conversion factor, $1 in 1860 equaled $20.41 in 2001.

One Chinese silver tael in the mid nineteenth century equaled between $1.50 and $1.60 in U.S. currency of the time. One British pound (£1) equaled approximately $5 or 25 francs.

A ballpark indication of the value of money in Victorian England can be discerned from working men's wages. A police officer in mid-nineteenth century London earned a little more than £1 a week, while a dockworker subsisted on the starvation wage of six pence per hour.

A chest of opium weighed approximately 170 pounds. Depending on supply and other politically influenced events, the wholesale cost of opium ranged from the firesale price of $200 per chest to $700 per chest during times of effective government interdiction, which were rare, and artificial scarcities created by war.

When romanizing the names of Chinese people and places, we have chosen to use the pinyin system of translation, except in cases in which the traditional or Wade-Giles translation would be more familiar to the Western reader. For example, the traditional or Wade-Giles translations have been retained for Amoy, Canton, Ch'iang Kai-shek, Chusan, Confucius, Hong Kong, Kowloon, Macao, Nanking, Peking, Sun Yatsen, Whampoa, Yukien, and the Yangtze River.

"Britain earned vast revenues from the opium trade by poisoning a substantial portion of the Chinese population."

—Martin Booth

"Suppose there were people from another country who carried opium for sale to England and seduced your people into buying and smoking it; certainly you would deeply hate it and be bitterly aroused... Formerly the number of opium smugglers was small; but now the vice has spread far and wide, and the poison penetrated deeper."

—Lin Zexu, high commissioner of Canton, in a letter to Queen Victoria,1839

"The use of opium is not a curse, but a comfort and benefit to the hard-working Chinese."

—1858 press release from the British firm of Jardine, Matheson & Co., China's biggest opium importer

"I am in dread of the judgment of God upon England for our national iniquity towards China."

—William Gladstone, 1842

Chapter 1

LORD ELGIN'S REVENGE

————————

*"All the diamonds in the world are as nothing
compared to what comes from the East."*

—Austrian Empress Maria Teresa

B y 1860, Great Britain had reached a military, literary, and artistic
ascendancy not seen in the Western world perhaps since Suetonius's
Rome. That year, Dickens published his masterpiece, *Great Expectations.*
Charles Darwin's *On the Origin of Species* was a bestseller despite its arcane
subject matter. Matthew Arnold was proofreading his gloss of Homer at
Oxford. And William Morris was about to launch the Arts and Crafts
movement. Also in that year, a Scottish earl—Britain's ambassador to
China—burned down the Yuan Ming Yuan, the Summer Palace of the
Xianfeng Emperor, outside Peking.

The destruction of the Summer Palace was the climactic act of the second of two Opium Wars (1839–1842 and 1856–1860) between Britain
and China. The man responsible for it was Britain's plenipotentiary to
China, James Bruce, the eighth Earl of Elgin, a direct descendant of Robert
the Bruce and son of the seventh Earl of Elgin, who had sent the
Parthenon's friezes to Britain.

Established in 1709 by the Kangxi Emperor, the Summer Palace was
said to have inspired the opium-fueled dream that the poet Samuel
Coleridge recorded in verse:

In Xanadu did Kubla Khan
A stately pleasure-dome decree:

> Where Alf the Sacred River ran
> Through caverns measureless to man,
> Down to a sunless sea.
> So twice five miles of fertile ground
> With walls and towers were girdled round:
> And there were gardens bright with sinuous rills,
> Where blossomed many an incense-bearing tree;
> And here were forests ancient as the hills,
> Enfolding sunny spots of greenery.

Under the lavish attention of Kangxi and his successors, the Summer Palace became more than simply the Chinese emperor's home away from his principal home, the Winter Palace within the walls of the Forbidden City in Peking. Indeed, the word "palace" hardly describes the reality at all.

Spread over some eighty square miles of carefully landscaped parkland, the Yuan Ming Yuan encompassed some two hundred buildings and a myriad of gardens in every Chinese style—many rivaling and even surpassing the formal greenery of Versailles. In the last half of the eighteenth century, the Qianlong Emperor in particular devoted himself to creating heaven on Earth there. Under his careful attention, the Summer Palace was designed to recreate the variety of landscape and architecture of the entire empire. And on its grounds and in its buildings, he collected the finest treasures of the Celestial Empire. As historian Jack Beeching described the incalculable value of the real estate lost to posterity: "The Summer Palace was the treasure-house of China—such a concentration of visual beauty, artifice and wealth as neither existed nor could once again have been brought into being anywhere else in the world."

A baroque jewel and a repository of priceless antiquities, the Summer Palace was actually a collection of pagodas, palaces, and pavilions housing libraries with original and irreplaceable manuscripts and fairly stuffed with priceless works of art—paintings, sculptures, porcelains, jades, and thousands of bolts of the finest silk, that precious commodity of the Middle Kingdom that had been coveted and exported to the West since the days of the Roman Empire. The Hall of Audience contained a rosewood throne from which the Emperor greeted foreign emissaries prostrate before him on the marble floor in a style already ancient in China when it was adopted by the Byzantine Empire in the first millennium A.D.

Not all the buildings were done in the Chinese style. The Qianlong Emperor, like most xenophobic Chinese, loathed the barbarians, but he was apparently intrigued by their architecture—or perhaps he simply wanted to include a representative example to demonstrate the all-encompassing nature of his Imperial rule. In any case, satisfying his whim to build a residence in "the manner of European barbarians," in 1747, two Jesuit priests and amateur architects, the Italian Giuseppe Castiglione and the French Michel Benoit, in collaboration with the German Ignatius Sickelpart and the Florentine Bonaventura Moggi, designed two neobaroque palaces with roofs of gold based on their recollection of Versaille's Le Grand Trianon. To complete the European flavor of the emperor's whimsy, the architects also created Disney-like *trompe l'oeil* streets that would have looked at home in Paris or Florence, a Potemkin village that deceived no one and delighted all.

The grounds of the Summer Palace were as impressive as the buildings and treasures they contained. The Qianlong Emperor had made six Imperial progressions through the empire, always visiting the most famous and beautiful scenery sites. On his orders, many of them were recreated in the Yuan Ming Yuan. Using the ancient rules of *feng shui*, a system of placement supposed to take advantage of and magnify the beneficial *chi*, or natural energy of the earth, Imperial architects transformed the flat landscape into a "Chinese fairyland,"as Beeching described it, with earth excavated to create artificial hills, and lakes surrounded by weeping willows and dotted with water lilies. Marble bridges with Palladian balustrades spanned the waters. Tiled pagodas rose from man-made islands in the lakes, which were stocked with goldfish. Herds of imported deer wandered the grounds, snuggling up to visitors like the denizens of a petting zoo, as tame and friendly as household pets because they had never learned to fear hunters. Disengaged emperors, forsaking real battles, played with their fleets of toy warships on the lakes. Miniature bonsai-like trees grew out of gardens of twisted rock. More than a country retreat, the Summer Palace was at once archive, museum, treasure-trove, and sybaritic paradise.

Into this enchanted landscape of art and architecture, on the sunny but frosty day of October 18, 1860, Major-General Sir John Michel led the British First Division through the East Palace Gate of the complex. On Lord Elgin's orders, Sir John's troops began systematically to burn the Yuan Ming Yuan. As many of the structures were made of wood, the Palace went up like a tinderbox. Darting between the flames, the soldiers were allowed free rein to take the gold and *objets d'art* that earlier looters had overlooked.

There was less loot than might have been expected, for the Palace complex had already been systematically stripped by the British and French armies two weeks before. On October 6, 1860, French soldiers had swarmed over the grounds like art-collecting locusts, followed a day later by British troops. Vandalism alternated with theft. "What they could not carry away, they smashed to atoms," wrote Robert Swinhoe, an eyewitness and interpreter of Chinese, in his memoir account, *Narrative of the North China Campaign of 1860.* Swinhoe's description sounds almost like a scene of housewives playing tug-of-war with marked-down clothing in the bargain basement of a department store:

> In one room you would see several officers and men of all ranks with their heads and hands brushing and knocking together in the same box, searching and grasping its contents. In another a scramble was going on over a collection of handsome state robes. Others amused themselves by taking 'cock' shots at chandeliers. No one just then cared for gazing tranquilly on works of art; each one was bent on acquiring what was most valuable. The silk warehouses on the right were burst open, and dozens rushed in over piles of valuable rolls of silk. Though plunderers were conveying them away by cartloads, still the ground was strewn with them. An officer would be seen struggling under the weight of old jars, furs and embroidered suits.

The looters lacked the means to cart off their treasures, and used bolts of silk embroidered with gold like giant plastic garbage bags to haul off this precious refuse.

The fastidious British inventoried what they took. An auction of the loot to transform it into more portable cash listed "white and green jade ornaments of all tints, enamel-inlaid jars of antique shape, bronzes, gold and silver figures and statuettes, immense quantities of rolls of silk, several of the beautiful Imperial Yellow, a kind prescribed by the Chinese law for use of his Imperial Majesty alone."

A Christie's catalog couldn't have described the consignment better or more enticingly.

The thrifty Scot in Lord Elgin was apparently more horrified by the economic loss caused by the vandals than the historical and cultural value of the antiquities. "Plundering and devastating a place like this is bad enough, but what is much worse is the waste and breakage. Out of £1 million of property, I daresay £50,000 will be realized." A bibliophile British interpreter among the troops realized the historical importance of the Imperial library and managed to save several wagonloads of books, which he dispatched to the British Museum, where they share ironic and symbolic turf with Lord Elgin's father's theft or preservation—depending on whether your viewpoint is Eurocentric or multicultural—of the Parthenon marbles. The son had grown up fending off the contempt aroused by the seventh Earl's expropriation of the ancient friezes and made a point of separating himself from the looters under his command. With perhaps unintentional irony, Elgin attempted to exculpate himself to his diary, "I would like a great many things the palace contains, but I am not a thief."

Despite such systematic looting, at the time Elgin's orders for destruction were carried out on the 18th, many delectable prizes of war still remained—a buffet of bronzes, enamels, clocks, silks, furs, and jade for the prize-hungry soldiers. One Indian officer made off with £9,000 worth of gold. The intruders also came upon the undisturbed living quarters of the Emperor and helped themselves to his cap, pipe, and satin pillows embroidered with dragons and flowers in the Imperial color of yellow. A French chaplain was shocked when he found the Emperor's pornography collection next to the sovereign's bed in a lacquer box.

Several artifacts that had been overlooked by the earlier looters had the symbol-laden flavor of a fictional account, but they were real. In an outhouse on the palace grounds, the British found eighteenth-century manufactures in mint condition, including two English-made carriages, astronomical instruments, an English shotgun, and two howitzers engraved with "Woolwich 1782." They had all been gifts for the Qianlong Emperor from King George III, presented by the Scots-Irish peer Lord Macartney, Elgin's predecessor as the first British plenipotentiary to attempt opening China to British trade. Macartney had presented them during an unsuccessful embassy in 1793. Rebuffing Macartney and spurning the gifts as inferior to Chinese manufactures, Qianlong had them deposited in a toilet.

Lord Elgin's decision to destroy the Summer Palace was controversial even within his own command. Despite the demolition orders, Sir John Michel simply refused to torch the exquisite Ya-tsing Pagoda: he was "struck by its simple beauty, and spared it as a work of art." The Major-General's humanitarian/antiquarian gesture was worthy of Alexander the Great saving the poet Pindar's home while decimating the rest of ancient Thebes. The discomfort of other officers is also apparent in their memoir accounts. "The world around looked dark with shadow," wrote Lt. Col. G.J. Wolseley, in his account, *Aktion, Narrative of the War with China in 1860.* "When we entered the gardens they reminded one of those magic grounds described in fairy tales; we marched [out of] them upon the 19th of October, leaving them a dreary waste of ruined nothings." Swinhoe too recorded the desolation: "The sun shining through the masses of smoke gave a sickly hue to every plant and tree and the red flame gleaming on the faces of the troops engaged made them appear like demons glorying in the destruction of what they could not replace. The Yuan Ming Yuan, or Round and Brilliant Garden, was fast becoming a scene of confusion and desolation, but there was as yet much spoil within its walls."

As the fire spread, the looters realized it was their loot going up in smoke, and the vandals became ad hoc conservators. But the method of their firefighting efforts combined destruction with preservation, as they used centuries-old tapestries woven with silver and gold to smother the flames. It took two days for the living museum to burn to the ground. Billows of thick black smoke that obscured the sun rose from the crackling forests of topiary and wooden structures while a northwest wind carried the choking cloud across the rooftops of the capital and deposited a blanket of ashes on them—as though advertising the Emperor's shame and humiliation to his subjects.

Lord Elgin set fire to the Emperor's palace in retaliation for the imprisonment, mutilation, torture, and/or murder of some twenty English and Indian POWS, including several British envoys who had been under the protection of a flag of truce and imprisoned at the Summer Palace.

In the second week of September 1860, about twenty French and British soldiers doing reconnaissance inside the Chinese lines had been surprised and seized by the Chinese. More ominously, two British diplomats, Harry Parkes, the Consul at Canton, and Henry Loch, Lord Elgin's private secretary, had been arrested while under flag of truce at the suburb of Tongxian outside Peking during negotiations with Prince Seng, the brutal Mongol commander-in-chief of the Imperial army and an implacable xenophobe. When the fearless Parkes refused to bow before his Mongol interrogator, Seng's soldiers repeatedly banged his head on the marble floor of the palace.

The prisoners' treatment got worse. They were kept in filthy cells jammed with common Chinese criminals, who surprisingly treated their high-born comrades with respect, unlike their warders. Over a three-day period, the Europeans were forced to kneel outside in the courtyard of the Summer Palace without food or water. Their hands and feet were bound with leather straps moistened to contract and cut into flesh. Their wounds became infected, and, bound, they were powerless to shoo away the maggots that began to gnaw on the open sores. Twenty of the thirty-nine European prisoners perished during their month of captivity, including Thomas Bowlby, *The Times of London's* correspondent in China, who had been captured while *shopping* behind Chinese lines. His death ignited a firestorm of bilious yellow journalism back home.

In his bestselling memoirs, Elgin's secretary, Henry Loch, later created first Baron Loch of Drylach for his pain and suffering, provided a heartbreaking account of the prisoners' confinement and torture. He described the suffering of a fellow prisoner, a Lt. Anderson, who had remained silent and stoic while the leather bonds tore into his wrists and ankles, but after he became delirious, begged his comrades to bite off his restraints. But when they tried to, the Chinese jailers beat them and kicked them away from Anderson. The Lieutenant died after nine days of confinement.

An even grislier account came from a Sikh cavalryman, Bughel Sing, in a deposition after the war. He testified that Anderson's hands swelled to three times their normal size and turned black from gangrene. Sing also said *The Times'* Bowlby "died from maggots forming in his wrists." The Chinese left the correspondent's corpse to rot for three days in the crowded cell occupied by his comrades, then they tied the body to a wooden cross and threw it over the city walls, where it was devoured by feral dogs and pigs.

A French prisoner went mad after maggots invaded his ears, nose, and mouth. A Sikh's hands burst under the pressure of the contracting leather bands. By the time of his death four days later, the Indian's hands had been completely eaten away. A single maggot, Sing said, multiplied at the rate of one thousand per day. Before an Indian Muslim prisoner died, his warders forced him to commit sacrilege by eating pork. Lt. Anderson persuaded the Hindu prisoners to eat beef when food was at last provided by their jailers.

In response to the Chinese war crimes, Elgin chose the Summer Palace as the target of his retribution carefully and after much soul-searching and anguish. In his mind, it was merely a personal possession of a wicked emperor—unlike the Winter Palace in the Forbidden City, which Elgin viewed as the national capital of the Chinese people. By burning the Summer Palace, he insisted he was conveying to the Chinese people that it was not they whom he blamed for the atrocities, but solely the emperor and his minions. The Earl posted a proclamation in Chinese throughout Peking providing a justification for his orders and the date they would be carried out. "That no individual, however exalted, could escape from the responsibility and punishment which must always follow the commission of acts of falsehood and deceit; that Yuan-Ming-Yuan would be burnt on the 18th [October 1860], as a punishment inflicted on the Emperor for the violation of his word, and the act of treachery to a flag of truce; that as the people were not concerned in these acts no harm would befall them, but the Imperial Government alone would be held responsible."

It's hard to understand why Elgin considered the Emperor personally responsible for the POW's torture and murder since it was well known and an international scandal that the ruler of China was an alcoholic opium addict who devoted himself to affairs of the harem and left matters of the state to his younger brother, two termagant wives, and a Byzantine court of dueling eunuchs and mandarins. Elgin's concerns for the feelings of the Chinese people were largely misplaced and displayed little real understanding of Chinese sensibilities. Apparently ignoring the ominous content of his placards, the Chinese were said simply to have laughed at their bad grammar. Although designed as a personal punishment for a debauched emperor and his corrupt court, Elgin's conscientious act of vandalism would only confirm to the Chinese people that the Europeans were indeed barbarians— and barbarians intent on dominating the Middle Kingdom. It was an act that would further poison relations between China and the West, and that would fuel Chinese determination to resist Western encroachment for the next century and a half.

A year later, Lord Elgin found himself in another treasure trove, the Royal Academy, whose members held a banquet in the Earl's honor. After dinner, Elgin delivered a speech notable for its lack of contrition. Beeching said that Elgin's speech "indicated that part of his mind once so tormented by what it met in China must have scarred over." A forensic psychologist might theorize that the Earl was in denial. Or maybe it was the rock-star-like adulation when he returned home as China's conqueror that turned guilt into self-congratulatory smugness.

While the leading scholars of his day smoked cigars and sipped port, Elgin said, "I am not so incorrigibly barbarous as to be incapable of feeling the humanizing influences which fall upon us from the noble works of art by which we are surrounded." The beautiful objects of art surrounding the peer at the Royal Academy reminded him of the beauty he had destroyed, and prompted him to shed crocodile tears of remorse. "No one regretted more sincerely than I did the destruction of that collection of summer houses and kiosks dignified by the title of Summer Palace of the Chinese Emperor."

Elgin's regret seemed inexplicable because he went on to dismiss the value of two thousand years of China's aesthetic achievements. "I have been repeatedly asked whether the interests of art are likely to be in any degree promoted by the opening up of China. I do not think in matters of art we have much to learn from that country. The most cynical representations of the grotesque have been the principal products of Chinese conceptions of the sublime and beautiful.

"Nevertheless, I am disposed to believe that under this mass of abortions and rubbish there lie some hidden sparks of a divine fire, which the genius of my countrymen may gather and nurse into a flame."

The cream of England's intelligentsia and academe stood and cheered the man who had burned down the Emperor's Summer Palace.

The issues that underlay both the violations of the flag of truce and Elgin's retaliatory destruction of the Summer Palace went much deeper than the treatment of war prisoners. They involved Britain's determination to force China into the modern, industrial global economy against their will, and to use opium as their major import to exchange for China's commodities of silk and tea—a tactic violently opposed by the Chinese. To this end, the British had imposed two wars on the Middle Kingdom in the space of two decades to try to force not only the sale of opium into China, but also Chinese recognition of Britain as an equal trading nation. But the real conflict was more than economic. In fact, the burning of the Summer Palace represented both a culmination and a new beginning in a much larger game of cultural confrontation—a confrontation between two great world civilizations, one new and one ancient, each believing itself to be the pinnacle of civilization on the planet—a game that had begun nearly a century earlier....

Chapter 2

DISASTROUS ETIQUETTE

—————

"I set no value on strange or ingenious objects and have no use for your country's manufactures."

—The Qianlong Emperor rejecting the gifts of
Britain's first envoy to China, Lord Macartney, 1793

Although the First Opium War began in 1839, the "first shot" in the conflict occurred almost half a century earlier, when Britain's envoy to China refused to bow down, literally "kowtow" in the Mandarin dialect, to the Qianlong Emperor, a custom accepted by every other nation doing business with the huge market that was China.

The envoy, Lord George Macartney, was a seasoned diplomat with an impressive résumé and a reputation for getting things done. A self-made man raised in genteel poverty in Ireland, he began his career in England as a barrister before entering the Foreign Service. Macartney was no inbred, dotty aristocrat, but a man who had risen to the top through merit. He brought all the skills of a well-trained civil servant and intellectual to the task of establishing a British embassy in China. To this point, his foreign assignments had all enjoyed success. China would prove to be his toughest and most frustrating posting in an otherwise fruitful career.

In 1764, Macartney was knighted at the precocious age of twenty-seven and sent to Russia as Envoy Extraordinary. It was rumored that he had been chosen for the mission not merely for his skills as a diplomat, but because of his good looks and the effect they would have on Russia's amorous Empress, Catherine the Great. After three years in Russia, Macartney returned to England with the Empress's affections, symbolized by her gift of a gem-studded snuff box. Urbane and well-spoken, Macartney became a

member of the social circle that included the leading intellectuals, politicians, and artists of his day: Dr. Johnson, Edmund Burke, and Sir Joshua
Reynolds.

In 1767, Macartney was elected to Parliament, where his rise was also
meteoric, and two years later he was appointed Chief Secretary of Ireland.
But after three years in that post, the lure of more exotic employment had
him traveling abroad again as the governor of the Caribbee Islands in the
West Indies. His success in the Caribbean was rewarded with elevation to
the Irish peerage as Baron Macartney. In 1780, Macartney received another
sweaty assignment as governor of Madras, India, where he served from
1780 to 1786. In 1792, he was created viscount and, a year later, sailed to
China, arriving in August 1793.

Viscount Macartney traveled with a simple brief from George III's government: establish a British embassy in the capital and get permission for
British ships to dock at ports besides Canton, the only harbor then open
to foreigners. Trade with China was booming and lucrative, but it had
become bottlenecked in overcrowded Canton. The British were so eager to
open up China, Macartney had instructions to offer an end to the importation of opium there from British-controlled India, which was officially
illegal in China but difficult to stop both because of enthusiastic customers
of the drug and the riches that the trade generated.

When Macartney landed on the coast of China, his retinue and baggage were transferred to Chinese junks by order of the Emperor before he
was allowed to move up the Bei He River en route to the capital, Peking.
It was a dreary journey along muddy shores dotted with mud huts and
tombstones. The Ambassador's ship had a large sign tacked to its mast by
order of the Chinese government, which spoke volumes about the relations
between Britain and China and anticipated the ultimate failure of the
embassy. In large black letters, the sign in Chinese said simply: "Tribute
from the Red Barbarians."

China had always felt superior to the rest of the world—and not without reason. After all, the Chinese had invented gunpowder, paper currency,
eyeglasses, and the printing press (which was first used to print money at
about the time of the Norman Conquest), among many other innovations
developed centuries before the West discovered them. (When Marco Polo
described "burning rocks" [coal] he had seen in China, his fellow Venetians

thought he was mad or a congenital liar.) China solipsistically called itself the "Central Civilization" and "Middle Kingdom," but neither term referred to a geographic location. The titles described the Chinese belief that the nation was the land around which all humanity was centered. The Emperor, known as the Son of Heaven and Lord of 10,000 Years, did not receive ambassadors, since that would suggest equal rank among the nations exchanging emissaries. Visitors to the court were called "tribute bearers" and "barbarians." In the eyes of the Chinese, foreigners did not come to negotiate; they came as subjects paying homage. "Barbarian" wasn't necessarily meant as an offensive term, since all foreigners received that designation, but it certainly involved a very conscious air of conde-scension. The term "tribute" also reflected the Chinese assumption that all other nations were inferior to China.

Macartney believed he was bringing gifts from one sovereign nation to another. The Chinese considered him a vassal paying tribute to the over-lord of a superior civilization. The gifts, which were transported in a junk behind Macartney's houseboat, represented the best of British technology and goods: telescopes, brass howitzers, globes, chime clocks, musical instruments, two carriages, and a hot-air balloon, complete with a bal-loonist. All in all, Macartney brought over six hundred gifts for the Emperor that required ninety wagons and forty wheelbarrows, drawn by two hundred horses and three thousand coolies.

Before his audience with the eighty-two-year-old Qianlong, Macart-ney met with the Viceroy of Pechili, the province in which Peking was located. Macartney was told to leave his "tribute" behind, where it was put on display at the Emperor's Summer Palace. Court officials were not impressed with most of the gifts, although they did admire the Wedg-wood pottery, a compliment indeed from a nation that had invented porcelain and given its name to "china." The humblest of the gifts intrigued the courtiers, when Macartney ignited sulfur matches with the flick of a finger. (The balloonist, alas, was never asked to take his craft aloft.)

The Emperor, Macartney learned from the Viceroy, would meet the Ambassador not in his Palace but in a horse-haired tent called a *yurt* outside the Imperial hunting lodge in Rehe in Tartary, a picturesque area north of Peking noted for its dramatic rock formations and waterfalls. The lodge, an architectural *hommage* to the Panchen Lama's palace in Tibet, had been built as a present for Qianlong's seventieth birthday in 1780. The choice of meeting place reflected another snub. An audience in the Imperial Palace (also called the Winter Palace) would have represented a meeting between equals. The temporary nature of the tent symbolized not only the Emperor's contempt, but also the hoped-for transitory nature of the visit. Hello, Milord. Good-bye, Milord.

At dawn on September 14, 1793, Macartney met Qianlong. The Emperor was in the twilight of his life and, though he did not realize it, his empire was also about to enter its declining years. During Qianlong's reign, which began in 1736, China had become the richest and most populous country in the world. During his reign, the empire doubled in size and area as its armies conquered huge swaths of Central Asia, Outer Mongolia, and parts of Russia.

Like his courtiers and government officials, Qianlong was a scholar, an accomplished calligrapher, and an enthusiastic patron of the arts. A voracious book lover, he collected more than thirty-six thousand volumes on the history and culture of China, compiled by fifteen thousand scholars. During six grand cultural tours of southern China, Qianlong commissioned court painters to immortalize the places he visited. He built eight ruinously expensive temples and the architectural masterpiece known as the Summer Palace.

Qianlong was a victim of his own success, however. Agriculture flourished during his reign as improved irrigation and American imports of sweet potatoes, ground nuts, and sorghum resulted in year-round harvests. But increased food production also led to a population explosion with which even Qianlong's agrotechnology could not cope, and by the time of Lord Macartney's embassy, starvation and poverty made a grim contrast to the beauty and luxury with which the connoisseur Emperor had surrounded himself and his court. Moreover, the cost of expansionism and building projects had almost bankrupted the empire.

Qianlong's court of backstabbing favorites, mandarins and eunuchs, was more twisted and vicious than a Byzantine emperor's. The chief intriguer, Heshen, was a handsome Manchu palace guard promoted by the smitten Emperor to the position of favorite and *de facto* prime minister thirteen years before Macartney's arrival. Heshen's nepotism was legendary. His placement of incompetent relatives in high government positions weakened the empire, as did his greed. Ruthlessly and rapaciously, he extorted money from other members of the bureaucracy. Even the army was undermined by lack of funds that went to increase his personal fortune, estimated at $1.5 billion by the time of his death in 1799.

While Heshen enriched himself as the Imperial favorite, Qianlong's court was also the scene of a long-standing rivalry between the so-called mandarins and the Imperial Court eunuchs. The mandarins, Chinese scholar-gentry officials educated in the Confucian classics and selected by competitive examination, theoretically administered the entire empire under the emperor's direction. For centuries, their rivals in greed and *realpolitik* had been the Imperial Court eunuchs, originally merely the emperor's personal attendants who were castrated so that they might safely be employed around the women of the Imperial household. Emperors often had a quasi-father-son relationship and affection for the eunuchs, many of whom served as their sovereigns' tutors and confidantes. At various stages of China's history, the eunuchs, who eventually numbered in the tens of thousands, not only came to dominate the Imperial Court, but also controlled the government throughout the country through a system of patronage and command of the palace guard. Eunuchs also sometimes dominated the army. Many commanders-in-chief came from their ranks, the most famous being Admiral Zheng He.

The low point of the eunuchs' power occurred in the fourteenth century during the reign of the first Ming Emperor, Hongwu. Exhausted by their intrigues and venality, Hongwu banned them from court and posted a notice in his throne room that said, "Eunuchs must have nothing to do with politics." When the eunuch Liu Jin was sacked after only four years at court, his personal fortune consisted of fifteen million pounds of gold and silver, jewels, armor made of pure gold, and a palace rivaling the Emperor's. The eunuchs proved far too valuable an asset, however, to be permanently suppressed. Unlike the mandarins, who generally came from well-to-do, landed families with potential provincial influence, the eunuchs were solely dependent on the emperors. Consequently, particularly for emperors worried about rivals, the Imperial Court eunuchs were indispensable.

After usurping the throne from his nephew, for example, Hongwu's fourth son, Yongle, restored the eunuchs to their positions and bestowed more power on them, using them as a counterweight to the mandarin bureaucrats. Thereafter, a silent war between the eunuchs, who tended to come from poor families in the north, and the mandarins, scholars from wealthy gentry families in the south, went on for centuries. It was partly palace intrigues between eunuchs and scholars that enervated the late Ming dynasty and made it ripe for takeover by invading armies from Manchuria in the mid seventeenth century. The Manchus too, however, ruling as the Qing dynasty, continued the policy of balancing the influence of the eunuchs with that of the mandarins until the Revolution of 1911 finally ended both Imperial rule and the interminable bickering between eunuch and mandarin.

———————

The octogenarian ruler that Lord Macartney greeted at Rehe was the fourth and greatest of the Manchu line, and the British diplomat dressed up accordingly. Over a scarlet suit, Macartney wore the sash, diamond badge, and star that represented his membership in Britain's exclusive chivalric order, the Knights of the Bath. His retinue of more than one hundred men at the meeting included Sir George Staunton, a baronet and a scholar, who wore the scarlet gown of an Oxford don, and Sir George's twelve-year-old son, also named George, a prodigy who spoke Mandarin and later noted that the ancient man before him "walked firm and erect." A generation later, the younger George would play a pivotal role in the worsening relations between Britain and China.

Before the British ambassador could discuss the purpose of his mission, however, there was the problem of bowing—kowtowing—to the Emperor. The ritual actually consisted of bowing, then kneeling, and then placing the supplicant's forehead on the floor *nine* times. For the sake of the mission and millions in trade, Macartney was willing to kowtow. But as the standard-bearer of the proudest and most powerful nation on Earth, Macartney demanded the same obeisance to his master by the Emperor's mandarin courtiers. Since George III couldn't be there in person, the Baron had thoughtfully brought along a life-sized portrait of the King. Macartney would kowtow to the Emperor—but the Imperial Court had to do the same to an oil painting.

The mandarins refused, and so did Macartney. No one bowed that day, and nothing was accomplished except a performance by little George Staunton. When the Emperor was told that the youth had learned to read and write Chinese during the long boat trip to China, he spoke a few words to the boy, who replied haltingly in the Emperor's native tongue. The Emperor was delighted with the precocious youngster and rewarded George with a yellow silk purse. The adults and their mission were another matter. Neither side would bow to the other, although in order not to set a dangerous precedent for other foreign supplicants, the courtiers who recorded the meeting wrote that Macartney had performed the kowtow.

Macartney's legation cost £80,000, which was paid not by His Majesty's government but by the British East India Company. He left China empty-handed with a parting assessment that compared the empire to "an old, crazy, first-rate man-of-war, which a fortunate succession of able and vigilant officers has contrived to keep afloat." The envoy accurately predicted that if and when less-gifted officials ran the government, the ship of state would drift until "dashed to pieces on the shore." Meanwhile, the Emperor insisted that the British continue to funnel all their trade through the clogged port of Canton; and there would be no British embassy in the capital of the Celestial Empire. The offer to end the opium trade never even came up.

China's intransigence was more than a matter of pride or a sense of superiority to "red barbarians." After the British mission left his country, the Emperor wrote a blunt letter to the King of England that showed none of the niceties of diplomacy and all the self-confidence of a self-sufficient empire: "Our ways have no resemblance to yours, and even were your envoy competent to acquire some rudiments of them, he could not transplant them to your barbarous land. Strange and costly objects do not interest me. As your ambassador can see for himself, we possess all things. I set no value on strange objects and have no use for your country's manufactures."

Despite the snub, Macartney came away from the meeting with a friendlier impression of the Emperor. "In his reception of us, Qianlong has been very gracious and satisfactory. He is a fine old gentleman, still healthy and vigorous, not having the appearance of a man more than sixty."

While Qianlong found King George's gifts useless, unfortunately for the British, they had a compelling "use" for China's most popular export, tea. Britain's love affair with tea and all its rituals began in 1664 when King Charles II received two pounds of black, strange-smelling leaves from China. Less than half a century later, tea had become Britain's beverage of choice with an annual consumption of twelve million pounds a year. By 1785, Britain was importing fifteen million pounds per year from China. While the British people became addicted to the mild stimulant, the British government became economically dependent on tea, because the Exchequer levied a whopping 100 percent import tax on it. Although China did buy some British manufactured and raw goods, tea was a much bigger seller in Britain than British calico, iron, and tin were in China. Between 1710 and 1759, the imbalance in trade was staggering, draining Britain of silver, the only form of payment China accepted for its coveted tea. During this period, Britain paid out £26 million in silver to China, but sold it only £9 million in goods.

British traders had to find something China wanted as much as the British wanted tea, and would be willing to pay for in silver. The solution to this predicament lay in opium. The British were not the first importers of the drug. Arab merchants had been selling opium cultivated in Asia Minor, modern-day Turkey, via caravan routes since the Middle Ages. It was used primarily for medicinal purposes as an analgesic. The infamous side effect of constipation caused by all opioids also prevented diarrhea caused by dysentery, which was endemic in China. The French and the Dutch picked up the trade in the seventeenth century. *Vereenigde Oost-Indische Compagnie,* Holland's version of the East India Company, began export from its base in Bengal, India, in 1659.

Initially, the British East India Company, the monopoly that controlled trade with India, tried to prevent British importation of opium into China since the illegal business interfered with the Company's legitimate trade. Based in Canton, representatives of the Company asked Warren Hastings, the Company governor of the newly conquered province of Bengal, to halt exports from India to China. Hastings readily agreed, calling the drug "not a necessity of life but a pernicious article of luxury, which ought not to be permitted…"

Hastings's idealistic commitment to "zero tolerance" soon gave way to financial and political realities. China only accepted payment for tea in Spanish silver dollars, which in the eighteenth century were the equivalent of today's American dollar, an international currency. Unfortunately, the supply of Spanish silver available to the British had dried up during the American Revolution, when Spain allied itself with the rebellious colonies. Britain had no alternative coinage acceptable to China, and its citizens were clamoring for their daily fix of tea.

Ten years after his condemnation of "pernicious" opium, Hastings relented and allowed the export of 3,450 chests of the contraband in two ships. Each chest of opium was the size of a small footlocker and contained 170 pounds of the drug. One of the ships was captured by French privateers en route, but the other arrived in Macao, Portugal's foothold on the south coast of China, in 1782. The trip was an economic disaster. Fearing reprisals by their government, Chinese merchants refused to purchase the contraband until one intrepid local businessman offered $210 per chest. To break even, each chest had to be sold for at least $500. The British merchants ended up dumping their cargo at a loss in Malaysia for the firesale price of $340. The fact that the opium found no eager buyers in China in 1782 suggests that it had not yet become a nation of addicts, although that would change dramatically in the next century. Indeed, fifteen years later, the British were importing four thousand chests per annum into China.

The Chinese government expressed its alarm at the opium invasion with a decree in 1799 that condemned the trade more forcefully than previous bans had. An Imperial edict proclaimed, "Foreigners obviously derive the most solid profits and advantages, but that our countrymen should pursue this destructive and ensnaring vice is indeed odious and deplorable." It was also inexorable. The East India Company paid lip service to the ban by forbidding British ships to carry opium. That didn't prevent the Company from selling opium in India to independent British and Indian merchants, who would then smuggle the drug into China. The profits were too enormous for the Company to ignore. It sold opium at auction in India for four times the amount it cost to grow and process. In 1773, opium earned the Company £39,000. Twenty years later, the annual revenue from opium sold in China alone had ballooned to £250,000. The popular drug was incrementally beginning to reverse the imbalance of trade between Britain and China. Between 1806 and 1809, China paid out seven million Spanish dollars for opium.

During the first two decades of the nineteenth century, opium addiction in China grew slowly. The East India Company kept the price artificially high, which meant that only the upper classes could afford it. It wasn't just profit motive that made opium expensive and beyond the budget of most Chinese. The drug was officially illegal, and the East India Company didn't want to antagonize the Chinese government by either bankrupting the Imperial treasury or rubbing the government's nose in the illicit trade by increasing imports and thus lowering prices. The five thousand chests of opium sold per annum during this period neatly balanced trade between the two nations without bankrupting the Chinese treasury.

Then, a technological innovation in Britain upset this equilibrium. The invention of the steam engine in the previous century had resulted in the mechanized production of cotton by factories in the north of England. Soon, the market was flooded with mass-produced textiles. The surplus found a ready market in India, whose merchants paid for the product in cash. But to pay for the ever-increasing amount of cotton, the Indians needed to cultivate and sell more opium. As a result, opium flooded into China, but its distribution remained bottlenecked at Canton. Britain wanted more ports opened to its merchant fleet and, to that end, sent another aristocrat in 1816 to negotiate with the Jiaqing Emperor. This legation would be even more disastrous than Lord Macartney's.

Marx apocryphally said that history repeats itself—first as tragedy, the second time as farce. Lord Macartney's embassy to China wasn't tragic, it was merely unsuccessful. However, the next visit by a representative of Britain, Lord Amherst, did have its farcical elements. William Pitt Amherst, Earl Amherst of Arracan, was born in 1773 at Bath, the son of General William Amherst and Elizabeth Patterson. His uncle on his father's side was Field Marshall Sir Jeffrey Amherst, who was created the first Lord Amherst in 1788 after a distinguished military career that included being named Governor-General of British North America after his successful capture of Ticonderoga and eventually Montreal from the French in 1860. William's mother died several years after giving birth to his sister, and their widowed father raised the two children by himself at St. John's on the Isle of Wight. In 1781, however, the General died and William and his sister went to live with their aunt and uncle at Lord Amherst's estate, Montreal (named after his victory over the French in

Canada), in the region near Tunbridge Wells. Lord and Lady Amherst raised the two children as if they were their own, and since Lord Amherst had no son of his own, the young William became heir to the title.

The future Lord Amherst was educated as befitted his class and station, first at Westminster and then at Christ Church, Oxford. After leaving university in 1793, William undertook the traditional "grand tour" of the Continent. Along the way, he proved to be an accomplished linguist and became proficient in several languages, including French and Italian. After returning to England, in 1797 he took the degree of M.A. at Oxford. The same year, his uncle died and William assumed the title as the second Lord Amherst. While on tour in Italy in 1794, William had become friends with the Earl and Countess of Plymouth. Following the Earl's death, in 1800 he married the widowed Countess in what was apparently a successful love match. With such family background and connections, it is not surprising that the still young Lord Amherst also became a favorite at Court, and from 1802–04, he was Lord of the Bedchamber to King George III.

In 1809, perhaps due to his language facility as well as his family background, Amherst was sent as Ambassador Extraordinary to Sicily during the Napoleonic Wars. In 1815, after the end of the wars, he was made a Privy Councillor. The following year, accompanied by his son Jeffrey, he was sent as Ambassador Extraordinary and Plenipotentiary to negotiate with the Imperial Government of China.

The China Amherst encountered in 1816 was quite a different place from the one Lord Macartney had visited a quarter of a century earlier. The old Qianlong Emperor, an able ruler, had retired, and his fifth son and successor, Jiaqing, combined weakness with obstinacy, which had led to a series of revolts. The land-based uprisings were put down, but pirates were not so easily suppressed, and they continued to control the coast of China. The last thing Jiaqing needed was a foreign power further weakening his already loose hold on the country.

This was Lord Amherst's first visit to the Heavenly Kingdom, but he had as one of his advisors a member of Lord Macartney's retinue—little George Staunton, now grown up and Chairman of the East India Company's Select Committee in Canton, a trade association of British merchants doing business in China. Sir George Staunton spoke the language—he also understood the Chinese world view and the symbolic significance of the kowtow. Staunton advised Amherst not to kowtow because it would establish him as a tribute bearer and an inferior—and inferiors do not negotiate with superiors.

In 1816, Britain was the world's greatest superpower, its position much like that of the United States's World War II. The nation had just defeated Napoleon, and its navy was all-powerful. Although other advisors urged Amherst to bow before the Emperor, Amherst accepted Sir George's advice. The stakes were high, after all—nothing less than equality between the two nations would be acceptable to the British.

The mandarin courtiers thought up a face-saving gesture that they hoped would satisfy both sides. They volunteered to clear the throne room and have Amherst kowtow to the Emperor's empty chair! Amherst agreed to bow and even genuflect, but he refused to put his face on the floor—and certainly not nine times. The Chinese officials were determined to get around the symbolically crucial bit of protocol. In a comic-opera scene, they woke the ambassador in the middle of the night and escorted him to a private room where the Emperor's throne had been relocated for a quick, surreptitious kowtow. They hoped that Amherst, half-asleep, would be too tired or disoriented to resist. As the ambassador went down on one knee, a courtier shoved him in an attempt to make him put his head on the floor. But Staunton grabbed Amherst by the elbow and caught him before he fell.

In the end, Amherst left China without even seeing the Emperor. Almost two decades would pass before Britain sent another official representative to China. In the intervening years, relations between British merchants in China and the Chinese government would continue to worsen.

In 1833, a reform-minded British Parliament abolished the East India Company's monopoly in China. With China open to all comers, within a year the amount of tea imported into Britain quadrupled. The trade in opium to pay for all this tea also dramatically increased. In 1830, eighteen thousand chests of opium were imported from India. Three years later, the number of chests had soared to thirty thousand.

The devastation wrought by opium in Chinese society can hardly be overstated. While the British didn't introduce the Chinese to opium, they were more efficient at supplying the drug than previous importers. Innovations in China's use of the drug also fueled the demand, which British merchants were only too willing to supply. Typically, opium had been swallowed. Then, in the eighteenth century, China's wealthy youth found a more potent way to ingest the drug. The parallels to cocaine use in this century are eerie. Inhaled, cocaine addicts its users, but not as powerfully and quickly as smoking its rock incarnation does. Similarly, the Chinese found that smoking opium, especially when mixed with another addictive drug, nicotine from tobacco, increased the intensity and prolonged the "high."

This expensive pastime of the idle *jeunesse dorée* gradually made its way down the socioeconomic ladder. Shopkeepers, servants, soldiers, and even Taoist priests were loading opium pipes and drifting off into weeklong escapes from productivity, responsibility, and consciousness. China's powerful elite were not blind to the mess that the foreign import had caused. One courtier estimated that four million Chinese were habituated. A British doctor in Canton suspected that the figure was three times that. The economy, government services, and standard of living all declined because of substance abuse.

Before its monopoly ended, a representative of the East India Company had handled all British affairs in China, the most famous representative being the Mandarin-speaking Sir George Staunton. Such an arrangement fit in with the Chinese principle that merchants in a region should be organized into societies, or guilds, each with a recognized leader who would be held responsible by the Imperial authorities for the guild members' activities as a whole. In January 1831, upon learning of the impending end of the East India Company monopoly and the advent of free trade among the British merchants in China, the current Viceroy of Canton ordered the British to appoint a *tai pan* or chief executive, who might still be held accountable by the Chinese authorities for British trade conduct in Canton.

Although the Chinese Viceroy's order was not followed through by his own successor, the British government too recognized the need to replace the role of the East India Company with some alternate arrangement. Consequently, the same Act of Parliament that threw the China trade open also authorized the government to establish "a British Authority" in China in the form of three Superintendents of Trade—a Chief Superintendent supported by two subordinates. The Chief Superintendent of Trade would preside over "a Court of Justice with Criminal and Admiralty Jurisdiction for the trial of offences committed by His Majesty's subjects in the said Dominions or on the high sea within a hundred miles from the coast of China." It was the beginning of British claims to extraterritoriality—jurisdiction over British subjects even within the territory of the Chinese emperor. To pay for this new administrative structure, the superintendents were given authority to impose a tonnage duty on British vessels trading within their jurisdiction.

The fateful appointment as Britain's first Chief Superintendent of Trade in China fell to Lord Napier, who arrived in Macao in 1834. Napier, like Amherst, was a veteran of the Napoleonic wars, having fought in the Battle of Trafalgar. At the age of forty-eight, the first Baron Napier of Meriston had no experience in trade and had spent his entire career up to this point in the military. Having reached the rank of captain, he retired in 1815, at the end of the Napoleonic Wars, to Selkirkshire, where he engaged in sheep breeding. In 1828, inheriting a Scottish barony, he entered the House of Lords and became well known as a supporter of progressive causes, including Catholic Emancipation, the abolition of slavery, the Reform Bill of 1832, and other causes that identified him as a proponent of free trade in opposition to monopolies like the East India Company. A devout Presbyterian and student of the Bible, Napier was something of a scholar *manqué* who shared an interest in mathematics with a forbear who had invented logarithms. Unfortunately, Napier's physical appearance was unprepossessing. Tall, thin, and gangly, he also had red hair, which coincided with the Chinese stereotype of the red-haired barbarian devil—although in person, the Chinese apparently considered the envoy a comical rather than threatening figure.

Napier's position in China was equivocal—and technically illegal. Foreigners were only allowed to reside in Canton during the tea-trading season, after which they were required to retreat to Macao. Napier arrived in the middle of July at the end of the tea season and stayed, arguing that the ban on foreigners in Canton only applied to traders, not to him as a government official.

The ambassador's assignment resembled his unsuccessful predecessors' brief. He was to protect British trade, open up more Chinese ports to British merchants, and—that persistent obsession—establish an official presence at the Emperor's court in Peking. Despite this long-term goal, however, the British government had apparently despaired of lodging an ambassador in the capital immediately and instead ordered Napier to set up his residence in Canton. He was told to present his credentials as Chief Superintendent of Trade to the Viceroy of Canton, Lu Kun, when he arrived aboard the frigate *Andromache* on July 15, 1834. Napier didn't even bother to request an audience with the Emperor—a sign of Britain's decreasing expectations about establishing traditional diplomatic relations with such a recalcitrant head of state and his bureaucrats. What he was told *not* to do was even more significant and would lead inevitably to two Sino-British wars. Officially, the government adopted a hands-off policy toward the private business that was the opium trade. "It is not desirable that you should encourage such adventures, but you must never lose sight of the fact that you have no authority to interfere with them or prevent them," his orders from the Foreign Office said. Anticipating the possibility of hostilities, the government also ordered him to locate and map places where British ships might securely shelter and replenish themselves on the southern coast of China.

On orders from the Emperor, the Viceroy refused to meet with Napier and issued an edict directing the emissary to follow the usual procedure and do business with the government through the Cohong, a group of Chinese merchants (individually known as the Hong merchants) who dealt with all foreign traders. Less than a week after Napier's arrival, Lu Kun announced, "The Barbarian Eye [Napier's Chinese nickname], if he wishes to come to Canton, must inform the Hong merchants, so that they may petition me."

Napier had a rude reception after arriving in Canton from Macao, when Chinese customs officials tore open his trunks and ransacked his papers. Nevertheless, he took up residence at the New English Factory. The European "factories" were actually complexes of living and business quarters, which would be called mixed-use buildings today. The Chinese rebuff continued when Napier sent his secretary-treasurer, John H. Astell, with a letter of introduction to the Viceroy. At the Petition Gate, on the edge of the factories where intergovernmental transactions traditionally took place, the letter was rejected on the grounds that it lacked a Chinese stamp required of all petitions to the Chinese government. Through Astell, Napier argued that his letter was not a petition and so required no stamp. A higher-ranking mandarin was summoned, but after an hour he still hadn't appeared and a threatening mob began to taunt Astell at the Petition Gate. Finally, the mandarin arrived and repeated his subordinate's orders. Worried that an international incident was about to occur that would harm their commerce, representatives of the Cohong begged Astell to give them the letter, which they promised to submit to proper government channels. Astell knew the symbolic importance of dealing directly with the government, however, and refused the offer of mediation. Two more Chinese government officials arrived, and they also refused to accept the letter. After three hours in the sweltering July heat, Astell finally retreated from the Petition Gate and returned to Napier at the New English Factory.

Lu Kun considered the standoff a huge diplomatic victory, and crowed in a letter to the Emperor: "It is plain, on the least reflection that in order to distinguish the Chinese from outsiders it is of the utmost importance to maintain dignity and sovereignty." Lu Kun issued a second edict, ordering Napier to leave Canton and return to Portuguese-held Macao, fifty miles to the south. To back up his command, the Viceroy ordered a temporary halt in all trade with Britain until his orders were obeyed, and Napier sailed back to Macao. Lu Kun's edicts actually delighted the cannier of the British traders, who now believed that some sort of intervention by the British government was inevitable.

The most powerful of the independent British trading companies was that established in 1834 by two Scotsmen, Dr. William Jardine and James Matheson. Born in Lochmaben, Scotland in 1784, Jardine had begun his career fresh out of medical school at the age of eighteen as a ship's surgeon in the East India Company fleet. Taking advantage of the Company policy that allowed employees to trade on their own account, by 1817 he had amassed enough wealth to go into business for himself. In 1820, he committed himself to the China trade, settling in Canton as one of the earliest advocates of free trade. Matheson, too, was a Scot, having been born in Lairg in 1794. After first trading in India, he had entered the Canton trade, where he became a vocal advocate of free trade. There, in 1827, along with his younger brother, he had founded one of the earliest of the English-language newspapers, *The Canton Register*, to espouse the principles of free trade and the end of the East India Company monopoly. Anticipating the end of the East India Company monopoly, in 1832 Jardine and Matheson joined forces to form Jardine, Matheson & Co., and in 1834 had shipped the first private loads of tea and silk from China to Britain. The company quickly became the most powerful and influential firm in the China trade and in the future Hong Kong; along with its colorful founders, it was the model for James Clavell's novels *Tai-Pan* and *Noble House*.

As the most respected and influential of the China traders, Jardine had Napier's ear and urged him to retaliate for the Chinese Viceroy's behavior. Jardine was delighted by Lu Kun's edicts, which he hoped would enrage British public opinion and lead to military intervention. Napier accepted Jardine's advice, echoing it in a letter to the Foreign Secretary, Lord Palmerston. "Three or four frigates and brigs, with a few steady British troops would settle the thing. The exploit is to be performed with a facility unknown even in the capture of a paltry West Indian island," he wrote on August 14, 1834.

There were two strikes against Napier's proposed military adventure. His instructions had explicitly stated he was not to interject the British government into the battle over the opium trade, and during the three months it took Napier's letter to arrive in London urging force against the Chinese, the Whig government fell. Under the new Tory ministry, the reactionary but isolationist Duke of Wellington took Palmerston's place as Foreign Secretary. Responding to Napier's advice, the new Foreign Secretary reiterated his predecessor's instructions and wrote: "It is not by force and violence that His Majesty [William IV] intends to establish a commercial intercourse between his subjects and China, but by other conciliatory measures so strongly inculcated in the instructions you have received."

Despite his liberal past, Napier seems to have held his Chinese counterparts in the same contempt with which the Chinese regarded all barbarians. Writing to Lord Grey, Napier described his Chinese opponents' mind-set in language that was at once both accurate and a case of projection. The Chinese people, he wrote, wallowed in "the extreme degree of mental imbecility and moral degradation, dreaming themselves to be the only people on earth, and being entirely ignorant of the theory and practice of international law."

On August 16, 1834, the Viceroy of Canton enacted a partial embargo on British imports. In a letter to Lord Grey, Napier once again called for military intervention and predicted a quick and easy success: "What can an army of bows and arrows and pikes and shields do against a handful of British veterans?" Meanwhile, Napier decided to bypass Lu Kun and make his case directly to the residents of Canton, whom he argued would be hurt by the trade embargo as much as the British. "Thousands of industrious Chinese…must suffer ruin and discomfort through the perversity of their government," he declared on a placard in Chinese posted in the city.

The declaration enraged Lu Kun, who countered with an edict that contained a violent threat and was noteworthy for its contempt of the enemy: "A lawless foreign slave has issued a notice. We do not know how such a barbarian dog can have the audacity to call himself a 'government official.' Though a savage from beyond the pale, his sense of propriety would have restrained him from such an outrage. It is a capital offense to incite the people against their rulers, and we would be justified in obtaining a mandate for his decapitation."

Lu Kun backed up the threat by embargoing all British trade on September 2, 1834, in an edict that called for but did not implement expulsion of all barbarians from China. "The Barbarian Eye is indeed stupid, blinded, ignorant…there can be no quiet while he remains here. I therefore formally close the trade until he goes." Lu Kun wasn't through. In yet another edict, he ordered all British residents of Canton to leave and relocate at Macao. He added an extra irritant by allowing the American, Dutch, and French merchants to remain and continue their lucrative business.

Napier was dining on indigestible salt pork from a British ship with Sir George Robinson, the Second Superintendent of Trade, when a Chinese servant appeared, crying hysterically and informing Napier of the Viceroy's new edict, posted on the door of the New English Factory, which was now surrounded by howling Chinese soldiers. Napier went to the entrance of the factory, tore up the placard, and ordered the soldiers to disperse, but they ignored his orders and continued to make threatening gestures and jeers. Napier retreated and returned to his dessert of plum pudding with Robinson. As a painting of George IV looked down on the diners, Napier told Robinson of his plan to send him to Captain Blackwood, commander of the *Imogene*, which lay at anchor in the Bay of Canton with the *Andromache* and *Louisa*, with orders for the three frigates to sail to Whampoa, twelve miles west of Canton.

Access to Canton was guarded by the two Bogue Forts thirty miles south of the city on the Pearl River. Napier knew the defenders would fire on the British ships, and he ordered Blackwood to fire back and destroy the forts' cannons. The forts showed how primitive China's military defenses were. The Bogue bristled with sixty cannons, but the guns were immobilized in masonry instead of gun carriages, bolted to the ground and incapable of aiming. Jack Beeching doesn't minimize the pathetic state of Chinese artillery: "They were more like fireworks than pieces of ordnance." As the frigates sailed blithely past the forts, the cannons fired over the heads of the invaders. Charles Elliot, the captain of the *Louisa*, considered the cannonade so harmless that he sat in a chair sunning himself on deck as he sailed past the antique artillery. The British frigates returned fire, but much more effectively than their opponents. All sixty cannons at the forts were knocked out of service. Only two British sailors were killed and five wounded in what came to be called the Battle of the Bogue.

But what the Chinese lacked in state-of-the-art technology, they made up for with crude force. Qi Long, the Governor of Canton, blocked the frigates' exit from the Bogue with a dozen stone barges, a cable drawn across the river, and hundreds of fire rafts loaded with gunpowder, all guarded by a fleet of Chinese warships. Unlike the impotent cannons, the fire rafts (rafts set on fire and set adrift toward enemy ships) posed a genuine threat to the *Imogene* and *Andromache*, which were made of wood and jammed with gunpowder. The frigates could continue on to Canton, but they would be unable to return. Like the British colony at Canton, they were stuck.

Although the British ships had provoked the fight by sailing to the Bogue Forts, Napier condemned the Chinese response, as ineffectual as it had been, and used the Chinese cannonade to justify an escalation in the conflict. "It is a very serious offense to fire on or otherwise insult the British flag. They have opened the preliminaries of war. There are two frigates [*Louisa* was a cutter] now in the river, bearing very heavy guns, for the express purpose of protecting British trade," he blustered in a letter to Lu

Kun. Left unsaid but easily inferred was the fact that the frigates were also there to provoke a fight the British knew they would win.

So, Napier was stuck in Canton. Adding to his troubles, he contracted a fever. His doctor, T.R. Colledge, advised him to return to Macao where the climate was healthier and better medical care was available. The Chinese agreed to let Napier go, but only under humiliating terms. Napier wanted to go to Macao in a British ship, but Lu Kun insisted that he sail in a Chinese ship under guard of soldiers and other ships. Gongs and firecrackers disturbed the peace of Napier, who by now was dying from the fever, as he made his way to the harbor. This was the same manner in which high-ranking Chinese prisoners were transported to their place of execution. Napier returned to Macao after a painful eighty-five-mile journey that took five long days, and died on October 11, a few days after his arrival. The British public didn't mourn the loss of the failed diplomat and referred to his ignominious end as "Napier's Fizzle." The isolationist Duke of Wellington perhaps best summed up the general view of Napier's critics: "The attempt to force upon the Chinese authorities at Canton an unaccustomed mode of communication with an authority of whose powers and of whose nature they had no knowledge had failed, as it is obvious that such an attempt must invariably fail, and lead again to national disgrace." British merchants in China, of course, viewed the matter rather differently: Jardine and eighty-five other merchants signed a petition to the new king, William IV, demanding revenge for Napier's humiliation and a strong military response.

Napier's replacement was John Francis Davis, his subordinate First Superintendent of Trade. A Chinese scholar and a former member of the East India Company, Davis, ironically, got along with the Chinese but disliked the aggressive, war-mongering British merchants, whom he thought were trying to goad Britain into a full-scale war. As a former employee of the British East India Company, he was also prone to look down his nose at the freebooting independent traders who had so effectively broken the Company's monopoly in the China trade. Within a few months, Davis resigned in disgust and was replaced in January 1835 by the Second Superintendent of Trade, Sir George Robinson.

Another former East India Company employee, Robinson too detested the British merchants, but managed to form a working relationship with them. He suggested a way to mollify the Chinese and restore relations. He sought permission to halt the opium trade and went so far as to recommend that the British stop cultivating the drug in India. For his efforts, Robinson was fired and replaced with a more belligerent Chief Superintendent of Trade, Captain Charles Elliot, in June 1836.

A Scotsman and avid watercolor painter, Elliot had volunteered for the navy at the end of the Napoleonic Wars and later fought pirates in Algiers and slave traders along the west coast of Africa, where he held the government title "Protector of Slaves." Retiring from the navy in 1833, Elliot helped draft legislation that outlawed slavery throughout the British Empire. The Foreign Minister, Lord Palmerston, called Elliot out of retirement and sent him to Canton. Like his predecessors, Elliot, a fervent Calvinist, also despised the opium trade, but shrewder than his predecessors, he did not make his objections known. In fact, his orders from the Foreign Office were to make sure Britain's drug of choice, tea, made it safely out of China and into the teacups of English drawing rooms for the ritual afternoon tea. Elliot chose to ignore the fact that opium paid for the tea.

In November 1836, five months after Elliot's arrival, the Daoguang Emperor issued an edict banning both the importation and use of opium throughout China. In December 1836, the new governor (or viceroy) of Canton's province, a venerable scholar of sixty named Deng Tingzhen, proclaimed, "The smoke of opium is a deadly poison. Opium is nothing else but a flowing poison; that it leads to extravagant expenditure is a small evil, but as it utterly ruins the mind and morals of the people, it is a dreadful calamity." Deng had nine prominent merchants, including the powerful William Jardine, arraigned on trafficking charges, followed by an order for their expulsion from China. The merchants ignored the order and went unpunished. Deng's failure to arrest the merchants may have had to do with his lack of enthusiasm for suppressing the opium trade, which he told a colleague would be as effective as a ban on tea.

Foreign importers, not only the British, but Americans and French as well, took the news of the ban with a huge grain of salt. Previous edicts against the drug had been issued and ignored. It was rumored that the Viceroy of Canton was involved in the opium trade himself, and that members of the Imperial Court profited from the trade in the form of bribes or as smugglers themselves. The opium trade had thoroughly corrupted the Chinese government as much as it had devastated its citizens' health. When the foreign merchants ignored his expulsion order, Deng responded by doubling the "excise tax," actually a bribe, charged for each chest of opium

But this time, the Emperor meant business when he said he wanted to end the opium business. Between Lord Macartney's arrival and Elliot's, the Imperial Treasury's silver reserve had fallen from seventy million taels to ten million (one tael in the mid nineteenth century equalled $1.50). The number of Chinese addicts at the time Elliot took office was estimated at four to twelve million, mostly men in what should have been their most productive years, between twenty and fifty-five years old. Perhaps fearing to take on the foreign importers directly, in 1837, Viceroy Deng destroyed the Chinese galleys in Canton that collaborated in the opium trade. Again striking at his own countrymen rather than foreigners, Deng arrested Chinese opium merchants, distributors, and even addicts throughout China. As a warning to foreigners, he ordered the execution of He Laojin, the proprietor of a popular opium den.

The execution of another Chinese smuggler was also planned, but this time it would take place just outside the foreign factories in Canton. The Chinese erected a scaffold in the form of a wooden cross right under the window of the American factory where the verdict—death by strangulation—would be carried out. Deng considered the provocative placement of the scaffold an object lesson: "To arouse reflection, that the depraved portion of the foreign community might be deterred from pursuing their evil courses; for those foreigners, though born and brought up beyond the pale of civilization, have human hearts." Enraged, the American consul took down the flag, but was in no position to do much else.

With an iron chain about his neck, the condemned man was about to be tied to the cross when his captors, with no sense of irony, gave him a pipe of opium to ease his ordeal. In an opium haze, he voluntarily lifted his hands so they could be secured to the cross. But before the execution could be carried out, eighty sailors from the Anglo-Indian ship *Orwell* tore down the scaffold and used its planks to beat the crowd of Chinese assembled to witness the execution. The Chinese government officials fled, but took the condemned man with them. At this point, a mob of six thousand Chinese gathered outside the factories and began to stone the American compound.

The sailors threw broken bottles at their attackers, and the shards of glass ripped through the feet of the Chinese mob.

After a request from Howqua, the leader of the Cohong, to the Governor of Canton to stop the riot, which was injurious to trade, Chinese troops dispersed the mob with whips, and the smuggler was executed at another site in Canton, far from the foreign settlements. A year later, foreign merchants and the crew of a British ship, which had just docked in Canton, broke up yet another execution. A Chinese mob attacked the ship, but was repelled by Chinese soldiers sent to protect the foreigners. After the danger ended, however, the Chinese troops remained outside the factories, whose occupants found their presence threatening. More ominously, the Emperor responded to the foreigners' interference with the executions by creating a new post, High Commissioner, and appointing a strong-willed diplomat untainted by participation in the opium trade to suppress the drug trafficking.

Chapter 3

ZERO INTOLERANCE

———

"The laws against the consumption of opium are now so strict in China that if you continue to make it, you will find that no one buys it."

—The High Commissioner of Canton to Queen Victoria, 1839

U ntil 1838, the prevailing attitude in the Chinese heirarchy had been that the evils of opium could best be resolved by suppressing its importation and distribution. However, as the problem grew, so did the debate within the Chinese government. Some scholar-officials actually recommended legalization of the drug. Decriminalizing its use, they argued, would permit them to regulate it and even tax it. Others, however, took a hard line. Not only did they insist that the drug traffic should be stopped, the also began to argue for serious efforts to halt or punish users. In 1838, the Daoguang Emperor called for recommendations from his governors general and other officials on the best approach to take to the problem. After hearing both sides of the debate, the emperor decided to follow the advice of the hardliners—notably that of the governor of Hubei and Hunan, Lin Zexu.

The High Commissioner, Lin Zexu, brought to his new job a sterling résumé and an impeccable reputation, having suppressed the opium trade in the provinces of Hubei and Hunan. Lin's nickname was "Blue Sky," because he was said to be as pure and unblemished as a cloudless sky. He was a reformer and a literary scholar, plump and above average in height with a bushy mustache and scraggly beard. He was the son of a poor teacher in the province of Fujian. Lin had grown up witnessing the devastating effects of opium, as many inhabitants of Fujian were users of the drug. Lin was also a master diplomat whom the Emperor employed for seemingly insoluble problems. During a peasant revolt in 1823, Lin single-handedly persuaded the rebels to lay down their arms. Now, the Emperor called on Lin to perform a similar feat of magic. Lin's memorial not only recommended suppression of the drug trade, it also called for serious efforts to root out the use of the drug in China. Lin's memorial was most repressive for its thoroughness.

The High Commissioner made a dramatic entrance into Canton, one calculated to impress spectators with his importance. He was carried in a litter by twenty bearers, but with a military escort of only six men. The paucity of bodyguards implied that the authority of the semi-divine Emperor was the only protection he needed. Lin got down to business immediately. From his base at the Yuanhua Academy, which was close to his target, the foreign factories, he issued an edict proscribing fifty-four local government officials who colluded in the opium trade with the foreigners. Other edicts demonstrated the extent to which opium had penetrated all levels of society. One ordered schoolteachers to stop their students from smoking opium and commanded that the teachers to set a good example by abstaining as well. Another edict condemned Chinese marines stationed along the coast, charging them with stopping foreign smugglers while participating in the trade themselves.

A man ahead of his time, Lin believed in rehabilitation as the best way to destroy the market. Eradicate the desire and you eradicate the trade. Based on his successful efforts as Viceroy in Hubei and Hunan, he felt that even long-time opium users could be saved. Without any of the loathing and suspicion of foreign ways and methods felt by his fellow mandarins, Lin sought help from the foreign Medical Missionary Society in Canton and inquired if the West had a safe drug that would wean addicts from opium. (The Medical Missionary Society may not have been the best place to seek help since the No. 2 man there was Dr. William Jardine, one of the biggest opium traders in China.) Along with these efforts to beat the addiction, however, Lin also advocated execution for those who failed to kick the habit after eighteen months.

In a memorandum to the Emperor, Lin had complained that Chinese customers spent one hundred million taels (one tael = 38 grams of silver) on opium, while the entire government budget was only forty million taels. The Viceroy warned, "If we continue to allow this trade to flourish, in a few dozen years we will find ourselves not only with no

soldiers to resist the enemy, but also with no money to equip the army."
Lin overdramatized the cost of the drug to the economy and military,
but underestimated the timetable when a combination of social devastation and economic ruin would bring China and Britain to war. Instead
of the Commissioner's "few dozen years," the conflict was about to
begin.

———·———

In 1839, Lin decided to approach the British government directly to halt
the pernicious traffic in opium. In a letter to Queen Victoria, Lin began
with an appeal to a universal sense of right and wrong: "The Way of
Heaven [Tao] is fairness to all. It does not suffer us to harm others in
order to benefit ourselves. Men are alike in this all the world over: that
they cherish life and hate what endangers life. Your country lies twenty
thousand leagues away; but for all that the Way of Heaven holds good for
you as for us, and your instincts are not different from ours." Lin's disconsolate message to the Queen has the ring of today's zero-tolerance
advocates and the same hopelessness of U.S. efforts to end the drug
trade.

Mixing in a bit of honey to sweeten his bitter barbs, Lin conceded
that British traders had behaved themselves by and large for more than a
century in their guest country. Perhaps to reinforce this behavior, he
added that many of the foreign merchants had become very rich from
their trade with China, the implicit message being: don't slaughter this
cash cow:

> There is a class of evil foreigner that makes opium and
> brings it for sale, tempting fools to destroy themselves,
> merely in order to reap profit. Formerly, the number of
> opium smokers was small; but now the vice has spread far
> and wide and the poison penetrated deeper and deeper. I
> am told that in your own country opium smoking is for-
> bidden under severe penalties.

Lin's mistaken belief that opium was proscribed in Britain was typical
of the Chinese unfamiliarity with barbarian cultures. Opium was very

popular in England, but in the less addictive form of laudanum, a tincture of red wine and usually only a grain or two of opium. Famous users included the poet Samuel Coleridge and the essayist Thomas De Quincey, who created a scandal and a bestseller with the publication of his autobiographical *Confessions of an English Opium-Eater* in 1821. The drug's most notorious victim, Robert Clive, the conqueror of India, apparently used laudanum to treat depression, or as Victorians called the modern malady, "choleric temperament," and suffered a fatal overdose in 1774.

Lin's letter to Victoria continued, "This means that you are aware of how harmful it is. So long as you do not take it yourselves, but continue to make it and tempt the people of China to buy it, you will be showing yourselves careful of your own lives, but careless of the lives of other people." Then Lin's lecture turned into explicit orders leavened with a threat if his demands were not carried out. "I now give my assurance that we mean to cut off this harmful drug forever. What is here forbidden to consume, your dependencies [India] must be forbidden to manufacture, and what has already been manufactured, Your Majesty must immediately search out and throw to the bottom of the sea." More carrot followed the stick. "Calamities will not be sent down on you from above; you will be acting in accordance with decent feeling, which may also influence the course of nature in your favor."

Lin also displayed his confidence in the new but as yet unproven policy that he helped create, which he believed would solve China's opium problem. "The laws against the consumption of opium are now so strict in China that if you continue to make it, you will find that no one buys it," Lin wrote—at a time when there were an estimated ten million opium addicts in China.

Unlike his prediction that the Chinese market for the drug was drying up, Lin's threat to confiscate the contraband would soon come true. If Her Majesty didn't dispose of the lucrative poison, Lin's minions would. "All opium discovered in China is being cast into burning oil and destroyed. Any foreign ships that in the future arrive with opium on board will be set fire to."

The letter concluded with a peremptory demand that reflected the Chinese view of barbarians as inferior, including their Queen: "Do not say you have not been warned in time. On receiving this, Your Majesty will be so good as to report to me immediately on the steps that have been taken at each of your ports."

Lin's personal translator had trouble rendering his master's letter in English, and the Commissioner once again showed his openness to barbarian culture by asking Peter Parker, an American linguist and eye doctor who ran a clinic in Canton and who was fluent in Chinese, to translate the letter. Parker did a better job, but still found the document impenetrable. "Some parts of it we could make neither head nor tail of," Parker said.

In Peking, the Emperor had accepted Lin's evaluation that while rehabilitation should be attempted, if it failed more severe penalties would follow. An Imperial edict enacted the most draconian rules to date. Addicts were given eighteen months to surrender their drugs and escape punishment. Foreigners who engaged in the trade would be beheaded, and Chinese dealers would be strangled. Corrupt officials who looked the other way in return for bribes would also suffer the death penalty. Even what today is called "drug paraphernalia" was proscribed. By the spring of 1839, the year the First Opium War began, sixteen hundred residents of Canton, from dealers to users to dishonest government bureaucrats, had been arrested, and forty-two thousand opium pipes were confiscated. Three thousand chests of opium were seized, and by mid summer, eleven thousand more were.

Lin's job, however, was far from done. Twenty thousand more chests lay in foreign ships anchored off of the long coast of China. In fact, there was a glut of opium, and more ships from India carrying the drug were making their way to China. Even the inexorable cravings of an addicted nation couldn't keep up with the supply from India. Some foreign merchants in China secretly welcomed Lin's confiscations because they hoped seizures would raise the price of the drug and eliminate the glut.

Lin's appeal to the British monarch was doomed from the beginning. The Queen, as a constitutional ruler, couldn't take any unilateral steps to stop the opium trade. In any case, Lin's letter never reached Victoria. The luckless bureaucrat had done the modern equivalent of "mailing" the letter via U.S. Post—sending it in a British ship called a mail packet. For reasons unknown, the letter got lost "in the mail" during its eight thousand–mile trip from China to England, and Queen Victoria never saw it. *The Times of London*, however, did manage to get hold of Lin's letter and print it—but to no avail.

Lin then launched into the practical business of making good on his threats to the Queen. He began interrogating native Chinese who participated in the opium trade: the foreigners' local liaisons, the Hong merchants; and the foreign merchants' employees—interpreters, clerical staff, and compradors, or local Chinese agents.

Word of Lin's interrogations reached the foreign merchants, and it slowly began to dawn on them that as far as the opium traffic was concerned, business would never be as usual in China again. But they wanted to know how Lin proposed to wipe out a strongly entrenched business with so many enthusiastic customers. His immediate method was not only to squeeze the foreign merchants, but also their Chinese trading partners, the merchants of the Cohong. The most important of the Hong merchants at the time was Wu Bingjian, known to the European merchants as "Howqua." The richest and most powerful of the Cohong merchants, Wu Bingjian was the third son of Wu Guorong, Howqua I, the founder of the family company. A shrewd businessman, Howqua II was heavily engaged not only in the tea and silk trade, supplying both the British East India Company and the American trading organization, the Boston Concern, but also in opium and many other ventures. He made a considerable amount of money by advancing money to weaker merchants in times of crisis, in exchange for considerable interest. He also exported a variety of goods on his own account and eventually, through an American factor, invested heavily in American railroads. By 1834, Howqua was not only the most important member of the Cohong, but also probably the richest man on Earth at the time.

Howqua now offered some advice and a prediction that must have sent shivers up the collective spines of the British merchants. Why not leave Canton and relocate in the friendlier port of Singapore, where merchants were revered as gods, not as criminal drug lords? Better yet, stay put...but turn their entire cache of opium over to the Chinese, who stood by ready with torches to send the product to heaven in a fiery confiscation. The alternative to these steps was even worse, according to Howqua. China would summarily end all trade with the foreign devils if they didn't stop selling their most lucrative product.

For someone so ignorant of British parliamentary government "twenty thousand leagues away," Lin was surprisingly well informed of the activities of the British closer to his own home. One of the biggest traders, Russell and Company, had announced they were getting out of the opium business, but their operatives continued covertly to ply the trade. As a sop to Lin, which fooled no one, the merchants volunteered to surrender one thousand chests, which belonged to the Hong merchants, not the foreigners. Lin saw through the ruse and commented, "This is a mere fraction. There are tens of thousands of chests." Lin had given orders to arrest one of the most prominent British traders, Matthew Jardine, but before this international incident could take place, Jardine took Howqua's advice and fled the country.

On March 18, 1839, Lin demonstrated that he would back up his written threats with dramatic action. The High Commissioner still refused to deal with the barbarians, summoning their Chinese partners, twelve Hong merchants, to the Yuanhua Academy, where he read aloud two proclamations, with orders to relay the information to their barbarian partners. First, the foreign merchants were to surrender the contraband on their ships and stop future importation. The second proclamation, which the unfortunate Cohong heard while kneeling before the commissioners, accused them, correctly, of being accomplices in the opium trade, and hurled insults and invective at them for their role in it. He cited the precedents of twenty-year-old laws that forbade foreign importation of the drug. And for more than those twenty years, the Cohong had served as middlemen and grown rich from their illicit collaboration, Lin railed. The Cohong were so enmeshed in the trade that they provided the wooden chests in which opium was shipped.

Almost as bad, but not as toxic to China, was the Cohong's participation in the export of silver to pay for the prized drug. They were not only poisoning the Emperor's subjects, they were draining his treasury. Lin exclaimed that he "burned with shame" for merchants he called "traitors." Then he gave them an impossible task with the ultimate penalty if they failed. Within three days, somehow the Hong were to stop a centuries-old enterprise, in particular, arrange the delivery of all opium to Lin for confiscation. The Commissioner strengthened his orders with a threat. If the Cohong did not succeed, he would ask the Emperor's permission to execute two of the twelve and impoverish their heirs by the confiscation of their wealth and lands.

Powerfully motivated by fear, Howqua and Lu Wenwei, known as Mowqua and the second most important member of the Cohong, immediately passed Lin's orders on to their foreign partners. The day after their audience with Lin, Howqua hoped to ensure compliance by forbidding the British merchants to leave China. Howqua gave the orders in person to the top merchants, Dent, Matheson, Green, Daniell, Wetmore, and the Indian Dadabhoy Rustomjee, followed by a reading of Lin's edicts so they couldn't claim to be unaware of the Commissioner's wrath and demands. The merchants responded to Howqua equivocally. Instead of compliance, they announced their plans to hold a meeting of the Chamber of Commerce in three days to *discuss* the issue—ignoring the fact that the Cohong had only three days before Lin would execute two of their number.

On March 21, 1839, forty members of the Chamber gathered to mull over Lin's ultimata. From the start of the proceedings, it became clear that the merchants had no intention of abandoning their business or surrendering the proscribed goods to Lin. They offered a transparent excuse for failing to obey the Emperor. The contraband, worth millions of dollars, did not belong to them! Actual ownership resided in opium manufacturers in faraway India. Let the Emperor pursue the perpetrators to the ends of the Earth—or failing that, their home bases in Bombay and Calcutta. The European merchants were merely middlemen, handling the drug on consignment—Russell smugly announced that he didn't own a single ounce of opium, even though fourteen hundred chests of the drug lay aboard his ships docked at Canton. Taking the dubious high ground, one merchant proclaimed, "What we do not own we cannot in conscience surrender!" The merchants had the audacity to tell the terrified Cohong that Lin was bluffing and not to worry about the imminent loss of their lives—without offering any evidence to back up their *sang froid*.

Only one trader, Charles King, berated his colleagues for ignoring the Cohong's plight, by putting "the pocket of a constituent [the opium producers in India] in competition with the neck of a neighbor." But profit trumped integrity, and by a vote of twenty-five to fourteen, the merchants told the Cohong to inform Lin that they would consider the Commissioner's orders, but they would need another six days—six more than the Cohong had before the executions.

It's hard to imagine the terror with which the Cohong relayed the news to Lin, who became enraged at the foreigners' defiance. Without Lin's approval or knowledge, the Cohong merchants returned to the traders with a gentle suggestion that maybe if they surrendered a bit of their contraband, Lin might be appeased and they (the Cohong) could keep their heads. This was the wishful thinking of the truly desperate.

Perhaps a pang of conscience—or genuine fear that Lin would make good on his threat of confiscation—prompted the Chamber of Commerce to hold a second meeting late in the evening of March 21, 1839. There, the assembly tried to assuage their guilt by making sure that the Cohong's situation was desperate. "Seriously and solemnly, are you in fear of your lives?" a merchant asked the twelve members of the Cohong, one by one.

The terror in the faces of the Chinese businessmen melted the hearts of the foreigners, but only a bit. Dent agreed to hand over a tiny portion of his opium and strong-armed his colleagues into surrendering another one thousand chests, worth only $300,000, a pittance compared to the millions of dollars' worth in the holds of foreign ships in Canton's harbor. Unmollified by the merchants' offer, Lin expanded the prohibition against the merchants' leaving China to the entire foreign community in Canton by stationing soldiers outside the factories.

Lin jumped the gun on his deadline. The day before the Chamber met, the Commissioner's men boarded the *Snipe*, a small vessel docked near the Bogue Forts, the gateway to Canton, and confiscated all opium aboard the ship. Lin was determined to cover both ends of the trade, importing opium and exporting silver, by stopping other ships that had dropped off opium from leaving Whampoa, a village eight miles east of Canton. He ordered the crews back to their factories, where he placed them under house arrest.

D-Day, Deadline Day, the 21st of March, came and went with no further confiscations or obstructions by Lin. The Commissioner now seemed to have had a failure of nerve or courage, because the day after he had threatened to execute some of the Cohong if the opium traders didn't hand over their contraband, he summoned one of the top foreign merchants to his palace for interrogation.

Having failed to bring Jardine to ground, Lin set his sights on almost as big a fish, Lancelot Dent, whom Lin alleged possessed six thousand chests of opium. Lin planned to behead Dent as an example and inducement to the other traders to surrender their stores, unaware or indifferent to the international repercussions of a summary execution of a wealthy merchant with strong political backers in Parliament. Since an appearance before Lin was far better than confiscation or execution, Dent at first planned to heed Lin's summons, but colleagues urged him not to, reminding him of the fate of the gunner of the *Lady Hughes*, who answered a similar summons and ended up spending more than two years as a prisoner of the Chinese until his execution by garrote in 1774 for the accidental killing of a Chinese sailor. Although the incident had happened more than sixty years before, fear trumped Dent's natural inclination to confront the hated Lin face to face. So the merchant equivocated, and through the luckless Howqua, sent word to Lin that he would obey the summons but only with a guarantee of safe conduct.

Howqua didn't bother or dare to relay Dent's demands; instead, with another member of the Cohong, he appeared outside the factories wearing an iron collar ordered by Lin and symbolizing the Cohong's fears that they would soon be garroted if Dent didn't appear before the Commissioner. The traders were unmoved by the sight of their Chinese collaborators' public humiliation and supplications at the factory gates. Some of the foreigners thought it was an act, or in the words of James Matheson, "the most complete exhibition of humbug ever witnessed in China."

The Cohong now enlisted the aid of three local magistrates, who turned up at Dent's factory, Baoshun, and basically staged a sit-in, refusing to leave until Dent accompanied them to an audience, and possibly an arrest and execution, by Lin. Dent stayed put, but tried to mollify the bureaucrats by sending them a handsome dinner. The men eventually left, but were replaced by various Hong merchants, until they too grew tired of the vigil and departed, disconsolate and terrified by their impending punishment by Lin at midnight.

Dent stalled by sending one of his partners, Robert Inglis, to a meeting with Lin's subordinates at the Temple of the Queen of Heaven in Canton. Lin did not detain Inglis, but continued to insist on Dent's surrender. Dent requested a safe-conduct pass before meeting with Lin, which was ignored. Soon, Dent's obstinacy turned to bravado as he tried to call Lin's bluff by getting word to the Commissioner that he would not resist arrest if Lin chose to send soldiers to enforce the invitation, but under no circumstances would he voluntarily deliver himself to possible imprisonment or worse. Again, Lin backed down. For reasons only the wily mandarin knew, he preferred diplomatic pressure to a violent seizure that could lead to a flat-out war. Lin was wise about the downside of fighting the foreigners, a wisdom his superiors in hindsight should have shared.

While the Imperial Commissioner hesitated and Dent and the other merchants grew bolder, Charles Elliot, the new Chief Superintendent of Trade, sailed toward Canton from Macao. A retired captain in the Royal Navy and son of the former Governor of Madras, the thirty-five-year-old diplomat was well connected. The Earl of Minto, First Lord of the Admiralty, and the Earl of Auckland, the Governor-General of India, were both first cousins. Elliot's decision to come to Canton had been prompted by a note smuggled out of the encircled factories alerting him to the presence of the soldiers Lin had placed there. Elliot was a pugnacious as Dent, perhaps even more so. He was ready to fight, he wrote in a letter to the Foreign Secretary, Lord Palmerston, before he arrived at Canton. "I have no doubt that a firm tone and attitude will check the rash spirit of the provincial authorities." Elliot was the typical myopic, uninformed foreigner, unaware or uncaring that while Lin was indeed a "provincial authority," all his actions were governed by the capital.

Before he arrived in Canton, Elliot sent word ahead to all British ships docked at the city to sail to the relative safety of Hong Kong. As the new Superintendent, in full dress uniform, sailed up the Canton River en route to the factories, to speed his trip he transferred to a small rowboat. The inauspicious craft, flying the Union Jack, landed near the factories on March 24, 1839, three days past Lin's deadline. The appearance of such an unprepossessing vessel must have offered little assurance to the beleaguered residents of the factories. But Elliot, despite his humble conveyance, would prove those fears unfounded. The terrified inhabitants of the factories had lowered the British flag before Elliot's arrival. His first act upon landing was to order the Union Jack back up. Then he proceeded straight to Dent's factory, where, holding the trader by the elbow, he escorted him to Elliot's headquarters in a nearby factory. Like the symbolism of the flag, Elliot's commandeering of Dent's person announced to the Chinese that the trader, and by implication *all* foreign merchants, were under the protection of Her Majesty's government. The factory residents cheered Dent and Elliot as they strode toward the Superintendent's bivouac, but their cheers rang hollow because symbolic patriotism seemed a pale rebuttal to the genuine menace of the Chinese soldiers outside.

That night, Elliot convened a meeting of British, American, Indian, and Hong merchants at the New English Factory. His news was not good, and he counseled a strategic retreat. Besides the soldiers outside, Elliot knew from his trip up the Canton River that the Chinese had positioned fire ships at the Bogue Forts, and he relayed this distressing intelligence to the assembled. Then he told them all to pack their bags and be prepared to move fast. He would try to secure passports for the refugees, but he was not optimistic and admitted that failure to secure safe passage out of Canton would turn the situation into a hostage crisis.

Elliot tried to leaven the bad news with good. "Thank God we have a British man-o-war, [although] small indeed she is outside!" This dubious protection would be augmented, he hoped, by the imminent arrival of two American fighting ships, the *Columbia* and the *John Adams*, even though they were expected in Macao, not Canton, where they were sorely needed because of the siege of the factories. Elliot's speech didn't appear to soothe the crowd very much, and received only muted applause and half-hearted cheers. Remembering his manners, Matheson took the podium and thanked Elliot. One wonders if the rest of the terrified merchants shared Matheson's gratitude.

The tenseness of the situation increased as the Chinese employees of the factories, first slowly, then pell-mell, began to flee the compound "as if they were running from a plague," William Hunter, a trader in the employ of Russell and Company, wrote in his diary. The stalwarts who didn't join the exodus were ordered out by the native Chinese translators, who seem to have formed a fifth column within the factories. Terrified bearers, cooks, butlers, and compradors left the coddled foreigners to fend for themselves.

———————

Meanwhile, Elliot busied himself writing a letter to Lin to secure safe passage out of Canton for the residents of the factories. To add to the menace of soldiers just outside his window, a flotilla of small boats containing more soldiers arrived and anchored at the factory docks. After the servants had cleared out, Lin forbade the European residents of the factories to leave the city and stationed soldiers outside the foreign quarter.

Elliot ended up sending his letter demanding passports to Deng Tingzhen, the governor general of the province and nominally Lin's superior. Like his adversary Lin, Elliot knew the psychological power of time limits, and offered Deng one of his own. If permission to depart was not granted within three days, Elliot said he would consider the entire foreign colony hostages, then added a vague threat that implied the powerlessness of his situation by saying he would "act accordingly."

The following day, March 28, 1839, the presence of the soldiers outside turned into a real siege, as they sealed off the factory area street by street. To increase the pressure on the foreigners, the Chinese endlessly banged huge gongs to keep the inhabitants in a sleep-deprived fog. Food was forbidden to be sent to the factories and only two buckets of water were allowed, although local purveyors ignored Lin and smuggled in some provisions and more water with the help of soldiers who had been bribed.

To underline the threat, five hundred additional soldiers began to drill outside the factory windows. The sight must have terrified the occupants, because the new soldiers were their former servants who had been transformed into an ad hoc militia. Perhaps to emphasize the defection of these erstwhile subordinates, they wore pointed hats with the name of their former factories scrawled on them. Worse, the once-ingratiating Cohong now left the factories and took up positions among the soldiers. To prevent escape from the rear, professional soldiers bivouacked out back, but the ferocity of their presence was lessened somewhat by the antiquated matchlock muskets, a century old, aimed at anyone attempting to flee.

The foreigners had to fend for themselves, and their efforts showed how much they had come to depend on the locals to take care of their basic needs. Powerful merchants found themselves sweeping and cleaning, drawing water from the communal spring, and cooking food so unpalatable that their culinary efforts would have been amusing if the need for them hadn't represented their cause—the absence of servants who, rat-like, had fled a sinking ship. Only the Indian merchants didn't suffer, since they had imported servants from their homeland. Dent borrowed a few of the Indians. The British presented the traditional stiff upper lip and killed time with games of cricket and leapfrog. James Matheson perhaps exaggerated the *bonhomie* by saying, "They suffered more from an absence of exercise and from over-feeding than from any actual want of the necessities of life," which was simply not the case.

The "servant problem" paled compared to the scarcity of food. Although in the past, the residents of the factories had imported preserved food like jelly and pickles and manufactures like soap and candles from abroad, perishable food had come from local markets, now out of reach. Loyal servants of Howqua smuggled in some food, but not enough to make up for the embargo.

Whether it was the lack of servants to care for him or the realization that the food shortage would soon turn into a famine, Elliot had a failure of nerves and backed off from his original demand for passports within twenty-four hours of having made it. He sent another letter to Lin with his apologies and a request for a parley with a government official. The weakness of his position was underlined by the fact that he made it clear he was willing to meet with *any* representative of the government, even an underling, which must have spoken volumes about the foreigners' weakness to the protocol- and status-obsessed Chinese.

The next morning, the Europeans woke up to find giant placards affixed to the walls reiterating Lin's demand that all opium supplies be surrendered at once. The Chinese intensified the sense of the factories' containment by nailing the gates of the factories shut. The residents were further unnerved by the sight of thousands of Chinese in adjacent buildings standing on roofs and staring at the captives, fish in a barrel waiting to be shot by matchlocks one hundred years old.

Elliot capitulated. Perhaps to save face, he ordered the opium traders to surrender their stores to him, not Lin. The superintendent sweetened the confiscation by giving his word that the British government would compensate the merchants for their losses, a promise he was not authorized to make. Meanwhile, the pressure intensified when the foreigners saw soldiers scuttling the merchants' small commuter crafts. There would be no escape by sea. The following morning, March 27, 1839, Elliot's confiscation orders were read throughout the factories. "Constrained by paramount motives affecting the safety of the lives and liberty of all the foreigners here present in Canton, and by other very weighty causes, I, Charles Elliot, Chief Superintendent of the Trade of British Subjects in China, do hereby in the name and on behalf of Her Britannic Majesty's government enjoin and require all Her Majesty's subjects now present in Canton forthwith to make a surrender to me for the service of Her said Majesty's government, to be delivered over to the government of China, of all the opium belonging to them, or British opium under their respective control; and to hold the British ships and vessels engaged in the trade of opium subject to my immediate direction."

Elliot also asked for an inventory of the drug supplies and promised that the government would fully reimburse them for the cost of the product, but not the lost profits. Then, almost Lin-like, Elliot added a stick to the carrot of reimbursement: if the merchants held back any of their wares, they wouldn't be reimbursed. Future negotiations would determine the amount of reimbursement.

Lin rewarded the foreigner's compliance by sending 250 cattle to the besieged and famished residents of the factories. Surrendering their opium was a win-win situation for the merchants, with Her Majesty's taxpayers back home picking up the tab for possibly saving the traders' lives and ridding them of a product of which there was already a glut.

A year later, safe at home back in England, some merchants complained to Parliament that Elliot should have turned over to Lin only a portion of their opium while claiming that the amount represented the entirety. But at the moment, these same men were delighted to escape with their necks, the image of the executed Chinese opium dealer still fresh in their minds.

Emboldened by the promised generosity of Parliament, some of the traders got greedy and drew up fantasy figures for their reimbursement, which, they imagined, would include their costs as well and even interest. The possibility of additional profit from interest and the inflated estimate of stores prompted them to turn over everything they had. Alexander Matheson, the nephew and employee of the great *tai pan*, James Matheson, gleefully described doing business with Her Majesty's proxies this way: "The money of the British government was as good as any other money we could get." Since Lin had made it clear that the vast market of China was now closed off to Matheson and his colleagues, the government's money was the only payment they could hope to receive.

The merchants were so happy to get the troublesome drug off their hands, there was no problem meeting Elliot's 6 P.M. deadline of March 27. Some eager traders surrendered their cargoes at 10 A.M. By nightfall, Elliot found himself the nominal owner of more than twenty thousand chests of opium, which the American missionary Elijah Bridgman, in a letter to his compatriot, the merchant C.W. King of Olyphant & Co., overestimated to be worth $20,000,000, although at the top price of

$600 per chest, the real value could not have exceeded $12,000,000. Elliot sent the entire lot to Lin at his headquarters, Consoo House. Elliot must have felt angered and betrayed by Lin's response to his fastidious compliance with the Commissioner's orders. Lin sent bricklayers to seal the entrances and exits to the factories. Communication with the outside world had to be smuggled out through messages wrapped inside cigars and shoes carried by Chinese intermediaries. Even this precarious correspondence dried up when one of the letter carriers was caught and tortured to death. Elliot wrote numerous letters to the Foreign Office, apprising his bosses back home of developments, but he had no way to send them. The act of letter writing may have allowed the powerless Superintendent to feel as though he were doing something, that he was exercising some kind of control in a situation over which, in reality, he had none.

Although Lin believed that the British had surrendered all their stores, he was still waiting for the other foreign merchants, the Indians, French, and American, to comply with his orders—and he held all the foreigners responsible, including the compliant British, until every last chest was surrendered. In fact, Lin now possessed all the foreign-owned opium in Canton. The French were not in Canton at the time. The Dutch didn't deal in opium. And the Americans and Indians disingenuously insisted that the opium in their possession belonged to others; they were merely consignees. Lin ignored the facts and lies and demanded that the other foreigners surrender twenty thousand chests, the same as their British counterparts had, even though such a vast amount did not exist.

The High Commissioner wasn't above doling out more carrots in his big stick negotiations. He offered the foreigners a step deal. When one-fourth of the inventory had been handed over, the Chinese servants would return to the factories. After half had been surrendered, passenger ships would be allowed to depart, which must have heartened the terrified residents. Trading (except, of course, in opium) would be allowed at the three-quarter mark. When all the contraband was in Lin's hands, he offered an anticlimactic reward that "everything [would] proceed as usual," without specifying what "usual" meant.

When the American trader Charles King protested his punishment because he did not trade in opium, Lin postulated collective guilt—and redemption. King's task, the Commissioner admonished him, was to persuade his colleagues to surrender *their* stores. He was his brother's keeper of opium. Canton's Dutch consul, Van Basel, made similar protestations of innocence to Lin and got the same lecture.

The Commissioner wanted his soldiers to carry the opium from the factories to Lankit, an island five miles south of the Bogue Forts and thirty-five miles from Canton. Elliot insisted on his men transporting the contraband to Lankit. Although Lin complained that Elliot was just complicating things, in a rare instance that contrasted with his usual intransigence, he allowed Elliot this small, face-saving gesture. On April 11, Lin and Governor-General Deng arrived at the Bogue. In his journal, Lin noted that fifty chests had been turned over at this point in the crisis. There was much more work to be done before Canton would be free of the devastating import.

The Jardine, Matheson & Co. clippers *Austin* and *Hercules* docked at Lankit first, where they transferred the cargo to chop boats. Choppy water forced the transactions to relocate to nearby Chuanbi. Aboard the *Louisa*, Elliot's deputy, Alexander Johnston, reassured the nervous traders that reimbursement by the British government would be made by handing out receipts for the surrendered chests. The hands-on, micromanager Lin was everywhere, inspecting everything. The process was slow and exhausting; it would be a long time before the quarter mark was reached and the pampered merchants allowed their servants back. On April 11, fifty more chests were confiscated, six hundred the following day, and one thousand the next.

The merchants who remained at the factories gradually got relief from the siege. Food, water, and animal feed were smuggled in. Lin's representatives donated pigs and chickens. On April 12, even though a quarter of the opium had not arrived at Chuanbi, Lin relented and let some of the serving staff return, but apparently not enough to keep the foreign quarters tidy. The factories became filthy, and water continued to remain in short supply since the servants who usually cleaned and carried water were pressed into more pressing duties, like guarding the factories. Desperate games occupied the besieged occupants as they killed time by going on rat hunts, for which there was an increasing number of quarry as the filth piled up in their deteriorating environment.

After three weeks, the surrender of opium had reached the halfway mark, but Lin, despite earlier signs of relenting on his draconian demands, failed to follow through on his promise to allow boats to carry away the residents of the factories. They were simply too valuable a strategic pawn as hostages. Sharing the anger of his cocaptives, Elliot ordered a halt in the surrender of the opium for three days. Lin explained his actions. The ships unloading the contraband had not been full, which led the Commissioner to suspect that the foreigners were retaining some of their contraband. Lin's suspicions were correct. En route to Chuanbi, where the chests were surrendered, some industrious traders had been selling opium to willing buyers along the way, which accounted for the partially filled ships.

Elliot's perseverance evaporated after three days as conditions at the factories worsened. He ordered the resumption of the handover—but at the snail's pace of less than one thousand chests a day. Elliot began to wish he hadn't promised to surrender one thousand chests per day, and Matheson complained to the Superintendent that he never should have offered so much to Lin in the first place. Traders made things worse by loosely packing their chests so that they appeared to be delivering more opium. The arrival of more opium from India helped fill the quota. Finally, on May 21, 20,283 chests of opium had been unloaded at Chuanbi. The delighted Emperor sent Lin two gifts: a roebuck venison, which according to court tradition symbolized a forthcoming promotion, and a beautiful scroll with calligraphy personally written by the Emperor that said "good luck and long life."

When news of the successful confiscation reached India, the price of opium plummeted to $200 a chest (it had gone as high as $600 in the past), since it was presumed that the huge market of China was now closed forever. James Matheson heeded the age-old wisdom of the stockbroker to sell high and buy low by sending $100,000 to India to buy opium at firesale prices.

When news of the siege of the factories reached London, Dent and Matheson's lobbyists went to work stirring up public opinion with pamphlets that exaggerated the plight of the "starving, imprisoned" residents faced with imminent "execution" by the bloodthirsty Chinese. In a case of unabashed jingoism, pamphlets and newspapers reported totally fabricated stories about "some thousands of acres laid down to poppy plantations" owned by the hypocritical Lin, despite the fact that the drug was not cultivated in China at this time.

The factories celebrated the return of their much-missed domestic staff, who cleaned up the area, brought in fresh supplies of water, and relieved the hopeless foreigners who had tried to cook for themselves. Soldiers continued to surround the factories, but gawking neighbors on the rooftops of adjacent buildings seemed to have lost interest in the plight of the hostages and ceased their vigil. Finally, on May 5, a month and a half after Elliot had sailed into Canton, Lin decided that his orders had been complied with and dismissed the soldiers outside the foreign quarter. Ships were allowed to depart, and a day after Lin relented, fifty anxious residents fled the country. Not everyone was allowed to leave, however. Those considered the main participants in the opium trade, Dent, Matheson, and Jardine, had to remain behind until Lin was satisfied that no opium had been held back.

On May 24, Lin believed that all the opium had been confiscated and ordered all merchants who had engaged in the opium trade to leave China and never come back. They sailed out of Canton under the command of Captain Elliot, who, now that he had done Lin's bidding, also found himself *persona non grata*. Symbolically, and with a bow to *faux pas* past, a life-size oil painting of George IV, which may have been brought to China for possible kowtowing, was carted and taken away by the fleeing opium traders. Terrified by the siege, most of the remaining British, including those not involved in the trade, such as missionaries and servants, also fled. The factories were soon decimated. By June, only fifteen Americans, six British, and no Indians remained in the city of Canton. The Americans, however, began secretly selling modern weapons to Lin and accepted on consignment the huge stores of tea that the fleeing British had left behind.

That same month, Lin prepared a conflagration that would show in symbolic and practical terms that he and the Emperor meant business when they set out to destroy the opium trade. Near Chuanbi, Lin had had three holes dug and lined with wood, then flooded with water from the river. Coolies dumped the contents of twenty thousand chests on the ground, then crushed the cakes of opium under foot to make it easier to dissolve in water. The opium was shoveled into the pits and stirred with shovels. The brew gave off a terrible stench as it flowed out of the basins and into the river, thence to the sea, carried away by ocean currents. It took three weeks of this backbreaking work to dissolve and disperse the opium.

Lin had his soldiers witness the destruction and make sure none of the opium was stolen by the workers before it could be destroyed.

The Commissioner was puzzled by the departure of all the British. After all, he had only ordered the British who engaged in the opium trade to leave and never return. Curious, he asked two American traders to meet with him at the site where the opium was being dumped. The Americans, who did not traffic in opium, presented a petition to Lin, asking him to compensate them for the money they had lost in trade during the siege of the factories. Lin sidestepped their request by saying he only received petitions in Chinese; the Americans' request had been in their native tongue. In either form, Lin was not interested in compensating any barbarians. He wanted his own questions answered. Why had all the British fled Canton? he inquired. And what was the best way to contact their Queen, since Her Majesty had still not replied to his letter, which he did not realize had been lost in the mail.

Although disappointed by Lin's refusal to compensate them for the lost trade, the Americans were impressed by Chinese efficiency and obduracy in confiscating the drug imported by foreign devils. "Have we anywhere on record a finer rebuke administered by pagan integrity to Christian degeneracy?" one of the Americans Lin interrogated, Elijah Bridgman, later wrote admiringly in the *Chinese Repository*, an English-language journal published in Canton.

Despite his concern about the exodus of the British, Lin was delighted with the outcome of his stern approach to the opium problem, which he considered solved for good. Lin couldn't have been more wrong. In a letter to the Emperor, he misinterpreted the mind-set of the foreigners and predicted no more trouble. "Judged by their manners, it appears that they feel a sense of shame. Henceforth," he said with glasses so rose-colored as to be opaque, "it seems that all will reform themselves and be greatly improved." Lin presumed the foreigners would get over their snit, and business—except for the opium trade—would return to normal when the new trading season began in the fall.

Fall came, but the British did not return to Canton. Enraged by their monetary losses and traumatized by the siege of the factories, they refused to return to the scene of their humiliation.

Chapter 4

CANTON
BESIEGED

———•+•———

*"The English are full of fright and threaten to clear out,
one and all."*

—British merchant to his sister in London

E lliot's compliance with Lin's orders to hand over the opium had been a feint, not a surrender. While Lin held Elliot's compatriots and others hostage, he had no choice but to comply. But once the foreigners, especially the civilians, were beyond Lin's reach and punishment, Elliot held the upper hand, and he had no intention of surrendering *that* to the Emperor's man.

The foreign colony was an obedient group. Just as they followed Elliot's orders to turn over their valuable contraband, the merchants now heeded his instructions to stay away from Canton. Anger over the confiscation and fear of future hostage situations were not the most compelling motives for Elliot's decision, however. On April 4, 1839, Lin had increased the threat to the foreign community by ordering a new bond to be signed by all merchants entering Canton, promising not to import opium. If contraband were found among the cargo, the entire crew was to be "left to suffer death at the hands of the Celestial Court." Lin had instituted the death penalty for engaging in the opium trade.

The unfortunate fall guys in the dealings between the barbarians and the Celestial Court, Howqua and Mowqua, had the unpleasant task of presenting the decree announcing the bond to promise not to engage in the opium trade to Elliot for his signature. Elliot refused to sign because he was certain that merchants would continue to traffic in the lucrative opium business. Mowqua and Howqua then took the bond before the Chamber of Commerce, which responded by dissolving itself. The luckless Chinese merchants tried Elliot a second time, but with no hostages to protect, the Superintendent of Trade was proving as obdurate as Commissioner Lin. In a letter to the Foreign Secretary, Elliot described his dramatic refusal, which seemed guaranteed to offend Lin and the Emperor: "I tore it up and desired them to tell their officers that they might take my life as soon as they saw fit, but that it was a vain thing to trouble themselves or me any further upon the subject of the bond."

Through Elliot, the British government promised to compensate the opium traders for the confiscation of their cargo a sum of £2.5 million pounds, a fraction of its value of £10 million to £20 million. But Parliament refused to pay for future confiscations. Indeed, there was talk that Parliament would demand that the Chinese government reimburse it for the lost wares, which showed how far apart the two sides were and oblivious to each other's sense of justice. Matheson reviewed the impasse and predicted, "I suppose war with China will be the next step."

Matheson was not a warmonger; he was a seer. The great merchant and other traders did not want war with China. Their legitimate trade in tea and cotton was almost as lucrative as the opium business, and war would snuff out their last source of legal profits. To prevent another hostage crisis, Matheson ordered all his clerks and the rest of the support staff out of Canton and onto his ship the *Hercules*, which was anchored at the mouth of the Canton River and could sail away at the first sign of trouble. He also ignored Lin's order never to return to China, and more ominously, resumed the importation of opium. In a letter to his agents at Bombay, where Jardine, Matheson & Co.'s ships were bursting with opium, he wrote, "I strongly recommend your losing no time in sending back the *Mahommedie* with a full cargo," a euphemism for opium.

While Matheson plotted business as usual, the rest of the foreign colony seemed to be suffering from post-traumatic stress disorder and feared another bout of Chinese encirclement. The trader Abbot Low wrote to his sister Harriet in London, "The English are full of fright and threaten to clear out, one and all."

On May 24, a hint of things to come occurred during a celebration of the Queen's birthday aboard Matheson's ship *Hercules*, which had arrived from India on its owner's orders and lay at anchor at the relatively safe distance of Macao. The Queen's birthday was celebrated with a great deal of rum, and the tipsy crew fired a cannon that struck a Chinese warship by accident. The ship fled, and the Chinese did not lodge a complaint.

In May, Matheson, Dent, twelve other British merchants, and twenty-four Indians sent a letter to Parliament complaining of the money they had lost from Lin's confiscation and demanding British troops be sent to extract compensation by the Chinese.

In June, Elliot allied himself with the war party among the merchants and asked the Foreign Secretary to send warships and troops from India to Canton. Fearing the cost of disruption in trade, Elliot hoped that the troops wouldn't be used for anything more than creating a threat that would bring the Chinese back to the *status quo ante*.

Not all foreigners took a bellicose attitude toward the Chinese, especially those without a profit motive, like the American missionary Wells Williams, who wrote home that he felt gratitude for Lin's confiscation and reiterated the devastation that opium had wrought upon Chinese society—including making it harder for Christian missionaries to attract converts if they were near-comatose. Williams projected his own high moral principles onto a nation more interested in profit than the perfection of men's souls when he predicted that once awareness of opium's insalubrious effects became widely known in Britain, the citizenry would rise as one and commend Lin's eradication efforts. "They will rather applaud the firmness of the Chinese," Williams asserted with misplaced optimism.

Opium was too lucrative to be ended by a single confiscation, no matter how dramatic. Within a month of Lin's seizure, foreign merchants had transferred their headquarters to the Portuguese colony of Macao, sixty miles southeast of Canton. A trade that had been overt now became covert. Communications between the merchants and their ships' captains referred to the various forms of opium by their colors, white and gray—never by the word itself. Ships carrying the drug continued to sail up and down the South China coast, avoiding Canton in favor of friendlier Macao. Government interdiction proved fitful and ineffective. In July, Chinese warships fired on the British ship *Ann* and managed to kill seven of her crew, but the ship avoided capture. The Chinese government had better luck intimidating its own citizens. In the summer of 1839, Matheson guessed that the Chinese were consuming one fifteenth of what they had been buying before Lin's bust. Ironically, Lin's actions had been a business boon to the foreigners. The decreased supply of opium made prices skyrocket. While Dent, Jardine, and Matheson reimmersed themselves in the trade, the American firm of Russell and Company obeyed Lin's orders and imported legal merchandise only.

By mid summer, the remainder of the British had left Canton at Captain Elliot's orders. He mollified the refugees by telling them to bide their time until British troops from India arrived. Most of the other foreigners followed suit until only a handful of American missionaries remained in the city. It seemed that Lin had not only cleared the city of the hated drug, but of the hated barbarians as well.

With no more hostages at stake, Elliot felt free to counterattack Lin, by diplomacy at first. On June 10, 1839, Elliot complained to Lin that the Chinese fleet was stopping British trading ships from going ashore for food and water. Without provisions, Elliot warned that the ships of the two nations might come into conflict. Lin backed off a bit and promised to relocate the Chinese ships, but only for five days, after which the British ships must leave the coast of China. Failure to comply would result in bombardment of the British ships by the Chinese. Lin, however, was bluffing, as the British ships were guarded by the heavily armed *Cambridge*, a merchantman rented by Elliot for £14,000 for eight months. Long after Lin's deadline, the Chinese ships continued to trail the British, but without incident.

Meanwhile, Lin occupied himself with an even more thorough cleansing of the barbarian detritus. On July 7, 1839, he visited the factories and supervised their dismantling. If the foreigners ever returned, they would find nothing to return to and be unable to resume their odious trade. Lin's order was both a symbolic purification and a practical impediment to reoccupation. On the same day that Lin began tearing down the factories in Canton, eighty miles southeast in Hong Kong, a drunken melee ended in tragedy and raised the simmering tension between the Chinese and Europeans to the boiling point.

At this time, Hong Kong was not a city, but a collection of sleepy fishing villages and a few coves used by pirates. As the typhoon season approached in mid summer, opium-carrying ships in Macao sailed forty miles northeast to Hong Kong's harbor, which provided better protection. There, at the end of June, soldiers aboard a Chinese warship arrested the comprador of the British ship the *Carnatic*. Enraged sailors on the *Carnatic* demanded the comprador's return, but their captain hesitated to inflame an already incendiary situation with violence. The sailors seethed and plotted revenge. It was only a matter of time before the resentment boiled over into action. On July 12, 1839, thirty seamen from the *Carnatic* and the *Mangalore*, both owned by Jardine, Matheson & Co., went ashore, joined by colleagues from other British and American ships. At the village of Jianshazui on the Kowloon peninsula north of Hong Kong island, the sailors got hold of a fortified rice wine called *samshu*, with which they proceeded to get blind drunk. Letting out steam after being cooped up in their ships for so long, the men turned into belligerent vandals, destroying a temple and fighting with the locals, one of whom, Lin Weixi, died a day later after a severe beating by the sailors.

Elliot was livid when he heard the news. He had hoped to bide his time and lay low until reinforcements from India arrived. Now a bunch of drunken, murderous tars had put the whole foreign community in peril with no protection from home. The industrious Superintendent rushed to Jianshazui and distributed bribes or reparations: $1,500 to the family of the victim, $200 for evidence leading to the conviction of the murderer(s), $100 as a sop to the rest of the villagers, and $400 to bribe government officials. These were enormous sums for subsistence fishermen, but a vain attempt to paper over murder or manslaughter with money.

Bribery was useless against the incorruptible Lin. When he learned of the sailors' rampage, he demanded that the culprit(s) be handed over to Chinese "justice," which the British presumed, based on the treatment of miscreant foreigners in China like the gunner of the *Lady Hughes*, Terranova, would amount to summary execution by strangling. Chinese law was positively Mosaic in its demand of an eye for an eye, a life for a life.

Lin also launched a propaganda war by posting notices throughout Macao making the unassailable point that if a Chinese had killed a foreigner, Lin would have had him executed immediately. The inference was clear: the murderers of Lin Weixi would receive the same punishment. The only problem was no one knew who had killed the villager or which blow had been fatal in the general melee. The British blamed the American sailors, whom they claimed had imbibed more *samshu*. In his proclamation at Macao, Lin quoted Chinese law that, "He who kills a man must pay the penalty of life." As required by the Act of Parliament that had established the office of Chief Superintendent of Trade, Elliot called a court of inquiry and charged five British sailors with riot and assault, but brought no murder or manslaughter charges. More ominously, he refused to turn over any of the indicted men to Lin. As Lin saw it, the arrogant British had unilaterally set up an extrajudicial institution that denied China's sovereignty.

With no military backup to cover his exercise of judicial authority, Elliot commenced the trial of six of the likeliest suspects aboard a borrowed ship, the *Fort William*, on August 12, 1839. In a gesture that was more bluff than gracious, Elliot invited Lin to send government officials to observe the trial. Lin didn't accept the offer; he retaliated. Three days later, the Commissioner promulgated an edict that forbade the sale of food and water to all British citizens in China on penalty of death. To the foreign community, it seemed like a replay of the factory siege and embargo.

The verdicts of the trial aboard the *Fort William* inflamed the situation. A jury of merchants that included James Matheson rejected murder charges against the *Mangalore's* boatswain, Thomas Tidder. Two sailors were convicted of rioting, fined £25, and sentenced to six months imprisonment—in England. (When they returned home, the prisoners were immediately set free on the grounds that Elliot's jerry-rigged tribunal had no jurisdiction—apparently despite the fact that under the Act of Parliament, he was expressly appointed to preside over "a Court of Justice with Criminal and Admiralty Jurisdiction for the trial of offences committed by His Majesty's subjects in the said Dominions or on the high sea within a hundred miles from the coast of China." It was a point the Chinese would have agreed with, but for different reasons.) On August 17, 1839, Lin ordered Elliot to hand over the murderer without specifying the perpetrator's identity. Even if Elliot had wanted to comply, the diplomat knew the uproar that the surrender of a British citizen would cause back home.

Cut off from supplies during Lin's embargo, the British soon found themselves once again without their Chinese servants. Portuguese hired to replace them also fled within a few days. Chinese warships began to sail into

Hong Kong Harbor. Wells and streams on the island were poisoned. Lin left Canton and arrived in Xiangshan, forty miles north of Macao. Rumors spread that the Imperial Commissioner would invade Hong Kong.

Matheson quickly boarded a ship, ready to flee at the first sign of attack. Elliot sent his wife and two-year-old son to the dubious protection of the *Fort William*, where the trial of the drunken sailors had taken place. A few days later, he joined his family aboard the ship. On August 24, 1839, Macao's governor, Don Adraio Accacio da Silveira Pinto, announced that the Chinese had ordered him to expel the British from the colony. The Governor secretly warned an employee of the merchant Lancelot Dent that the Chinese planned to surround every dwelling in Macao that housed British subjects and seize them. Pinto himself wanted the British to leave before Lin turned his attention and wrath on the Portuguese residents of Macao.

The same day, tensions increased when two ships belonging to Jardine, Matheson & Co., the *Harriet* and *Black Joke*, arrived in Macao. *Black Joke* lived up to its name and more so. There was blood all over her decks, and the crew had disappeared. The *Harriet* had towed the ghost ship into the harbor. It was soon learned that the night before, unidentified Chinese had boarded the ship as it passed the island of Lantao, eight miles east of Hong Kong, and massacred the entire crew except a sailor who had jumped overboard and saved himself from drowning by clinging to the ship's rudder. The Chinese marauders spared the single civilian passenger on the *Black Joke*, an Englishman named Joe Moss, but they cut off his left ear and stuffed it into his mouth, then left him to die of his wounds. After ransacking the ship's wares, they were about to burn the vessel when the *Harriet* showed up, whereupon the intruders fled.

Moss informed Matheson of the atrocity and speculated that the attackers had been pirates and not acting on government orders. The by-now-hysterical residents of Macao didn't believe Moss's theory and feared that the same government animus that had led to the massacre would soon be directed toward them. Governor Pinto grew so alarmed by the attack on the *Black Joke* that he ordered all British citizens to leave Macao within twenty-four hours. Rumors spread that soldiers camped outside the colony were about to attack, and the threat seemed more real when the Chinese servants of the British refugees fled the city. To protect his guests during their exodus, Governor Pinto generously placed soldiers around those British who had not already fled to the dubious safety of ships in the harbor.

The *Black Joke's* fate, the rumors, and Pinto's decree were effective. The desperate refugees didn't need to be coaxed; within twelve, not twenty-four, hours, 250 of them, everyone except a nursing mother and a gravely ill woman, had boarded eighteen ships in the harbor—though foul weather kept the ships momentarily in port. A day later, psychological and military relief arrived at Macao in the form of the *Volage*, a gunboat from India bristling with twenty-six cannon. The *Volage* not only brought armaments, but good news. Another fighting ship, the *Hyacinth*, with eighteen guns, would arrive shortly. The following day, the wind and rain abated, and the flotilla of refugees set out from Macao for the Kowloon peninsula above Hong Kong.

Lin was exhilarated when he learned of the exodus. "No doubt they have on their ships a certain stock of dried provisions; but they will very soon find themselves without the heavy, greasy meat dishes for which they have such a passion," he wrote to the Emperor. The Chinese frowned on beef eaters because oxen were needed to plow the land and feed the exploding population.

On September 1, 1839, Lin received a letter from the Emperor that demonstrated the Imperial Court's demonization and ignorance of the foreigners, which only made Lin's job of dealing with them that much harder. The Emperor wanted to know if it was true that the barbarians bought thousands of female children and used them in their diabolical rites. Lin wrote back that the foreigners employed Chinese adults as plantation workers and miners, and a handful of youngsters worked with them, but no black magic was involved in their employment.

The Emperor also inquired about the claim that imported opium contained human flesh, which the Emperor suspected might explain the drug's preternatural addictive power. Lin knew that rumor to be preposterous, but it amounted to *lèse majesté* to contradict the Son of Heaven, so the diplomatic diplomat replied that opium might contain the flesh of crows and second-handedly of humans, based on his knowledge that Indian importers of opium allowed crows to eat human corpses as a ritual means of disposing of the dead.

Lin decided to visit Macao and thank Pinto for complying with his orders to expel the British, although the real purpose of his trip was to demonstrate that the Chinese controlled Macao and that the Portuguese only leased the island and adjacent mainland. Pinto sent a representative to greet Lin on the outskirts of the colony and received him with full honors, including one hundred Portuguese soldiers. When Lin arrived, he was followed by heavily armed Chinese troops. The pleasantries that followed belied the presence of men on both sides armed to the teeth. Lin gave Pinto and his officers gifts of silk, fans, tea, and candy; Pinto's enlisted men received beer, mutton, wine, and $400 in cash (silver). Lin's munificence belied the contempt in which he held his hosts and that he confided to his diary. Lin seemed to echo the Imperial court's view of foreigners when he wrote, "The bodies of the men are tightly encased from head to toe. They look like actors playing the part of foxes. They have heavy beards, much of which they shave, leaving only one curly tuft. Indeed, they do really look like devils."

If Lin's entourage were meant to intimidate, it had minimal effect on the foreigners who remained at Macao. American merchants still in Macao noticed that although armed to the teeth, the Chinese soldiers' weapons—bows and arrows, pikes, halberds, and matchlock rifles—were vintage sixteenth-century arms. The anachronistic display of antique power hinted at the outcome of any conflict between the museum-piece quality Chinese military and the modern British army. It would be the Medieval Era fighting the Industrial Age. As Lin toured Macao, oblivious to the mismatch, he felt encouraged by the sight of ceremonial arches decorated with silk and flowers to commemorate the expulsion of the barbarians.

The Commissioner decided to expel the refugees from their new sanctuary in Hong Kong by cutting off their water supplies. There were now seventy British ships with several thousand aboard in Hong Kong's harbor, and the mass of refugees was growing restless, for good reason. Elliot, also in Hong Kong, suspected that men aboard three Chinese warships in the harbor had been poisoning wells and stopping food from arriving. He sent three ships, the *Louisa*, the *Volage*, and the *Pearl*, to attack the Chinese warships that patrolled the harbor.

Before the attack began, Elliot made one last stab at diplomacy. He sent an interpreter and missionary, the Reverend Dr. Karl Gutzlaff, who had translated Elliot's demands into Mandarin, to deliver them to the local official. The demands included a threat of reprisals if food shipments were not restored and a plea for the locals not to poison the colony's springs that furnished drinking water. The officials were polite, but insisted that they lacked the authority to renew victualing. Elliot ratcheted up the negotiations by threatening to bombard the Chinese warships if provisioning didn't resume by 2 P.M. Two o'clock came and went with no response from the Chinese, so Captain Henry Smith of the *Volage* fired on the nearest Chinese ship. It was the first shot of the First Opium War, and the Chinese named it the Battle of Kowloon.

The outdated cannon aboard the Chinese craft aimed too high and missed the British ships, but the British soon ran out of cartridges and tried to escape, with the much larger Chinese ships in pursuit. Fortunately, the wind died and with it the ability of the warring parties to continue the fight, which ended in a stalemate. Frustrated, Elliot called off the attack, and the Chinese ships sailed back into Hong Kong Harbor when the wind returned, renewing the threat to the beleaguered British. The following day, Elliot sent a face-saving report to the Foreign Office. "The violent and vexatious measures heaped upon Her Majesty's officers and subjects will I trust serve to excuse those feelings of irritation which have betrayed me into a measure that I am certain, under less trying circumstances, would be difficult indeed of vindication."

For millennia, the Chinese had rewritten history to suit political aims and save face. This revisionist double-think happened again when the commander of the Chinese ships reported to Lin a great victory over the British interlopers, including the sinking of enemy ships and inflicting fifty casualties. (There was, in fact, no British loss of life or ships.)

The captain of the *Volage* begged Elliot to let him confront the Chinese ships in Hong Kong Harbor again, certain of victory over the decrepit fleet. Elliot refused, fearing the outbreak of a wider conflagration without the Foreign Minister's approval. Despite the Chinese claims of victory, the damage done to the Chinese ships seems to have made the Imperial government reconsider its treatment of the refugees. A few days after the battle, food suddenly appeared in Hong Kong, and signs warning that the wells had been poisoned disappeared, which, since the toxins remained, seemed a dubious and dangerous concession to the enemy.

While Hong Kong simmered, Macao erupted in new conflict. A Spanish brig, the *Bilbaino*, was set ablaze by the Chinese. It was a tactical and technical mistake. Earlier in the day, a British ship had sneaked into Macao and unloaded its stores of opium, then sailed away just as the *Bilbaino* arrived. Lin's men confused the two ships with disastrous results, torching the noncombatant Spanish vessel. Pinto armed his ships in response, and Elliot volunteered to send the Governor of Macao ammunition, which was not needed because the Chinese backed off. The crisis settled into another poisonous stalemate.

Lin now had another problem, a personal one, in the form of an excruciating hernia. Chinese doctors failed to alleviate his pain, so the Commissioner visited the offices of Dr. Peter Parker, a Yale-educated medical missionary. Parker fitted Lin with a truss that ameliorated his pain and gave the mandarin five additional trusses to take with him, Parker's entire supply. As he convalesced, Lin spent his time reviewing the troops and overseeing war games. He also began writing a poem that showed how much he underestimated the military superiority of his opponents and which provided an ironic interpretation of the outcome of the Battle of Kowloon: "A vast display of Imperial might had shaken all the foreign tribes/And if they now confess their guilt we shall not be too hard on them." It was wishful thinking in meter. If the war games gave him any comfort, it was of the delusional kind: the Chinese engaged in mock battles that consisted of exchanges of arrows and spears, as once again the sixteenth century collided with the nineteenth.

In Hong Kong, Elliot was encouraged by the arrival of the warship the *Hyacinth*. The beleaguered Superintendent welcomed the extra firepower, but it didn't turn him into a hawk. He realized that the only permanent solution to the conflict between Britain and China was the eradication of the opium trade, and to that end, he ordered all British and Indian importers of opium to leave Hong Kong. But there was simply too much money to be made, and few of the opium traders complied with Elliot's orders. Elliot's attempt at compliance with the Chinese ban on opium seems to have softened Lin's hard-line stance. The unpunished sailors who had gone on the drunken rampage in Jianshazui continued to rankle the Chinese, but perhaps out of weariness or fear, while Lin continued to demand the surrender of the culprit(s), his demand was becoming more *pro forma* than heartfelt. Finally, the anger caused by the murder, which had set off the current hostilities, dissipated when a sailor from a Jardine Matheson ship was drowned, and the Chinese volunteered to let the dead sailor be identified as the murderer of the Jianshazui villager.

As tension subsided, one sticking point to the resumption of British trade was the bond Lin continued to demand that all merchants sign, promising not to import opium on pain of death. Elliot and his bosses in London blanched at the thought of imposing the death penalty for engaging in a business they knew would continue, however *sub rosa*.

While Elliot balked, some of his countrymen undercut his resolve to resist the bond. In October, when a British cargo ship, the *Thomas Coutts*, sailing from Bombay under the command of a Captain Warner, reached the mouth of the Canton River with its cargo of cotton and no opium, the captain broke ranks and agreed to sign the bond since he wasn't in the opium business and the death penalty imposed by the bond was irrelevant to him. The captain was emboldened by a legal opinion he had secured in Bombay that said Elliot's ban on signing the bond had no force in English law. He offloaded his cargo and sailed away without incident, but with a new mission—as Commissioner Lin's courier. Lin was delighted with Warner's defection and felt he could trust the captain, to whom he gave a copy of his letter to Queen Victoria deploring the devastation of opium coupled with threats if the trade did not stop.

Warner made good on his promise. Upon his arrival in London, he handed the letter over to the eponymous co-owner of the *Thomas Coutts*, who asked for an appointment with Lord Palmerston so he could deliver Lin's complaint. When Palmerston's office refused to see him, he forwarded Lin's letter to *The Times of London*, which unlike the Prime Minister, was interested in the message and published it.

Lin was shocked then delighted when he learned that another British vessel was also willing to sign the bond. Encouraged by this crack in British resistance, Lin decided the corpse of the drowned sailor would not do as the Jianshazui perpetrator after all, and renewed his demand that the murderer be handed over for Chinese justice. Failure to comply would result in the expulsion of the entire British colony, Lin warned.

In the fall of 1839, thirty-eight British trading vessels with members of twenty-eight trading companies aboard remained in Hong Kong Harbor.

Accommodations were cramped, and shipboard life was expensive to maintain. Elliot begged Governor Pinto to let his charges return to Macao, but by now the British had become dangerous pariahs, and Pinto declined, fearing that the Portuguese's lucrative trade in opium, amounting to £20,000 per annum, would be put at risk and Portugal dragged into the impending war.

Elliot's hands were tied. He could not hand over the Jianshazui culprit, even if he had been so inclined to surrender British judicial sovereignty, so he prepared for war. A letter he received from Palmerston on October 20, 1839, informing him that by early next summer, sixteen British ships with four thousand troops aboard would arrive and rescue the ship-bound hostages in Hong Kong Harbor, reinforced Elliot's bellicosity. In the meantime, he decided not to wait for these promised reinforcements to arrive because he feared other British merchants not engaged in the opium trade would follow the example of the *Thomas Coutts* and sign the bond. Indeed, the British *Royal Saxon*, carrying rice from Java and recently arrived in Canton Harbor, was rumored to be the next defector willing to sign the bond.

Elliot reasoned that fresh military actions would poison relations between the two nations and make it impossible for potential defectors to treat with the Chinese. Lin's next action provided him with a justification to renew hostilities: toward the end of October 1839, the Imperial Commissioner ordered all British ships to leave Canton within three days. Elliot quickly set sail for the Bogue aboard the *Volage*, with the *Hyacinth* behind him.

When the ships reached Chuanbi near the mouth of the river on November 2, 1839, they ran into a Chinese fleet consisting of fifteen war junks and fourteen fire ships commanded by the old and revered Admiral Kuan. During the next day, Elliot and Kuan exchanged a series of notes, each trying to ferret out the intentions of the other. Kuan threatened to seize the ship in which he incorrectly believed that the Jianshazui murderer was lodged. Kuan wrote Elliot, "All I want is the murderous barbarian who killed Lin Weixi. As soon as a time is named when he will be given up, my ships will return into the Bogue. Otherwise, by no means whatsoever shall I accede." Kuan's demand was a smokescreen for his real goal—expelling the British from Canton.

Elliot failed to persuade Kuan that his presence was not intended as a military threat. The Admiral's fleet began to maneuver into a position from which it could attack the British merchant fleet that was gathered just below the Bogue. As Kuan maneuvered, the *Royal Saxon* arrived on the scene on its way to Canton. With Elliot anxious to prevent a repitition of the *Thomas Coutts* embarrassment, Captain Henry Smith of the *Volage* fired a warning shot across the *Royal Saxon's* bows to prevent the ship from entering the river. Smith simultaneously warned Kuan not to approach the British ships. Unintimidated, but still wary of provoking a full-blown conflict, Kuan anchored his ships in position between the British warships and the merchant fleet they were supposed to be protecting. Smith, anxious about the tactical position in which he found himself, pressed for an attack, but Elliot hesitated.

The following day, November 3, 1839, Elliot gave in to Smith's pressure. The British ships approached the Chinese warships and began to fire broadsides into them. The stationary guns aboard the Chinese vessels could not be aimed effectively and fired over the masts of the British ships. A lucky volley hit one of the Chinese warship's magazines, and, after exploding, it sank. The Chinese began to panic as the *Volage* continued to score hits at close range. Three more Chinese ships sank. Crews on other ships jumped overboard. The entire Chinese fleet sailed away, except for Kuan's flagship, which suicidally stayed and returned the British fire. Kuan's single ship posed a minimal threat, and Elliot, impressed by the old man's courage, ordered Smith to discontinue the barrage, allowing the damaged Chinese flagship to sail off. The way to Canton was now clear.

The sea battle came to be known as the Battle of Chuanbi, and the results of the altercation did not bode well for the Chinese in any future naval conflict. Twenty-six Chinese ships, the largest fleet the Chinese could muster, were bested by two small British warships. The British suffered no fatal casualties (one sailor was wounded). The medieval had once again collided with the modern, and the outcome seemed preordained.

While the *Royal Saxon* sailed on to Canton, Elliot returned to the relative safety of Macao and waited for the inevitable Chinese response of outrage and indignation generated by the first blows struck in what would be christened the Opium War by *The Times of London*.

Chapter 5

THE BLACK HOLE OF CANTON

"Her Majesty's government by no means disputes the right
of the government of China to prohibit the importation
of opium into China."

—Lord Palmerston, British Foreign Secretary, 1840

As news of the sea battle in China reached England, the government remained in denial about the cause of the friction, which was the opium trade. On May 2, 1839, John Trotter, a member of the Board of Control, which would later be called the Secretariat of State for India, dismissed the misery caused by the drug. "During the nearly nine years I was attached to the Benares Agency [in India], I never knew one solitary instance of impaired health amongst natives resulting from the use of the drug, not even in the factories, where the people passed twelve hours a day in an opium atmosphere and ate as much as they could consume."

So why were British and Chinese warships slugging it out in a mismatched battle at the mouth of the Canton River? In a letter to a British officer stationed in India, Captain C.R.D. Bethune of the India-based ship the *Conway* offered an explanation for the war, which to modern ears sounds like a classic case of projection. Bethune wrote that the Chinese government didn't care about the health of its population. What it really cared about was the depletion of its silver supplies to pay for the drug, ironically the same concern that had propelled Britain into the business. "I don't think they care two pence about the immorality of using opium," Captain Bethune wrote.

British merchants and opium cultivators in India suffered huge financial losses as the price of the drug plummeted after Lin's confiscation, with a chest of opium falling from 750 rupees to 300. On June 4, 1839, the Bombay Chamber of Commerce sent a petition to the Queen demanding compensation for the opium that Lin had confiscated in Canton, as Elliot had promised the government would. The Bombay businessmen demanded not only compensation, but military action to ensure no further seizures would take place.

The Chamber of Commerce in Calcutta also expressed concern about the catastrophic loss of business, but couched its concerns in a humanitarian way, sending reports back to London that the foreign colony was on the brink of "rapine and massacre," an exaggeration of Lin's actions in Canton, which included a siege, but no rapine or massacre. Members of the Calcutta Chamber played on the hysteria still aroused by the memory of the Black Hole of 1756, in which 123 British imprisoned in a tiny jail cell by a Bengali potentate died of neglect, and warned of similar atrocities in China.

Meanwhile, a group of lobbyists who had formed in Canton during the siege of the factories arrived in London to add a human presence to the provocative correspondence from India's business centers. It was an impressive lobby consisting of Robert Inglis, Dent's partner; Hugh Hamilton Lindsay; James Matheson's nephew, Alexander; the former captain of the *Hercules*, Alexander Grant; John Abel Smith, a Liberal MP and a partner in an opium-exporting firm; and William Jardine himself. Together, they represented what today might be called Big Opium. Like modern lobbyists, they enlisted the help of friendly journalists. Matheson wrote to Jardine, "You may find it expedient to secure the services of some leading newspaper to advocate the cause and [use] literary men to compose the requisite memorials in the most concise and clear shape."

While the lobbyists were united in their support of the opium trade, they could not agree on the best methods to save it from dissolution by the zealous Lin. Matheson had refused to sign a declaration composed by Dent that not only demanded compensation for the confiscated opium chests (with which Matheson concurred), but included a justification for the opium trade (which Matheson thought better left implied than stated since a powerful coalition among the English clergy allied itself with Lin in condemning the trade). Dent eventually came around to his colleague's reticence about the morality of the trade. "Quite irrelevant, opening up questions and vindicating things that require no vindication," Dent wrote to Jardine.

Because of opposition within Britain to the opium trade, Matheson remained pessimistic that Parliament would intervene to save the beleaguered opium traders of Canton. He suspected that Lin was aware of the anti-opium party in Britain, and believed it added to his obduracy. "He [Lin] perhaps knows enough of what I must be excused for terming the senseless clamor of the High Church party against the traffic, to hope for the cooperation of our Government in his designs," Matheson wrote to his ally, the MP John Abel Smith. Matheson, perhaps blinded by profit or racism, remained oblivious to the pernicious effect of the drug, claiming that no Chinese had "in the least been bestialized" by its use, and insisting that the narcotic was on a par with (and as harmless as) the British love of champagne and brandy. Matheson wanted to impress that "fact" on the Foreign Secretary. Fortunately for Matheson, Palmerston was not intimidated by the Anglican Church's denunciation of the opium trade, his base of power being the merchant class, not the prelacy.

As the pro- and anti-opium lobbies pressured Parliament, pamphleteers composed denunciations of the "abominable vice" of opium trafficking and use. While a hostage in the Canton factories, merchant Charles King of Olyphant & Co. wrote to Captain Elliot gently begging him to help end the trade. King's letter was turned into a pamphlet. A radical Anglican vicar, Algernon Thelwall, composed a more forceful tract, "Iniquities of the Opium Trade with China," a diatribe based on a wealth of facts about the misery caused by the drug that he had culled from Canton's English-language journal, the *Chinese Repository*. Thelwall's pamphlet received national attention when it was reprinted in the *Times of London*. Palmerston, however, remained unmoved by the condemnation and offered a cynical reason for the clamor in England against Demon Opium. In the margin of his copy of Thelwall's pamphlet, the Foreign Secretary attributed the anti-opium activism to unemployed lobbyists—"...most probably the work of anti-slavery agitators whose occupation is in a great measure gone," referring to the abolition of slavery in the British Empire in 1834! The troublemakers were out of work and needed gainful employment, Palmerston believed, and his plan of action was inaction. He would simply ignore the problem, hoping that indifference would make it go away.

The opium merchants were determined to change Palmerston's do-nothing approach. A parade of China notables made the pilgrimage to his office, including John Abel Smith; George Larpent, chairman of the London East India and China Association; and Sir Alexander Johnston, a government bureaucrat from Sri Lanka who brought with him desperate letters from Canton. Jardine and Captain Alexander Grant of the *Hercules* brought maps of China to their meeting with Palmerston and offered unsolicited advice on where to attack the ossified Chinese army. Not all of Palmerston's importuners were hawks on China. Larpent told the Foreign Secretary that if the Chinese were indeed sincere about abolishing the opium trade, Britain would need to find a new source of revenue to pay for Chinese tea. Unfortunately, Larpent had no substitute product to offer, and he and his trade group were in the minority. Most of the opium traders believed that the Chinese show of might against the factories had to be met with a commensurate show of arms by Britain.

At the center of the controversy in Canton, Captain Elliot added his voice—and letters—to the war party soon after the naval Battle of Chuanbi. "It appears to me, my Lord, that the response to all these unjust violences should be in the form of a swift and heavy blow unprefaced by one word of communication," he wrote to Palmerston on November 16, 1839. Despite his hawkishness, Elliot aligned himself with the High Church's condemnation of the opium trade as demonstrated by his letter to Palmerston: "No man entertained a deeper detestation of the disgrace and sin of this forced traffic on the coast of China. [There was] little to choose between it and piracy. As a public officer I have steadily discountenanced it by all the lawful means in my power, and at the total sacrifice of my private comfort in the society in which I have lived for years." Elliot couldn't know it at the time, but his handling of the crisis would also lead to public discomfort and his personal disgrace.

Palmerston's original indifference gave way to a plan of limited intervention. At a cabinet meeting on April 24, 1840, he read aloud Elliot's letters, which insisted that all it would take to solve the "China problem" were one warship, two frigates, three steamers, and some small armed vessels, which would be enough to blockade the coast from Peking to Canton. Francis Baring, Chancellor of the Exchequer, cooled the war fever by inquiring where the money was to come from to finance this small-scale action, especially since the government was already pledged to reimburse the China merchants for the £2.5 million worth of opium that had been confiscated.

Further complicating the strategy against China was the weakness of Prime Minister Melbourne's Whig government, which held power by a tiny majority. With the government threatening to fall at any moment, was this really a good time to launch a foreign adventure, no matter how limited in scope? Plus, the Exchequer was basically broke. Unbalanced budgets had produced huge deficits of £1 million pounds or more per annum for the past three years. Melbourne believed that a weak Parliament would never grant the funds to reimburse the traders for the £2.5 million of lost opium, much less an even more expensive war halfway around the world.

Goaded by his Secretary of State for War, however, the legendary eighty-nine-year-old historian Thomas Babington Macaulay, Melbourne came up with an ingenious way to fight a war against the Chinese—make them pay for it. After a brief conflict, which Melbourne expected would be a quick and efficient rout, China would be forced to pay reparations, which would serve as reimbursement for the opium chests it had confiscated. The plan had a neat tautology to it. Ignoring searing editorials in the *Times*, which described the Palmerston plan as "suicide," the Foreign Minister sent orders to Elliot to prepare for war.

Mindful of public opinion, especially religious radicals, the Foreign Secretary paid lip service to the evils of the opium trade while hatching plans to ensure it survived and thrived. In a letter to Elliot, he wrote, "Her Majesty's government by no means disputes the right of the government of China to prohibit the importation of opium into China." Officially, the might of the British navy would be sent to China not to promote the opium trade, but to protect the British colony there from another hostage situation orchestrated by Lin. Palmerston's letter accused the Chinese of trying to exterminate the British merchants "by the cruel process of starvation." British honor would be avenged. If the opium trade, which had provided a windfall of tax revenue for the government, flourished because of this military action, it would only be a natural offshoot, not its cause. In another century and another place, Palmerston would have made a brilliant casuist and courtier.

Jardine and his colleagues were elated by Palmerston's decision, not caring if higher principles motivated him as long as they could continue to do business as usual. In the meantime, Jardine asked the government to reimburse him and his associates for the opium lost to Lin. The weak, bankrupt government ignored Jardine's petition. Millions for defense, not one penny for compensation. The cash would come from the Chinese after their defeat, the skeptical merchants were told. Palmerston explained to the Canton traders that Parliament would not vote the reimbursement money, and he made sure by not even bringing the subject to a vote. The government could not risk falling just to satisfy some out-of-pocket drug dealers.

Chapter 6

THE BATTLE
IN BRITAIN

———·+·———

*"A war more unjust in its origin, a war calculated in its progress to cover this country with a permanent disgrace, I do not know and I have not read of...
[Our] flag is become a pirate flag, to protect an infamous traffic."*

—Opposition MP William Gladstone, 1840

The British believed a quick victory inevitable. The merchant Bennet Forbes said in January 1840, "Chances are five to one that we are all out of Canton in three months." Tension fueled by threats increased among the foreign community. Abandoning dangerous Canton for the dubious safety of Macao, Elliot became alarmed by the appearance of signs posted all over town announcing the imminent arrival of Chinese soldiers to expel the foreigners. Although the military didn't materialize and the expulsion didn't take place—perhaps because Captain Smith's warship the *Hyacinth* patrolled the waters off Macao—Elliot thought it expedient to send his wife and son to Singapore when he returned to Canton. There, on February 14, 1840, Jardine's clipper *Mor* arrived from England with a letter to Elliot from Palmerston. Its contents, which he was ordered not to reveal, delighted Elliot, for they promised the imminent arrival of land and naval reinforcements in Canton.

Back in England, Palmerston's letter to Elliot was not revealed, and Parliament remained Sphinx-like about its intentions toward China, as exemplified at its opening in January 1840 when Queen Victoria gave a Delphic speech that simply said "attention was being paid" to the China problem. Palmerston promised that no British taxes would be used to reimburse the opium merchants for their confiscated chests, but that was as close as he got to any specifics. An interview he gave the *Times* after the opening of Parliament was a masterpiece of obfuscation. Thoroughly unsatisfied, Sir Robert Peel, the leader of the Tory opposition, introduced a bill of censure that condemned the government's military response to the opium crisis in China.

During the debate on Peel's motion, a thirty-year-old Tory MP, William Gladstone, the future Prime Minister, delivered a career-making speech that denounced the opium trade. Gladstone's zealousness came from personal acquaintance with the havoc wrought by the drug. His beloved twenty-four-year-old sister, Helen, had been prescribed laudanum during a painful illness and had become addicted to the elixir. Her dependence on laudanum became well known and created a scandal in God-fearing, drug-hating, laudanum-swilling Victorian England. At the time of his speech, Gladstone had just returned from a trip to Italy with his sister, where he sought unsuccessful treatment for her addiction. He then suffered a nervous breakdown, but recovered enough to participate in the Parliamentary debate.

Referring to Macaulay, the Secretary of State for War, who had urged escalating military action in China, and had said, "I beg to declare my earnest desire that this most rightful quarrel may be prosecuted to a triumphal close [and] that the name not only of English valour but of English money may be established," Gladstone countered:

> Does he [Macaulay] know that the opium smuggled into China comes exclusively from British ports, that is, from Bengal and through Bombay? That we require no preventive service to put down this illegal traffic? We have only to stop the sailing of the smuggling vessels…it is a matter of certainty that if we stopped the exportation of opium from Bengal and broke up the depot at Lintin [near Canton] and checked the cultivation of it in Malwa [an Indian province] and put a moral stigma on it, we should greatly cripple if not extinguish the trade in it.
>
> They [the Chinese government] gave you notice to abandon your contraband trade. When they found you would not do so they had the right to drive you from their coasts on account of your obstinacy in persisting with this

infamous and atrocious traffic...justice, in my opinion, is with them [the Chinese]; and whilst they, the Pagans, the semi-civilized barbarians have it on their side, we, the enlightened and civilized Christians, are pursuing objects at variance both with justice and with religion...a war more unjust in its origin, a war calculated in its progress to cover this country with a permanent disgrace, I do not know and I have not read of. Now, under the auspices of the noble Lord [Macaulay], that flag is become a pirate flag, to protect an infamous traffic.

Palmerston's rebuttal speech in the House of Commons blamed the buyers, not the sellers, for the epidemic of opium use in China. "I wonder what the House would have said to me if I had come down to it with a large naval estimate for a number of revenue cruisers...for the purpose of preserving the morals of the Chinese people, who were disposed to buy what other people were disposed to sell them?" Palmerston added that the practical effect of halting British opium exports to China would include Turkey and Persia picking up the slack and servicing the millions of Chinese who were "disposed to buy." Palmerston also quoted in his speech a recent petition he had received, cowritten by William Jardine and backed by his fellow opium traders: "Unless measures of the government are followed up with firmness and energy, the trade with China can no longer be conducted with security to life and property, or with credit or advantage to the British nation," the petition said. Palmerston's practicality trumped Gladstone's moral misgivings, as Peel's vote of censure against the government's handling of the Opium War was defeated in the House of Commons by a close vote of 271 to 262.

———·—·——

News of Palmerston's military preparations in Calcutta for an attack on China was leaked to the British press in March 1839, and the *Times* announced, "War Declared on China." British hawks floated a trial balloon urging that after hostilities had brought China to heel, the country would be transformed into another British Raj and an even bigger jewel in the British crown. The *Bombay Gazette* conjured up the fantasy that many believed would become lucrative reality: "Only imagine the brother to the Sun and Moon [the Chinese Emperor] a pensioner on our Government for half a million a year while a British Ministry manages his affairs." The Son of Heaven would become another compliant *maharajah* or *Aga Khan*. If India was a gold mine for the British, many hoped that China would be a platinum lode. Paternalism and profit were an intoxicating combination.

A month after the Whigs eluded the vote of censure, another debate over the "China question" began in the House of Commons in April 1840. Sir James Graham, an opposition MP, entered a motion that excoriated the Prime Minister's management of war preparations, but did not condemn the coming war itself. It was not a House divided over war, but the proposed means of prosecuting it that the Tories lambasted, having discerned the public sentiment and realizing that a pacifist position would weaken the party and prevent its return to power, which seemed imminent as Melbourne's government equivocated. Graham saved his special venom for the Foreign Office, which he accused of abandoning Elliot during the siege of the factories and Lin's opium confiscation. Graham said it was unfair that the British had been forbidden to trade with China while other opium importers, especially the Americans, picked up Britain's trade, costing the treasury millions of dollars in opium taxes.

Graham harangued the House for three days while ignoring the issue of the morality of the opium trade itself. Only Gladstone continued to be distressed by the drug's destructiveness, and he once again revived the ugly subject that business interests and jingoists had tried to ignore. Gladstone pointed out that everyone knew the addictive, devastating properties of the drug. The Chinese prohibition and confiscation of it were not an abrogation of British authority and fiscal interests, but a justified execution of Chinese sovereignty. Gladstone, horrified by military preparations in India, repeated his earlier rhetoric, claiming that they would lead to "a war more unjust in its origin, a war more calculated in its progress to cover this country with permanent disgrace."

Gladstone would turn out to be a better Prime Minister than seer. Treading on dangerous waters that could have sunk his blossoming Parliamentary career, he even defended the Chinese poisoning of wells that supplied the factories in Canton as a justified means of expelling the opium traders. But towing the Tory line and the party's sense that the military die had already been cast in the public mind, Gladstone stopped short of demanding that military preparations in India cease.

Palmerston replied that Graham's condemnation of the government's handling of the situation in China had nothing to do with mismanagement and everything to do with trying to get the Whig government, with its razor-thin majority, to fall. A bald power grab masqueraded as just criticism of government ineptitude, he said. Palmerston pointed out that China's real objection to the opium trade was fiscal, not moral or health-related. The Chinese government, he noted, allowed cultivation of opium in its own country, although the Foreign Secretary failed to mention that homegrown production was infinitesimal compared to the transshipment of the drug from India. China's real concern, Palmerston said, was the outflow of silver from China to Britain to pay for opium. His speech deracinated Graham's motion of censure, and the Tories failed to carry it—but by only nine votes.

The debate also played itself out in the House of Lords, where Lord Stanhope, in a lonely minority position, reiterated Gladstone's flat-out condemnation of the opium trade and the government's complicity in it. A member of his own party, however, the Duke of Wellington, undercut Graham's position. The hero of Waterloo remained a hawk into his seventies, and senescence hadn't mellowed the Iron Duke, who had also voted against Catholic Emancipation and extended suffrage. Even a stroke had failed to take the fire out of the old warrior. He rose in the Lords and gave a speech praising Elliot's bravery in saving the British colony in Canton, honest businessmen who, he said, had suffered unbearable wrongs at the hands of the Chinese, whose punishment he now clamored for.

Melbourne found himself in the unusual position of agreeing with a member of the opposition and claimed that opium smoking was no more dangerous than downing a bottle of fine wine, then undercut his own argument by conceding that if it were indeed a scourge, the Chinese were addicted anyway and if the British didn't sell them the stuff, someone else would. At least half of Melbourne's assessment was accurate, and it was convincing enough for the Lords to vote down Graham's motion to ban the trade. During the debate, the *Times of London* coined an evocative term for the hostilities in China—"Opium War"—which would give the two conflicts their historical name.

The Times failed to note that another opium war was going on right at home—a war for men's souls (and health) rather than the monetary considerations that fueled the troubles in China. For not all opium from India ended up in China: three hundred chests a year were diverted to England with the same disastrous effects as in the Middle Kingdom. Anticipating Marx's famous equation that religion was the opiate of the masses, in this case, opium was the opiate of the underclass in England's grim and grimy industrial cities, where workers on payday lined up outside the chemist's (pharmacy) for the inexpensive palliative to their industrial hell at the reasonable price of one and two pennies per packet—Huxley's brave new world of *soma* therapy. The temperance movement took no joy in the recent decrease in alcoholism because the anti-alcohol lobby knew that opium had taken up the slack.

But the general public remained unconcerned about the drug's addictiveness. Despite its popularity with the working masses, it seemed like a genteel drug, prescribed by doctors for everything from sore gums to gangrene. And as ingested in England, it had none of the stigma of smoking the drug, which was associated with opium dens in China that were considered dormitories of vices other than addiction, such as prostitution, venereal disease, and drug-facilitated rape of white women "shanghaied" by agents of the Yellow Peril. Opium in the form of laudanum seemed like what today would be a prescription drug available at the corner chemist. Sweet old ladies measured out their doses in teaspoons, just like other medicinal drugs, and spent their declining years in a euphoric daze. They never thought of themselves as addicts, though many of them were. Some accidentally overdosed as their tolerance and need for more of the drug increased, the great Robert Clive of India in the previous century being opium's most famous casualty.

Meanwhile, entrepreneurs in India thought they had found a solution to the opium problem. Ironically, opium created more problems in India than the entrepreneurs hoped to solve. Seeds from the tea bush in the Fujian Province of China were smuggled out of the country and cultivated with brilliant results in a greenhouse in Calcutta. If the British could grow their own tea in British-controlled India, there would be no need to use opium as barter to pay for tea produced by China. Indian tea would liberate the British from the fiscal tyranny of China. Unfortunately, tea production was a labor-intensive enterprise. While tea flourished in the literally hothouse conditions of Calcutta tended by industrious botanists, in the fields of Assam, attempts to grow tea were a disaster. The workers needed to pick the leaves were all debilitated by opium use and in no condition to perform the complex task of tea production. China's problem had been transplanted to India. One man's poison was also another man's poison.

Even sound monetary arguments failed to sway Parliament to enact legislation against the drug's cultivation. A year before the First Opium War began, C.S. Bruce, a retired ship captain and now a tea producer in India, warned that opium was destroying his tea harvester's work ethic. News of Bruce's prescient warning, delivered to the Agricultural and Horticultural Society of India, never made it to Britain, where it might have added support to Gladstone and Stanhope's call for abolition.

Chapter 7

DRUGS AND GUNS

———————

*"I am glad to say that our Chief Superintendent seems
completely weaned of his hostility to the drug traffic."*

—Opium trader William Jardine
on Britain's highest-ranking official in China

When Lin's ill-fated letter to Queen Victoria arrived in England, where it found its way onto the pages of *The Times*, it had no effect. Lin's quaint language and impotent threats seemed risible and gave rise to a popular stage farce that recreated the siege of the Canton factories with the surrounded British merchants brandishing comical, larger-than-life pistols and dressed as pirates. The Opium War in far-off China was a source of mirth and entertainment in London and no cause for concern. Even Parliament had brushed it off.

In China, on the other hand, Lin's efforts at opium eradication brought him a reward from Peking in the form of a promotion, from High Commissioner to Governor-General, replacing Deng Tingzhen. The promotion seems to have made Lin even more industrious in his crusade against the barbarian scourge. Sounding more like a Prussian theoretician than a Chinese mandarin, Lin wrote, "Only by knowing their strengths and their weaknesses can we find the right to restrain them." Keep your friends close, and your enemies closer, the original importers of opium, the Arabs, liked to say. While he shared the rest of the nation's contempt for all things foreign, Lin forced himself to learn about the enemy in order to destroy them. He read Vattel's *Law of Nations*, Thelwall's monograph condemning the opium trade, and back issues of the English-language journal the *Canton Press*. All court officials, called mandarins, had been trained as literary scholars, and Lin called on the discipline and intellectual curiosity of Vattel, the researcher and man of letters, in his quest for knowledge about the ways of the foreigners, with the ultimate goal of finding a way to defeat them. Lin was a scholar with a practical agenda.

The new Governor-General planned to put his knowledge to use. Lin bought the British warship the *Cambridge* for use by the Chinese navy and moored it at the mouth of the Canton River, virtually daring the British to pass by en route to Canton. But the *Cambridge* was a paper tiger and epitomized the technology gap between the two powers. Before acquiescing in the sale of the *Cambridge*, Elliot ordered all its cannons removed and sent to India. Lin countered by purchasing guns elsewhere—but they didn't work. In addition, the complexity of handling the sails of a modern vessel was still beyond the skills of Chinese sailors, and the *Cambridge* had to be towed to the Canton River, where it served as a dubious threat because it couldn't move. Lin could only hope for deterrence rather than confrontation.

By mid spring 1840, limited battles between Chinese and British ships carrying opium flared. Elliot decided to map the Yangtze River and borrowed an opium ship and its captain from Matheson. Elliot repaid Jardine by making the merchant his confidant, and showed the Scottish trader his correspondence with Palmerston. Matheson loaned Elliot the *Hellas*, captained by Frederick Jauncey, a veteran of a naval battle off of Shanghai in 1832. Matheson was no altruist when it came to selfless government service, and he ordered Jauncey to sell opium during his trip along the Yangtze.

The *Hellas* soon saw battle. On May 22, 1840, while it lay becalmed off Namoa, one hundred miles east of Canton, Jauncey found himself among what he thought were Chinese merchant vessels, until eight of them began to fire on his ship and hurl pitch at her. An attempt was made to board the *Hellas*, but after four hours of fighting, the attack ended when a favorable wind appeared, allowing the British ship to escape, but not without injury to Jauncey and his men. The captain suffered a broken jaw and almost lost an eye to enemy fire, but there were no fatal casualties.

At the end of May, the *Hellas* limped into Macao, where Jauncey and his crew disembarked for medical treatment. On June 8, the Chinese, encouraged by their success at Namoa, sent a fleet of fireships loaded with gunpowder and pitch among the British ships anchored at Capsingmun, forty-five miles east of Macao. Some of the British vessels fled, but the *Druid, Volage,* and *Hyacinth* used grappling hooks to tow the fiery intruders away from the rest of the fleet, and no ships were lost.

The very next day, June 9, 1840, the military assistance Palmerston had promised Elliott began to arrive in Chinese waters from various parts of the British Empire. A scarcity of sailors, who were massing in the eastern Mediterranean to fight the French and the expansionist ruler of Egypt, Mohammed Ali, had slowed the preparations of the China expeditionary force. Nevertheless, by the end of the month, some seventeen men-of-war had assembled, including three line-of-battle ships sent from England—the *Wellesley, Blenheim,* and *Melville*—as well as four armed steamers sent by the East India Company—the *Atalanta, Enterprize, Madagascar,* and *Queen,* later joined by the *Nemesis* from England. Not least, a small armada of twenty-seven troopships also arrived bearing three fighting regiments—the 26th Cameronians, the 18th Royal Irish, and the 49th Bengal Volunteers—as well as a corps of Bengal engineers and a corps of Madras sappers and miners: all to save China from the Chinese.

The vessels brought more than military reinforcements. Spying a chance for free military protection, civilian-owned transports filled with opium, more than ten thousand chests in all, sailed with the war party, flooding the Chinese market and lowering prices, an ironic development since military muscle had been sent to protect the trade, not cause a stampede of price cutting. Nevertheless, the large British military presence now in China allowed the opium business to thrive. Smugglers offloaded the drug at Lintin in broad daylight. The *Canton Register* published opium prices. Vessels packed with the drug followed the British warships, which allowed them to trade with impunity. (The military buildup in Canton had another sad effect. British ships that had cruised the west coast of Africa to stop the illegal slave trade were transferred to service in China, with the result that slave smugglers in Brazil and the American South had free rein to engage in their odious trade in human chattel.)

As the armada drew closer, fears among the foreign community in China that the Anglican High Church and its anti-opium lobby in Britain would prevail in Parliament evaporated. British merchants correctly felt that the fleet represented government approval of their business. Jardine, in particular, was overjoyed by developments, since he had only requested two ships-of-the-line. He also wrote to a colleague that the government's chief representative in China had at last come over to their side: "I am glad to say that our Chief Superintendent [Elliot] seems completely weaned of his hostility to the drug traffic." In fact, Elliot still questioned the morality of the trade, but he was a soldier first, a moralist second, and he followed orders, not his conscience.

Singapore had been chosen as the gathering place and launch site for the invasion of China. Marines practiced by storming the island's undefended beaches, with sailors in the rear. Chinese warships from a safe distance offshore observed the accumulating power of the British Empire with fear as they compared their antiquated junks to the state-of-the-art floating fortresses massing at Singapore. The opium vessels that accompanied the British warships took advantage of the military protection and sold a great deal of the drug—but at the depressed price of $350 per chest. War made business safe, but not necessarily lucrative.

By June 1, 1840, enough ships had arrived in Singapore to launch a credible offensive, and the fleet sailed out to open sea. On June 16, the first ship, the steamboat *Madagascar*, entered the Gulf of Canton, followed a few days later by the bulk of the fleet. When the *Wellesley* approached Macao from the northeast, Captain Elliot went on board and met with the head of the expeditionary force, Commodore Sir J. J. Gordon Bremer, where among other things they discussed Jardine's recent proposals. Jardine had written Palmerston urging him to commit top-of-the-line warships to a blockade of the entire east and part of the southern coasts of China, and the seizure of the island of Chusan near Shanghai. The merchant wanted the British navy to blockade the mouth of the Bei He River, which flowed into the Yangtze, which was connected to the Grand Canal, which led to Peking and provided the waterway for food shipments to the capital. Chusan was a critical depot for the Chinese. Taxes were paid in grain, and in a typical year, Chusan, an island of fifty-one square miles, saw more than a quarter million tons of grain pass through en route to feed the capital.

With the Emperor's sacrosanct capital threatened and deprived of its food source and revenue, the British merchants envisioned quick victory followed by a generous peace settlement. Not as hawkish as the traders on the scene, however, Palmerston had balked at Jardine's demand for major involvement and instead approved a partial blockade of the coastline and the commitment of a few hundred soldiers instead of the thousands Jardine had suggested. Palmerston's "diplomacy by other means" was at present more diplomatic than belligerent. The move against China would be incremental, rather than overwhelming from the start.

The British Admiralty's Sir John Barrow dismissed Jardine's counsel out of hand. He believed that threatening the Chinese capital would make its residents and ruler dig in to defend their last bastion rather than bring them to the negotiating table. Barrow wanted military efforts to center around the Gulf of Canton, shelling the city and seizing nearby Hong Kong. Elliot recommended a middle ground: take Canton, then with their rear protected, the British could proceed to the Bei He River and threaten the capital. Elliot also called for a blockade of Shanghai, a crucial hub of China's rice market, which would hurt the economy and make Peking more amenable to negotiations. Elliot preferred an attack on Shanghai rather than Peking because the latter would cause the government to lose face and become intransigent. Cutting off Shanghai would intimidate but not emasculate the Chinese.

Elliot awaited the arrival of his cousin, Admiral Sir George Elliot, who had been named his coplenipotentiary, but the title belied the actual scope of their power and actions, which were limited and dictated by voluminous instructions from London. Sailing on the *Wellesley*, Sir George brought with him a peace treaty with orders to make the Chinese agree to every article of it and to continue hostilities until they did. Palmerston also wanted to know, rather irrelevantly, if rumors were correct that Lin had sold the twenty thousand confiscated chests of opium instead of dumping them in the river.

Sir George arrived in late 1840 and ordered a blockade of the Gulf of Canton, but didn't personally stay to enforce it. Leaving behind five warships, with the bulk of the fleet he hurried north to avoid the approaching monsoon season. The British merchants in Canton were dismayed. They wanted a frontal assault, not a prolonged blockade, to free the city for trade.

With both Elliots aboard the *Wellesley*, the fleet approached Chusan, using ships from Dent and other merchants to guide them. Sir George also bore a demanding and condescending letter from Palmerston to the Emperor, informing him of Britain's intention to blockade and seize Chinese ports as a response to the Chinese siege of the Canton factories. As for the suffering wrought by opium on Chinese society, which had prompted the siege, Palmerston suggested that if the Emperor wanted to stop the trade, he should convince his subjects to stop using opium. After all this bluster, Palmerston offered a *douceur*. To avoid any more "unpleasantness," the Son of Heaven was invited to send negotiators to a shipboard meeting with the two Elliots, whose heavily armed vessel represented a threat to Peking as it lay at anchor at the mouth of the Bei He River.

The Elliots decided to deliver the letter as they approached Namoy, three hundred miles north of Canton. They sent Captain Thomas Bourchier aboard the *Blonde*, flying a white flag of truce. As Bourchier entered the harbor, a ship bearing mandarins pulled up and boarded the *Blonde*. Bourchier explained to the bureaucrats what his white flag meant and threatened to blow the city to pieces if the Chinese did not respect the truce, not a good opening move for a plan that sought to broker a peace deal. Bourchier appeared to be bluffing. When a menacing crowd formed on the beach, the Captain didn't make good on his threat to shell the city and sailed off instead.

The *Blonde* anchored a few hundred yards from the shore. The next day, Bourchier noticed cannons being mounted on a nearby fort and aboard Chinese warships. Bourchier's translator, Robert Thom, boarded a small boat and rowed closer to shore. He held up a placard that repeated Bourchier's threat of retaliation if his ship was fired upon. Thom began to shout the printed warning to the crowd on shore, which by now had turned into a mob whose howls drowned out the translator's threats. Some of the people on shore began to swim out to Thom's boat. An arrow and gunshots narrowly missed him, and Thom stumbled and fell. Cannon from the fort and warships began firing and hit six of the sailors aboard Thom's boat.

When the translator returned to the *Blonde*, Captain Bourchier made good on his threats and began to shell the warships and the fort. Bourchier continued to lecture and hector the mob. He composed yet another letter, explaining that Her Majesty's government had no quarrel with the Chinese people, only their ruler. Bourchier dispatched a courier with the message in another small boat, but once again, as the craft approached the shore, gunfire made it pull back. The dangerous scene became farcical when the Captain put a message in a bottle like some forsaken castaway and threw it overboard. A fisherman retrieved the bottle from the water. Then, before sailing away towards Canton, in a fit of impotent pique, Bourchier set fire to a nearby Chinese trading vessel.

On July 1, the armada anchored in the harbor of Dinghai on Chusan Island, about one hundred miles southeast of Shanghai. Dinghai, the capital and port of Chusan, was home to forty thousand people. A five-sided wall, twenty-two feet high and fifteen feet thick, studded with towers and surrounded on four sides by a canal, protected the city. The fifth side had the protection of a steep hill next to it, with a joss house (shrine) at the top of the hill. Chusan's defenders, sixteen hundred in all, were a tragic joke. Staffed by subsistence fishermen and sailors, the militia was armed with spears, bows and arrows, and matchlocks; they only practiced once a year.

Twelve Chinese warships had followed the British fleet, but kept a safe distance. Sir Arthur Gordon recognized a pennant flying from one of the ships indicating a high government official aboard. The British wanted to talk to him. This time, unlike their hostile reception at Amoy, the Chinese invited the British aboard their flagship. Bremer and his interpreter, Karl Gutzlaff, rowed over. The high personage aboard the Chinese flagship was not a naval officer, but the commander of the local garrison. Bremer was blunt and to the point: surrender Chusan or face the consequences. The Chinese were unintimidated and chose the latter. Bremer didn't live up to his threat, and instead of blasting the antiquated Chinese vessels out of the water, he invited the Chinese commander and his subordinates aboard the *Wellesley*, where the enemy was wined and dined, perhaps in a futile attempt to soften the commander's resolve. The courage of one Chinese officer, examining the seventy-four-gun *Wellesley*, impressed Gutzlaff, who quoted him as saying, "It is very true you are strong and I am weak. Still I must fight."

After dinner, Bremer repeated his demand for surrender, and gave the commander twenty-four hours to comply. In the meantime, the Chinese on shore began to prepare for battle, stuffing "sandbags" with rice and buttressing Dinghai's walls with them. When the twenty-four-hour grace period expired with no surrender, Bremer drew the *Wellesley* closer to shore. It was a temporary bluff. He didn't have the manpower to launch an amphibious assault until midday, when a half-dozen British warships arrived on the scene.

At 2 P.M. on July 5, Bremer fired a single cannonade from one of the *Wellesley*'s seventy-four guns at a tower of the fort in a small fishing village, which served as a buffer for Dinghai a mile inland. The Chinese responded in kind with a single shot. Bremer returned volley after volley for ten minutes. Lieutenant Colonel George Burrell, commander of the 18th Brigade, then led the landing party in small ships.

Inexplicably, the Chinese guns ceased fire as the assault team approached the shore. The British made good use of the unilateral cease-fire by blowing four Chinese warships to bits and damaging others. The British guns demolished the fort's tower and sea wall. "The crashing of timber, falling houses and groans of men resounded from the shore. Even after [the bombardment] ceased, a few shots were still heard from the unscathed junks. We landed on a deserted beach, a few dead bodies, bows and arrows, broken spears and guns remaining the sole occupants of the field," a member of the landing party reported. The men landed on shore without a fight because there was no one to fight. As the deserted beach suggested, the Chinese defenders had fled almost as soon as the gunfire began, and the gallant commander of the village, Brigadier Zhang, who had vowed to fight to the end despite the uneven forces, retreated on a litter, unable to walk because both of his legs had been severed by the guns of the British ships. The local magistrate and several subordinates committed suicide after the rout.

A detachment of Indian soldiers set up four artillery pieces on the hill with the joss house overlooking Dinghai. From this superior position they began to shell the defenseless inhabitants, who fled the bombardment. The British suffered no casualties during the landing and artillery attack.

Viscount Jocelyn, the expedition's military secretary and a protégé of Lord Auckland, the Governor-General of India, described the planting of the flag by the joss house: "The first European banner that has floated as conqueror over the Flowery Land." The landing and taking of the hill had lasted less than forty-five minutes. It was an augur of the entire campaign between the two mismatched sides.

The town of Dinghai was a mile from shore, and as the men under Colonel George Burrell approached its formidable pentagon of walls, artillery began to soften the town's defenses. The besieged residents responded with their artillery so ferociously that Burrell decided to wait until the next day to continue the assault. During the lull, British soldiers in the fishing village came across jars of the local brew called *samshu*, fortified rice wine laced with garlic and aniseed. The soldiers spilled so much of the *samshu* as they drank it that the streets overflowed with the brew. Soon roaring drunk, the men rioted and began to loot the village. In fact, the Hindi word *lut* was coined at the time to describe the invaders' behavior. "A more complete pillage could not be conceived. The plunder ceased only when there was nothing to take or destroy," the *India Gazette* reported. By nightfall, many of the men had passed out after imbibing huge amounts of the fortified liquor. Around midnight, a fire and explosions caused by abandoned gunpowder turned Dinghai into a firestorm that the British were unable to contain. They ended up abandoning the blazing village for fear that sparks would ignite the powder in their guns.

The next morning, July 6, 1840, the attackers were encouraged by the sight of townspeople fleeing Dinghai and hoped that the town would surrender peacefully. Viscount Jocelyn and half a dozen men approached the south wall with no resistance from the defenders. The rice bag–reinforced walls were only two stories high, and the invaders easily scaled them with ladders. Within minutes, they were over the top and the conquerors of Britain's first Chinese settlement, a deserted town that once held forty thousand inhabitants. Two thousand Chinese died in the fight for Dinghai, while the British lost only nineteen. The Reverend Dr. Gutzlaff, with a staff of turncoat mandarins, was named Civil Magistrate of the new British government on Dinghai.

Exploring the neighborhoods, the soldiers found caches of antiquated weapons and armor, including arrows and padded cotton jackets used as armor that reflected the unevenness of the opposing sides and heartened the invaders. The men began to help themselves to relatively worthless objects like pipes, statuettes, fans, and ornaments. Even the aristocratic Jocelyn found these souvenirs of conquest irresistible, and years later in his autobiography justified the pilfering as "lawful loot."

After the looting, the invaders behaved themselves, except for several rapes committed by Indian soldiers. "No one has been killed in cold blood that I am aware of, and only one or two cases of rape have occurred—perpetrated it is said by the sepoys," the interpreter, Robert Thom, wrote Matheson. The few remaining Chinese in Dinghai also engaged in looting. When it appeared that the Chinese would run off with the town's provisions, which were needed for the troops, Lt. Col. Burrell posted guards

around the town with orders to shoot, and they did. Several Chinese looters were killed. Apparently ignoring the culpability of his own side, Thom
wrote of the indigenous thieves, "A more subtle, lying, and thievish race it
never was my luck to live amongst."

Food in the town soon ran out, and foraging parties looked for provisions in the surrounding countryside. The looters now became traders and
paid cash for livestock ($20 for cows, $5 for goats). Unafraid of the occupiers, the local farmers seemed to find the British amusing and laughed at
their interpreters as they suffered with the local dialect. The laughter hid
real dangers for the intruders. During a shopping trip to the countryside,
a comprador named Bu Dingbang was seized by Chinese soldiers and tied
to a pole by a rope around his neck. Jocelyn and forty soldiers searched for
the missing comprador, but when a group of Chinese soldiers almost captured them, they retreated and left the comprador to his fate.

On July 11, David Jardine and Donald Matheson reached Chusan and
discovered that Admiral Elliot had forbidden opium ships from landing on
the island. Smugglers persisted and began to unload opium at the firesale
price of $100 per chest, which some said was an inducement to lure new
buyers and future addicts. With the Chinese navy paralyzed by the presence of British warships, the opium trade flourished. By November 1840,
forty-three opium ships were using Chusan as an offloading point. Twelve
thousand chests of opium at bargain prices had been brought through
Chusan by the end of the year.

In the wake of the medical and societal problems caused by the infu-
sion of opium, medical missionaries followed and tried to undo some of
the drug's damage. William Lockhart, a representative of the London Missionary Society, organized a treatment center at Chusan that was ironically
protected by British soldiers, who indirectly protected the opium smugglers as well by neutralizing the Chinese navy. The clinic soon overflowed
with sixteen hundred addicts over the rest of the year.

The leader of the troops, Colonel Burrell, proved to be a menace to his
own men. Despite the abandoned homes in Dinghai, he refused to quarter his men there for fear of alienating their absent owners. Instead, the
men were billeted in a malaria-invested paddy field. With temperatures in
the nineties, the martinet colonel ordered the men to keep the top buttons
of their heavy serge uniforms tightly fastened. In all, nearly five hundred

men, far more than the casualties of the invasion, died of dysentery or malaria. Lord Auckland in India fired Burrell, who was replaced by Sir Hugh Gough. Amid the heat and disease, Gough found a despairing corps. One officer wrote home, "We are playing at war, instead of waging it."

Meanwhile, Elliot tried to send Palmerston's letter to Jinhai, twenty miles to the northwest of Dinghai at the southern tip of the Yong River, but the local government sent it back unopened. On July 27, the *Blenheim* sailed into Dinghai, followed three days later by the *Wellesley*. Elliot now had enough firepower to proceed to Peking, five hundred miles to the north.

Chapter 8

DIPLOMACY BY GUNBOAT

———·••·———

*"It is notorious that [the Emperor] entertains the utmost dread
of our enterprising spirit."*

—Charles Elliot in a letter to Lord Palmerston, 1840

China had excellent internal communications, and within a week of the fall of Dinghai, Peking had learned of the disaster. The Emperor had no equivalent of a Secretary of State, so the bad news came directly to him. Despite the speed of communication, its clarity was poor. Afraid of enraging the Son of Heaven, his mandarins sent news of Dinghai's capitulation in memoranda that downplayed the seriousness of the incursion. Lulled by flowery letters from sycophantic courtiers, the Emperor responded to the crisis with firm inaction. Instead of accurate assessments of the danger, the government officials told the Emperor what they thought he wanted to hear, and the memorials dwelled on the alleged weaknesses of the invaders, which reflected more the ignorance of the courtiers than the real strength of the fleet advancing on the sacrosanct capital. Yukien, governor of Jiangsu Province, home of the crucial mouth of the Yangtze River, sent the Emperor heartening accounts of the barbarians soon to be in their midst. "Take our fort at Woosung. From the bottom upward there is the stone base, then the clay base, and finally the fort itself. It is an elevation far above the level of the barbarian ships. If they shoot upward, their bullets will go down and consequently lose force. Moreover [the British] are stiff and their legs straight. The latter, further bound with cloth, can scarcely stretch at will. Once fallen down, they cannot again stand up. It is fatal to fighting on land." The Governor also criticized the British for lacking bows and arrows.

Within ten days, Elliot's fleet approached the mouth of the Bei He River, only seventy-five miles southwest of the capital, but couldn't find the actual mouth. The water near the Bei He was too shallow for the men-of-war to dock, and for five days the ships sailed in search of a shallow harbor as Chinese warships passed by out of range of the British ships' guns. Elliot pursued one of the ships in the Madagascar, captured its pilot, and forced him to guide the fleet to where the pilot said were mud flats that flanked the mouth of the Bei He.

As they approached the promised flats, nothing was visible. High tide had obscured them, but Elliot guessed their location from poles stuck in the mud, and the fleet at last entered the Bei He. Two forts called Dagu guarded the mouth, but their guns remained silent. They appeared deserted and decrepit. Elliot was still looking for someone to receive Palmerston's letter; he found a likely candidate when he came upon several warships guarding a vessel commanded by a mandarin a mile upriver. The vessel didn't flee, and Elliot sent a sailor aboard to deliver the letter to the official. The mandarin replied that he had to send the letter to a higher-ranking bureaucrat, but added that his superior was only a short distance away. Elliot didn't mind waiting. A jeering crowd appeared on shore, and several British ships sailed closer to Elliot's vessel for protection. The captain's patience was rewarded by the arrival of a message from Qishan, the Governor of Chihli Province, in which Peking was located. Palmerston's letter had been forwarded to the Emperor himself, Qishan's message reported, but Elliot would have to wait for a reply.

The following day, Chinese ocean-going merchant vessels sailed into view. Elliot had the ships boarded and searched for food and water. A British sailor who was looting instead of finding provisions was caught by the captain of one of the Chinese merchant ships, and the Chinese shot and killed him. There was no retaliation by the British. Despite the looting, the Chinese treated the invaders like honored guests. On May 13, 1840, one of Qishan's men went aboard the *Wellesley* bringing food and drink for the British, since the Chinese had been informed that the barbarians loved "greasy animal flesh." For several days, the governor sent gifts, then announced that Palmerston's letter had been received in Peking, but regretted there would be another ten-day wait while the court mulled over its contents.

During the delay, bad water from Chusan wells caused an outbreak of dysentery in the British fleet. Elliot scattered the entire fleet, a perilous decision considering the war-like nature of their mission, but they had to find fresh water. Some ships searched as far away as one hundred miles. The ten-day consultation deadline came and went. When the ships returned with water (the *Wellesley* also managed to round up cattle during her peregrinations), Elliot decided it was time to "speed up" the mandarins' examination of Palmerston's letter. Elliot ordered the *Modeste* and the *Madagascar* to begin firing at the Chusan forts. Before the shelling began, however, a messenger from Qishan arrived, inviting Elliot to meet him on July 30, three days hence. The meeting would be the closest to Peking in the history of nonrelations between the two nations. The symbolism must have been obvious to both sides, encouraging for the British, irritating and foreboding for the Chinese, as well as humiliating.

The Chinese again greeted the invaders with ritualized courtesy, elegant surroundings, and a great deal of food. On a mud flat near the southern Chusan fort, Qishan, in a modest blue silk robe and white satin shoes and a straw hat with peacock feathers that symbolized the Emperor's special favor, greeted Captain Elliot, Viscount Jocelyn, and several sailors and marines. Qishan's arrival before the British was yet another sign of courtesy by the protocol-obsessed Chinese. In still another act of hospitality, the Chinese had built a floating dock on the mud flat so Elliot and company wouldn't have to dirty their boots on the muddy flats and could sail right up to the meeting place, a huge canvas tent with a smaller and elegant silk one within it. Qishan led Elliot to the smaller room, while Jocelyn and the fighting men were plied with multiple courses of food. Bored and stuffed, Jocelyn tried to leave the tent and explore the area, but he was politely invited to return for yet another round of food and drinks. For entertainment and perhaps as an inept show of Chinese military might, the guests watched while Chinese soldiers showed off their talent with bow and arrow and eighteenth-century-era guns.

As he was also wined and dined and plied with Chinese delicacies, Elliot spent six hours reviewing Palmerston's demands, the process slowed by Elliot's interpreter, John Morrison, whose facility with the Mandarin tongue was shaky. During their polite exchanges, a bit of tension arose when Qishan brought up that bugaboo dating back to the previous century. Qishan referred to both the Macartney and Amherst embassies as tribute bearers. Elliot immediately corrected his guest and insisted the previous emissaries had been ambassadors of a status equal to the Emperor's, not inferior barbarians bearing tribute. A supple diplomat, Qishan changed the subject.

The British occupation of Chusan was unacceptable to the Emperor, Qishan said, and Elliot agreed that the British presence there was temporary, merely a base for further operations. The latter represented an unveiled threat that Qishan decided to ignore. The defining issue of opium importation was not so easily handled. Qishan demanded a promise from Queen Victoria (the Chinese still could not digest the concept of a constitutional sovereign who could be overruled by representatives of [some of] the people) that Britain would cease exporting the poison to China. Elliot said he didn't have the power to grant such a concession and argued two obnoxious and erroneous points: if the Chinese wanted the opium trade to end, they should stop using it. Then fudging figures, he claimed that half of China's opium came from sources other than British possessions. Qishan didn't argue with Elliot's specious statistics or his simplistic solution to substance abuse in China.

The governor was more forceful when the subject of reparations came up. Palmerston wanted restitution for the twenty thousand opium chests seized, and the Chinese were to reimburse the invaders for the cost of invading their nation! Abandoning decorum, Qishan called these demands absurd. He grew alarmed when Elliot began to write in the margin of Palmerston's letter Qishan's reaction to the payment of reparations, and explained that the objection was only his "opinion"—many of the Emperor's other advisors might have different ones.

Now, as the talks hit their nadir, Elliot felt new optimism. As the interpreter Morrison droned on, stumbling over Qishan's words, it began to dawn on Elliot that Peking had made a 180-degree turn in its attitude toward the barbarian drug dealers. Lin had fallen out of favor at court, Qishan said. Eighteen months earlier, during the siege of the British factories, Elliot had thundered with impotent rage as well as unintended irony, as millions of dollars worth of opium was dumped in the sea, "Great moral changes can never be effected by the violation of all the principles of justice and moderation." The siege and the seizure were "hastening a career of violence which will react upon this empire in a terrible manner." Now,

Qishan seemed to share his indignation, although with less enthusiasm. He agreed that the British colony had been mistreated and unnecessary violence employed by Lin. But Qishan's moral indignation didn't translate into financial restitution. Giving the British precious silver for reparations was a nonstarter. However, Qishan sweetened his bitter refusal by mentioning that the Emperor planned to fire Lin and punish him for his excesses—an ominous prospect for Lin in a country where bureaucratic failure was often a capital offense. Lin would get his, but Her Majesty would not get hers—Chinese silver.

After six hours of niceties, no progress had been made. Qishan did surprise Elliot at the conclusion of their meeting by shaking hands instead of bowing. The Chinese weren't learning the ways of the West fast, but they were learning. In parting, the governor hinted that he might be Lin's successor as plenipotentiary and planned to travel to Canton, where he now urged Elliot and his forces to return. Qishan explained that Canton, as the center of foreign trade, was the logical place for the foreigners to be, but both men knew that the real reason was Qishan wanted the British menace as far away from the capital and the Emperor as possible.

Admiral Elliot felt the fleet was unprotected in Bei He Bay, and urged his cousin to end negotiations and leave. Also encouraged by the news of Lin's imminent dismissal, Elliot and the fleet sailed away. The abrupt departure weakened the British position and led the Chinese to believe that the invaders would not continue the war. This inaccurate deduction made future negotiations more difficult as the Chinese hardened their position.

But the British departure was only temporary. By September 1840, the menacing ships once again patrolled the waters at the mouth of the Bei He River. Elliot knew how much this show of forced terrified the Chinese, writing to Palmerston, "It is notorious that [the Emperor] entertains the utmost dread of our enterprising spirit."

Chapter 9

THE ECONOMICS OF ADDICTION

———•+•——

*"But as they have no mode of raising money for the expenses
of the war unless from the drug sales in China, we think [the British
government] cannot avoid giving it some toleration."*

—Memo to associate by opium trader James Matheson, 1840

Despite Lin's efforts and threats, the opium trade in Canton continued to thrive. Interdiction had failed, and the increased availability of opium drove prices down. By the fall of 1840, Jardine, Matheson had sixty-five hundred chests to trade in Canton, with thirty-seven hundred more chests aboard the firm's ships. The firm dwarfed other merchants: Dent had a mere eight hundred, the entire Portuguese contingent only six hundred, the Indian merchants three hundred, Innes one hundred fifty. The price of a chest fell to $400. It was a buyer's market, and the Chinese, despite severe government sanctions, remained enthusiastic buyers and consumers.

That was the opium bazaar in Canton. In recently conquered Chusan, Admiral Sir George Elliot forbade the sale of the drug, no doubt sensitive to Chusan's closeness to Peking and his desire not to antagonize the Emperor. Matheson was displeased by the ban, but his ire was tempered by cynicism and the awareness of the economic power the trade exerted over all parties. In a memorandum, Matheson wrote, "We look with some uneasiness to Admiral Elliot's prohibition of the drug trade at Chusan as indicating the same sort of disaffection which gave us so much alarm and trouble on the part of Captain Elliot. But as they have no mode of raising money for the expenses of the war unless from the drug sales in China, we think they cannot avoid giving it some toleration."

Once the funds Sir George had brought from England were exhausted, he had to raise money by selling bonds—a form of loan. The only people in China who would buy these bonds were the opium traders who knew the importance of British military protection. Admiral Elliot realized his fiscal dependence on the opium traders, and his prohibition of the business in Chusan was more symbolic than practical or effective. Vessels were allowed to offload opium near Chusan without interference from British warships patrolling the waters off the occupied town. Wrongly, the Admiral hoped his official ban would mollify the Emperor while at the same time allow funding of his presence there by bonds purchased by the opium *tai pans*.

The Emperor hesitated to replace Lin, which emboldened the Governor-General to attack the other half of the opium problem, consumers. He could be just as harsh with his own citizens as he had been toward the barbarians, even worse. In an edict, Lin gave drug users a limited time to wean themselves from the drug. "While the period is not yet closed, you are living victims. When it shall have expired, then you will be dead victims." Strangulation would be the fate of unrehabilitated users, Lin announced. Zero tolerance.

Foreigners without an economic stake in the trade, typically missionaries, shared Lin's abhorrence of the drug trade, if not his violent strategy to eradicate it. Dr. Charles Hobson, who ran a hospital in Macao, wrote an article for the English language journal, the *Repository*, describing the effects of the drug on users. Hobson's denunciation was based on personal experience. A Chinese man named Choo was sent by Hobson's sponsor, the London Missionary Society, to England to be trained as a Christian preacher. It was hoped that Choo would symbolize the possibility of peaceful coexistence between the two nations and become an attractive proselytizer as well. But the Missionary Society had placed their confidence in the wrong man. Upon returning to China, ready to preach the Gospel, Choo was unmasked when a fellow missionary, William Milne Jr., smelled opium in Choo's room. Choo insisted Milne was wrong, and perhaps because of his importance to the evangelical movement in China, the issue was not pressed—until the telltale odor once again emanated from Choo's quarters, which this time were searched and a thimbleful of the drug discovered. Choo said the opium

The Economics of Addiction 105

belonged to a friend. After a series of interrogations by his fellow missionaries, Choo confessed that the drug was his, but then became defiant. The missionaries were not only willing to forgive him, they begged him to mend his ways because of his symbolic importance to the evangelical movement. Choo compared his drug use to the British fondness for alcohol and tobacco. His colleagues decided to give him one more chance and laid out a set of rules Choo had to adhere to. Choo ignored the rules, and apparently his drug use led to absenteeism from not only prayers but prompted long absences from the missionaries' communal home. The last straw came in August, when Choo was found smoking opium in bed. He was expelled from the house.

Choo and other native addicts not only got opium from traders, but the merchants also gave their customers arms with which to resist government soldiers who tried to seize their drugs. These addicts were known to fire on government boats when attacked. It was hoped that conversion to Christianity would be accompanied by a rejection of drug use, but as it turned out, the power of faith was no match for chemical and psychological addiction.

But the missionaries remained optimistic that the opium menace could be eradicated with the right government effort. Elijah Bridgman wrote, "We doubt not that nine-tenths if not every one of them [addicts and traders] would abandon it at once and forever, provided it were disowned and disapproved of by their government, and a well-regulated and honorable commerce in all other articles opened and ratified with the Chinese."

Proselytizing efforts by the missionaries were further hampered by what the Protestant ministers considered the materialistic, nonspiritual values of the Chinese, ignoring the fact that the indigenous religions provided enough emotional succor so that foreign interlopers and their ideologies and creeds were unnecessary and ignored. Williams described his strolls with a friend in Canton, trawling for indifferent converts. "We often walk together and discourse sweet communion." Sometimes the two missionaries would stop passersby and deliver an impromptu sermon. The Chinese were polite, but changed the subject, inquiring about the price of Western clothing and remarking how large Western noses were compared to Chinese. Williams called the Chinese shallow.

While Williams scolded, other missionaries condemned the Chinese and exhibited the classic cultural racism of invaders and occupiers. The

French priest Jean-Henri Baldus wrote home, "I think that in all things the Chinese are decidedly inferior to the Europeans." Baldus was repelled by the ubiquitous presence of prostitutes, who solicited him on the street, the Chinese obsession with cockfighting, and the general sloth of the people in this most industrious nation. While the Chinese returned the insult by disdaining the barbarians as inferior tribute bearers, Baldus prided himself and the West on its unequivocally superior military prowess. "They [the Chinese] have acquired a considerable respect for English guns since encountering a few."

In 1840, Lin stepped up his campaign to stop the opium trade at its source, or at least the most important source of the problem, the market for the drug. A system of neighborhood spies was set up to denounce users, who were jailed or placed in sanitariums, both of which soon filled to capacity. Lin's interdiction efforts against the opium vessels that made lightening drops in the dead of night were much less successful, and the presence of the smugglers' ship at a safe distance from the shore and Chinese warships represented a constant affront to the Governor-General's authority.

Although Jardine had begged for a blockade of the entire coast of China, the cost-conscious Palmerston ordered more selective patrols near the Gulf of Canton, Amoy, Chusan, and the mouths of the Yangtze and Yellow Rivers in February. Two months later, the Foreign Secretary decided to punish the Chinese with a general order to seize all Chinese ships and property aboard. Besides punishment, seizure had a practical effect. The ships' cargo was sold to finance the British campaign.

In June 1840, a selective but effective blockade of the coast began in earnest. Within a month, the British had seized seven large trading vessels and confiscated their cargo. The Chinese responded by putting a price on the head of all British military personnel. The ascending amounts reflected the Chinese love of hierarchy, even when it involved political assassination: $5,000 for a ship's captain, $100 for an enlisted man taken alive, but only $20 for his corpse (actually, the victim's head would suffice for reimbursement). Commandeering a British ship would net the lucky privateer $10,000.

When it was difficult to find men in uniform, the Chinese turned to civilians, regardless of whether they engaged in the opium trade or not. In July 1840, the missionaries Williams and Hobson, while proselytizing in Macao and in the company of a merchant, were set upon by Chinese thugs who clubbed the men, gravely injuring Williams' leg and Hobson's arm. An American was pulled off his horse and pummeled, while two British officers were attacked with knives. All the victims escaped. Others were not so lucky. On August 5, 1840, Vincent Stanton, the tutor of a British merchant's children and a former divinity student at Cambridge, together with the missionary David Abeel, made the dangerous mistake of swimming in Macao's bay. Stanton went ahead of Abeel, and when the latter arrived at the beach, the tutor had vanished. A search that included dredging the bay turned up nothing. A few days later, the foreign colony learned that Stanton had been kidnapped on the shore and sent to Canton.

Amid all the turmoil in China after the British military expedition arrived, Macao, as a Portuguese stronghold, seemed the last safe place, psychologically at least, for foreigners. The seizure of Stanton destroyed this false sense of security and enraged the foreign residents. Captain Smith appealed to the Portuguese governor, Pinto, who expressed sympathy but took no action. Adding to the crisis atmosphere, eight Chinese warships docked at Macao. The hysterical foreign colony feared they would suffer Stanton's fate, whatever that was.

As it turned out, Lin had masterminded the abduction. The Governor-General had been unable to stop British ships from blockading the coast, so he targeted an accessible victim, whose importance was more tactical and psychological than practical. Pressured, Pinto sent a local Chinese man to confer with Lin, but the man came back empty-handed. The British felt they had lost face by using an intermediary from another power, and a decrepit power at that—Portugal.

Less than two weeks after Stanton's capture, the British replied with might. The *Hyacinth*, *Larne*, *Enterprize,* and *Louisa* sailed into Macao's Casilha Bay, bristling with four hundred Indian and British soldiers. The British ships fired on the Chinese vessels, which tried to return fire, but their antiquated guns couldn't reach the British ships. The Chinese soon deserted their crafts and the batteries on shore while British ships continued to fire for an hour. Then Captain Smith sent sailors in small boats to seize the guns on shore and destroy them. A pitiful skeleton crew aboard a Chinese junk fired on the British ships, but all it took was musket fire from the British to silence the outgunned Chinese. The Chinese ships fled as Indian troops and British marines scaled the walls of Macao, then stopped to burn everything in the vicinity of the walls before returning to their ships and sailing out of Macao. There were only four casualties on the British side, none fatal. The Chinese, who not only rewrote history but current events as well, sent reports to the Emperor of a great victory with many British dead and their ships sent to the bottom of Casilha Bay. Many of the Emperor's missteps throughout the conflict were not strategic mistakes, but actions based on bad intelligence.

The next day, the missionary Abeel noticed a change in the atmosphere in Macao. Before the battle, Chinese had screamed at him "foreign demon" whenever he went out. Now, the locals averted their eyes and rushed away. There were more dramatic examples of the change in climate in the Portuguese foothold. Not a single Chinese soldier remained in the city, and no war vessels returned, much to the relief of noncombatants, who found the Imperial army and navy as annoying a presence as the new invaders. The naval battle had saved Macao, but had no effect on the fate of the luckless Stanton, who remained imprisoned in Canton. The defeat at Macao, however, so traumatized the Chinese that they did not disturb the peace of the Portuguese colony for more than a century.

Chapter 10

CRUCIFIXION AND CAGES

————•————

"Mine was scarcely a yard high, a little more than three quarters of a yard long, and a little more than half a yard broad."

—Ann Noble, describing the wooden cage
she was placed in by her Chinese captors

S tanton's seizure had distressed the foreign community, but news of the torture and execution of a French Lazarist missionary, Father Jean-Gabriel Perboyre brought the Europeans to the point of hysteria. Determined to bring Christ to the Chinese, Perboyre had carried his mission into Hubei Province—in violation of Chinese law. Apparently betrayed by one of his own converts, Perboyre had been captured in September 1839. After a year of torture and interrogation, the devout priest was publicly executed on September 11, 1840.

The execution took place outside Wuchang, a city on the Yangtze River. The Chinese probably had little interest or knowledge of the Christian Bible, so it may have been just a coincidence that the martyred priest's death was Christ-like. Perboyre was executed along with several common criminals, tied to a cross before being ritually strangled. A secondhand account by the French missionary François Maresca claimed that a miracle occurred after Perboyre's execution. Instead of displaying the twisted countenance of a strangulation victim, Perboyre, who was left on the cross after his death, appeared to be still alive but sleeping, an expression of peaceful bliss on his face, perhaps the contentment of a martyr for the faith, secure in the knowledge that the manner of his death guaranteed instant access to Heaven. The corpse had been stripped bare, except for a loincloth—another Christ-like touch. Before Perboyre's burial, devout Christians who venerated it as a relic stripped even this last article of clothing from the corpse.

Foreigners began dying in other parts of China as well at this time, but not as violently as the French missionary. The British conquerors of Chusan had become besieged victims and began to die of starvation when villagers refused to sell them food and hid their animals from the occupiers to prevent confiscation. In desperation, some soldiers began robbing Chinese fishermen of the day's catch. Then, perhaps on orders from Peking, at the end of summer, the residents of Chusan vanished. The occupiers held possession of a ghost town.

The Indian soldiers ate moldy rice from Chusan's stockpiles, but the British turned up their noses at the local food, preferring something arguably worse, bread made from sour, worm-ridden flour stored aboard their ships. Also from the ships, pickled beef and pork had become so rancid that even the iron-stomached Brits couldn't tolerate it. The spoiled meat was sold in Singapore to be used as manure.

The occupiers' drinking water was another nightmare of taste and disease—its source, the rice fields outside Chusan, was contaminated by sewers and almost opaque because of the mud content. In a letter to Matheson, Thom, the translator, wrote about the water problem and other burdens that were decimating the troops. "Even the natives hold their noses [because of the water's smell]. Unless we can manage to get the canal and town cleared out, I fear that we shall be getting some contagious distemper among us. The climate moreover is moist and mosquitoes swarm in amazing numbers. Let no man come here without mosquito curtains, else he will bitterly repent of it." Chusan lay at the same latitude as New Orleans and shared its humid climate. The mosquitoes, their victims didn't realize, were the vector for malaria, which contemporary medical science attributed to dirty air (*mal'aria* in Italian) emanating from rotten vegetables. An outbreak of dysentery caused even more fatalities than malaria, starvation, and contaminated food and water combined. Twelve soldiers died in August 1840; the casualty list doubled the next month. Ten times those numbers had to be hospitalized. In mid September, a third of the men were too ill to fight.

Desperate for provisions despite the danger, the occupiers foraged further and further inland. Two of the foragers became separated from the rest of the party and found themselves surrounded by a mob, which stoned one of them to death and took the other prisoner to Ningbo, where he was interrogated, then put on display in a wooden cage and chained at the hands, feet, and neck in a space so cramped that his knees touched his chin. After six days on display, the prisoner, still in the cage, was taken to a prison where he saw a ghastly reflection of his own sorry state.

The largest group of captives came from the 281-ton brig the *Kite*, a commercial vessel that had been converted into a troopship. When the *Kite* ran aground on a sandbank on September 15, 1840, Captain John Noble's five-month-old baby was trapped and drowned below decks, while the captain, his wife, Ann, and twenty-six crew members, clinging to the capsized brig, were taken prisoner by the Chinese, who immediately put the survivors in chains. The wretched procession made its way to the prison at Ningbo in the rain. Villagers along the way taunted them, and one ripped the wedding ring off Ann Noble's finger. En route, the prisoners were placed in wooden cages, which Mrs. Noble later described in an article in the *Repository* along with her terrifying trip to prison. "Mine was scarcely a yard high, a little more than three quarters of a yard long, and a little more than half a yard broad. The door opened from the top. Into these we were lifted, the chain around our necks being locked to the cover. They put a long piece of bamboo through the middle, a man took either end, and in this manner we were jolted from city to city to suffer the insults of the rabble, the cries from whom were awful." Mrs. Noble failed to mention that the prisoners were also spat upon while villagers reached through the bars of the cages and tore at the captives' hair. Two marines who struck back at the mob were pulled from their cages and beaten to death. At the prison in Ningbo, thirty miles east of Chusan, they were lodged in cells but remained in cages within the cells. Three died of dysentery during their captivity. The stench from loose bowels in the uncleaned cages overwhelmed the captives. Their warders exhibited a strange racism. When the European captives were let out of their cages, their chains were removed. But when the Indian soldiers were briefly released, they were kept fettered. One of the English prisoners speculated that it was the Indians' habit of eating rice with their fingers that enraged the Chinese and merited the harsher punishment. Modern historians believe the Chinese discriminated against the Indians because they were darker skinned than their European comrades.

Elliot was horrified when he learned of the captives' treatment, especially since one of them was a woman. The Superintendent went to Ningbo aboard the *Atalanta* to negotiate the prisoners' release. He was told that all the prisoners would be set free immediately—after the British surrendered Chusan.

Although there was no way Elliot would ever abandon such a strategic stronghold as Chusan, he did not reject the offer outright. Because the Chinese believed both parties were negotiating in good faith and hoped for the return of Chusan, they began to treat the prisoners more humanely. The captives left their cages and cells and were lodged together in a temple. Their rations improved, and they received warm clothes and permission to send to Chusan for food and more clothing. Ann Noble and several officers were interrogated about troop movements and the presence of opium and guns aboard the *Kite*. (There was no opium, but the Chinese found two cannons among the ship's wreckage.) One interrogator asked if Noble, who was pregnant, was engaged in the opium trade. Her captors somehow came to believe that she was Queen Victoria's sister, and she was given a servant and bedroom furniture commensurate with her high birth and rank. The Chinese devotion to hierarchy operated even in prison.

The prisoners were joined by a Captain Peter Anstruther, an officer in the Indian army, who had been seized by Chinese peasants on September 16, 1840, a day after the wreck of the *Kite*, while he surveyed Chusan. Bound hand and foot to a long bamboo pole, he was ignominiously transported to Ningbo, where he joined the *Kite* crew. Anstruther charmed his captors with his sense of humor and courage, as well as his talent for portrait painting. High-ranking mandarins sought out this "court painter" and paid for his work with a dozen pork pies per painting. The Roman alphabet also seemed to fascinate the Chinese, and they solicited handwriting samples from their captives. Most of the British fared well in captivity, but a handful of marines, already sick with dysentery contracted in Chusan's dangerous paddies, died in the Ningbo prison.

While their physical environment improved, the psychological condition of the prisoners deteriorated as the Chinese resorted to threats. At one point, the British were told they would all be executed two days hence, and their death would be long and lingering. The deadline came and went with no execution. Anstruther's jailers told him his heart and liver would be cut out and offered as a religious sacrifice in propitiation for Chinese soldiers killed by the British. Anstruther again impressed the Chinese with his courage as he ignored the threats, probably because he knew human sacrifice was not part of the Chinese liturgy. On the other hand, the governor of Zhejiang Province, in which Ningbo was located, had a reputation for sadism, and the British could never be certain that he would not carry out his elaborate threats.

The British in China were incensed by their fellow nationals' captivity and demanded an invasion by sea of Ningbo to free them. Instead, orders went out to seize any Chinese warships the British came upon. Public opinion both in England and among the foreign colony in China was also enraged by this laissez-faire attitude toward the captives, and in October 1840, Captain Elliot met with Qishan at Chinhai, ten miles northeast of where the prisoners were held, and demanded their immediate release or he would end the peace negotiations begun at Chusan. The mandarin treated Elliot with deference, but promised nothing. Elliot noted with amusement the presence of Chinese cavalry, which he had never seen before, accompanying the mandarin and armed only with bows and arrows. During a second meeting, Qishan justified the imprisonment by accusing Anstruther of drawing reconnaissance maps and mentioned that other captives had injured Chinese citizens. (The set-to had occurred when the prisoners had tried to seize food and water.)

A compromise arose from the meetings between Qishan and Elliot, but the terms would not satisfy the British for long. The invaders agreed to stop seizing Chinese vessels and blockading ports. The prisoners would remain where they were, but their living conditions would improve. As a sign of good faith, on December 10, 1840, Qishan visited Vincent Stanton in prison, where he found him immersed in the Bible. Qishan was impressed with the divinity student's piety, freed him, and invited him to be his guest at his palace for a few days before releasing him to Elliot. But the fate of the other captives remained unresolved, and as tensions increased, more troops from India arrived, along with a futuristic weapon that symbolized the technology gap between the two combatants.

Chapter 11

STEAMED VICTORY

———•+•———

"In fact you have been as if your arms were tied, without knowing what to do. It appears that you are no better than a wooden image."

—The Emperor telling Lin Zexu why he was firing him

S team was the nuclear power of the nineteenth century. Relatively clean, efficient, and more reliable than wind or oars, steam power made its worldwide naval debut in the First Opium War. The *Nemesis*, a 660–ton steamship, was launched on the Mersey River in 1839, and made its way to Liverpool before beginning the voyage to China at the height of the Ningbo hostage crisis. An exemplar of state-of-the-art technology, the *Nemesis* was the first steam-powered vessel to round the treacherous Cape of Good Hope. Twelve years before its more famous counterparts the *Monitor* and *Merrimac* clashed during the American Civil War, the *Nemesis* also boasted a hull of iron. But fueling this coal-guzzler was a nightmare, and its journey was slow as it made frequent stops to take on more coal in order to feed its Rabelasian appetite of sixty-five tons per week. As the *Nemesis* steamed up Africa's eastern coast, a violent storm nearly sent it to the bottom after a long rip in its seams almost tore the ship in half. When the *Nemesis* reached Sri Lanka, her captain, William Hall, an early advocate of steam power and much experienced in the operation of steamships, received orders to proceed to Canton. On November 25, 1840, the *Nemesis* arrived in Macao. After a brief meeting with the Portuguese governor Pinto, Hall crossed the Gulf of Canton and set anchor in Danggu, twenty-five miles northeast of Macao, where it rendezvoused with the man-of-war the *Melville*.

The *Nemesis* arrived just in time to have an intimidating effect during the next parley between Qishan and the two Elliots. They met in Canton on November 29, 1840, aboard the *Melville*. Qishan, who cast aside protocol and status by agreeing to meet on the enemy's turf, the *Melville*, brought with him encouraging news. The old anti-opium warrior, Governor-General Lin, had been fired by the Emperor after sending his boss a letter conceding that the opium trade hadn't been eradicated yet, though assuring his master that eventually it would. The failure annoyed the Emperor in particular because Lin's letter arrived at the same time as British ships began to blockade the Bei He River and threaten the capital. Somehow, the English-language *Repository* in Canton got a hold of the Emperor's frosty response to Lin and printed it. The revelation in the press must have delighted both Elliots and the entire foreign colony, because it revealed their troublemaker's fall from power and influence. "Externally you wanted to stop the trade, but it has not been stopped. Internally you wanted to wipe out the outlaws, but they are not cleared away," the Emperor complained to Lin, whom he said had also "caused the waves of confusion to arise...[and] a thousand interminable disorders. In fact you have been as if your arms were tied, without knowing what to do. It appears that you are no better than a wooden image."

In a letter responding to the Emperor's, Lin painted a brighter picture than his boss's assessment of the impasse. He pointed out that the invaders had been decimated by dysentery and other diseases and predicted that the cost of maintaining troops so far from home would soon lead to their departure. Lin begged the Emperor to hold on and not appease the barbarians. He urged military action instead of diplomacy because the British would never be satisfied with compromise. "The more they get the more they demand, and if we do not overcome them by force of arms there will be no end to our troubles. Moreover there is every probability that if the English are not dealt with, other foreigners will soon begin to copy and even outdo them." The Emperor lashed back, "If anyone is copying, it is you, who are trying to frighten me, just as the English try to frighten you!"

In mid October, the Emperor fired Lin. As the disgraced official left Canton in a litter, hundreds of supporters blocked his path, begging him to stay while they cheered him and gave him presents, which the honest minister returned. If it was any consolation, at a farewell supper Lin learned that his predecessor Deng had also been recalled to Peking. When Lin arrived in Whampoa en route to the capital and possible execution, he got a reprieve that must have been a relief and an irritant at the same time. Lin was ordered to remain in Canton and assist Qishan in the negotiations with the barbarians.

Captain Elliot was certain that the zealous Lin's dismissal and humiliation indicated that the Emperor planned to make peace. Unfortunately, at this pivotal turn of events, Elliot lost the help of Admiral Elliot, as the elder man, citing heart problems, resigned and sailed back to England.

To inject military muscle into the negotiations, the British began to mass troops and men-of-war at Canton. Unlike his predecessor, Lin, Qishan appeared to be in a conciliatory mood. On December 4, 1840, he apologized for the cannon attack on the British ship the *Queen* at the Bogue Forts the previous month, and a week later ordered the release of Stanton. But the others remained in prison, and upon his release Stanton revealed that captives were being beaten.

Elliot began the negotiations by demanding the opening of four more ports to trade—Amoy, Fuzhou, Ningbo, and Shanghai,—the surrender of an unspecified island, reimbursement for the confiscated opium, which still obsessed the British merchants and their vocal Parliamentary lobby, and reparations to pay for Britain's military outlays in China. An optimistic Elliot wrote Palmerston on December 1, 1840 that all these demands would be secured within ten days. Three days after this self-imposed deadline passed, Elliot backtracked in a letter to Lord Auckland, conceding that he had failed to get the concessions, but predicted imminent success, this time declining to set a time limit. Then he gave Auckland the bad news. Any success would be "far short of the demands of the government. But we shall have sown the seeds of rapid improvement without the inconvenience of indefinitely interrupted trade; and we shall have avoided the protraction of hostilities, with its certain consequence of deep hatred." Elliot added the hope that a quick peace settlement would stop the Russians and French from joining the fray and sharing the spoils.

Qishan agreed to pay $5 million over twelve years. Elliot wanted $7 million in six years and the surrender of Amoy and Chusan as permanent British possessions. They split the difference over reparations and agreed to $6 million. The cession of Chinese territory was not so easily settled.

Qishan flat out refused Elliot's territorial demands. Elliot offered to forgo Chusan in favor of another port to be chosen later. Qishan ignored the offer, and Elliot resorted to threats, reminding the Emperor's ambassador, "There are large forces collected here, and delays must breed amongst them a very great impatience." To back up the threat, Elliot ordered Indian soldiers to go ashore for drill and target practice.

The New Year (1841) came and went with no movement toward a settlement on either side. An opium ship slipped into Canton, carrying not only the contraband, but a rumor that the Emperor had decided on war. Elliot decided to preempt the enemy, and on January 5, 1841, began preparations for an attack. Still hoping to avert hostilities, Elliot informed Qishan that if an agreement couldn't be reached within the next two days, war would recommence. He even set a specific time, eight in the morning of the 7th.

As promised, on the morning of January 7, 1841, fifteen hundred Indian soldiers and one hundred British marines, sailors, and infantry aboard the *Nemesis, Enterprize,* and *Madagascar* landed without a fight at the mouth of the Canton River, the gateway to Canton. The Anglo-Indian force, backed by artillery aboard the *Calliope, Hyacinth,* and *Larne,* as well as the *Nemesis* and four smaller steamers, attacked Chuanbi Fort while the guns of the *Samarang, Druid, Modeste,* and *Columbine* targeted the walls of Tycocktow Fort across from Chuanbi. Eight thousand men inside the fort's tower returned fire, but stopped after a few minutes. The Chinese cannon had been tied down and couldn't be aimed at the invaders. The British and Indians took advantage of the cease-fire, and two companies of marines went over Chuanbi's earthen walls at 9:30 A.M. The muddy flats in front of the fort slowed the artillery pieces that the men dragged along behind them. The Manchu Dynasty's elite corps of Manchu troops waved flags and banged gongs, but volleys from the British men-of-war soon knocked out their guns. The Manchus believed propaganda that the British killed all prisoners, so they resisted until most of them were dispatched by the invaders. "A frightful scene of slaughter ensued, despite the efforts of the [British] officers to restrain their men," an English participant recalled. By 11 A.M., the yellow Chinese flag was lowered by the invaders, and the British Union Jack flew in its place. Six hundred Manchus died, and another one hundred, apparently not taken in by propaganda, surrendered. The British had only thirty casualties, none fatal, and their injuries were caused not by the defenders, but by the accidental explosion of an overheated artillery piece.

The Chinese defenders fled the city, but a flanking move by Major Pratt of the 26th regiment forced the refugees back into the fort. Ships' artillery shelled the city, killing many of the defenders. The *Nemesis* and other British ships went in for the kill, setting ablaze eleven Chinese warships at anchor in the mouth of the river and using Congreve rockets as incendiaries.

The Chinese artillery at the fort and aboard war junks did not return fire. To escape the deadly bombardment, some defenders jumped into the water, where gunfire from British ships killed many of them. Others inside the fort were burned and disfigured when their antiquated matchlocks' gunpowder exploded—their misery compounded by British gunfire. The British took very few prisoners. Years later, a staff officer, Armine Mountain, wrote, "The slaughter of fugitives is unpleasant, but we are such a handful in the face of so wide a country and so large a force that we should be swept away if we did not deal our enemy a sharp lesson whenever we came in contact." In contrast to the slaughter of the Chinese, the British suffered no fatalities and only twenty-four wounded.

The successful seizure of Chuanbi was followed by a naval battle that was more like a rout, at Anson's Bay, to the east of Chuanbi. There, the steamship *Nemesis* demonstrated that it was a navy unto itself by firing on fifteen Chinese war junks. A rocket from the *Nemesis* had the blind luck of hitting one of the junk's powder magazines, and the ship was blown to pieces. At the sight of this ferocious new technology and its devastating effects, the fourteen remaining junks began to flee, but not fast enough for some of their terrified crew, who jumped overboard. The *Nemesis* didn't pursue the junks, but steamed up river where it found two more junks and another village that had been deserted as soon as the news of the massacre at Chuanbi made its way upstream. The *Nemesis* torched one of the junks, seized the other, and then rejoined the fleet.

Three other forts remained near Chuanbi. On the next day, just as British ships were about to shell the forts, a physician under a white flag of truce arrived with an offer from Admiral Guan, the commander of the Chinese troops, asking for a three-day cease-fire to allow him to confer with Qishan. Captain Elliot had been horrified by the massacre at Chuanbi, and to the fury of his men, who wanted to capitalize on their quick victory by marching on Canton, he accepted the cease-fire. Elliot displayed a conflicting combination of pacifism and belligerence in a letter to James Matheson after agreeing to the truce. "I hope we shall settle without further bloodshed. The Commissioner [Lin] knows we can take much more than he would like to lose whenever we please." Elliot channeled his men's bloodlust into demolishing the walls of the Chuanbi and Tycocktow Forts.

Qishan and Elliot parleyed at the Lotus Flower Wall, twenty-six miles south of Canton. Elliot showed up with an intimidating entourage of fifty-six Royal Marines, a fifteen-member fife-and-drum band, and Captain Rosamel, commander of the French corvette *Danaide*, anchored in Canton Bay. Elliot's invitation to Rosamel was both a diplomatic courtesy and a clever political ploy to keep an eye on the French, whom he feared would try to share in the British spoils without having fought for them.

While the Chinese feted Elliot's men with wine and mutton, and the British entertained their "hosts" with a musket drill that was part show, part threat, Qishan and Elliot conferred aboard a boat in the middle of the Canton River. By January 20, 1841, they had agreed to what would be known as the Chuanbi Convention. In light of the annihilation of the Chinese forces, the British were surprisingly magnanimous about the terms, which in the hands of a more vengeful power could easily have devolved into a *diktat*. The British agreed to buy Hong Kong for $6 million, ambassadors at last would be exchanged, all contact between the two powers would be direct and official, there would be no more linguistic squabbling about "tribute-bearing barbarians," and trade would resume. The British also agreed to return the forts they had captured, including all of Chusan Island. To pay for the war and save Palmerston from a budget battle in Parliament that might cause the government to fall, the Chinese were forced to pay $6 million, neatly neutralizing their gain from the sale of Hong Kong. Qishan presumed that the Emperor and his court would agree to the indemnity because they planned to extort the sum from the Hong merchants, which they in fact did. (Howqua alone coughed up the enormous sum of $820,000 as his contribution to the indemnity.) Far from home and burdened by slow communication, Elliot couldn't know that the Chuanbi pact would infuriate Palmerston, who still wanted the instructions he had given Elliot followed, namely reimbursement for the twenty thousand confiscated opium chests and the cost of the war. The Emperor was even more outraged, especially by the cession of Hong Kong, and recalled Qishan to Peking. Impotently, the Emperor, still operating in an alternate universe, however celestial, also ordered Elliot to report immediately to the capital for his execution.

Palmerston was as displeased as the Emperor, although British civil servants were not so ruinously punished. When the Foreign Minister learned the terms of the Chuanbi settlement, he complained, "After all, our naval power is so strong that we can tell the Emperor what *we* mean to hold, rather than that *he* should say what he would cede." The repatriation of the hard-fought-for Chusan particularly irritated Palmerston because he wanted a strong British presence near the mouth of the strategic Yangtze River, which Chusan provided. Palmerston also at last put the ugly source of all the hostilities on the table when he insisted on the "admission of opium into China as an article of lawful commerce." Elliot, the anti-drug advocate, had not even brought the subject up during his meetings with Qishan. Palmerston was also displeased with the $6 million indemnity, wanting more for the trouble the Chinese had put his invading troops to. And he wanted more ports open to British ships. When Elliot finally received Palmerston's written response to the Chuanbi Convention, the news was not good. The British government would not ratify the agreement.

On January 20, 1841, the same day that the Chuanbi Convention was signed, the Emperor ordered Qishan to stop negotiating with the barbarians because military reinforcements were being sent to Canton from the interior. Thousands of troops would be under the command of a geriatric commander whose days of military glory were far behind him. The seventy-year-old Yang Fang was an unlikely choice for *generalissimo* and China's last hope of wrestling sovereignty back from the encroaching British. Yang was stone deaf and gave orders to his men in writing. On the diplomatic front, the Emperor enlisted a cousin, Yishan, who also made his way from the capital to Canton.

Unaware of these hostile developments and the Emperor's rejection of the Chuanbi agreement, Elliot felt the current situation calm enough to send for his wife and young son in Singapore.

On January 26, 1841, the British, under the command of Lieutenant Colonel George Burrell of the 18th, occupied Hong Kong as part of the

Chuanbi settlement. Despite his personal opposition to the opium trade, Elliot agreed to let the British use the island for offloading the drug. Matheson wrote Jardine, "Elliot says that he sees no objection to our storing opium there, and as soon as the [Chinese] New Year holidays are over I shall set about building." James Matheson prized the island and transferred his headquarters there, building a huge stone fortress in case the Chinese ever repented the cession.

Despite its barrenness, Hong Kong was a brilliant new jewel in Her Majesty's crown because of its deep harbor and a native population too small to oppose their new British masters. (The British were happy to let go of dangerous Chusan, where Captain Stead of the troopship *Pestonjee*, unaware that the Chuanbi Convention had ceded the island back to the Chinese, was disemboweled by the locals after landing there.)

On February 1, 1841, Elliot unilaterally proclaimed Hong Kong British territory and the residents subjects of the Crown, neither of which assertions had been agreed to in the Chuanbi Convention. A week later, eight Protestant missionaries from Macao arrived on the island. British justice was also installed and practiced with the cruelty that was more appropriate for shipboard discipline than a civilian population, and included flogging. "None of the Chinese ever stood more than six blows of the cat [whip], when they invariably fainted," a resident of the island wrote.

Elliot met again with Qishan at Second Bar, an island twenty miles southeast of Canton, this time in the company of a French ship's captain. Qishan refused to put the Imperial seal on the Convention of Chuanbi. By now Qishan's position had become untenable. The Emperor was furious with the mandarin for ceding Hong Kong, and he had already been fired when Elliot met with him, which may explain why no progress was made. Qishan did not inform Elliot of his removal from office, but ascribed his refusal to illness.

As Chinese soldiers began to mass around the Bogue, Elliot decided to use arms again when diplomacy failed. On February 26, 1841, the *Melville*, the *Queen*, the *Wellesley*, the *Druid*, and the *Modeste* began to shell forts on Wangtong and Anunghoi islands on the Bogue. The stationary guns of the forts were set at such a high elevation they only damaged the topsails of the British ships. Within fifteen minutes, the Chinese stopped firing at the fleet as marines, sailors, and Indian soldiers landed on the beach on the southern portion of Wangtong. "Opposition there was none. The unfortunate Chinese literally crammed the trenches, begging for mercy. I wish I could add that it was granted," the leader of the troops, Edward Belcher, reported in the *Repository*. The Indian soldiers began executing the prisoners. When Belcher tried to save the prisoners, "two were shot down whilst holding my shirt, and my gig's crew, perceiving my danger, dragged me away exclaiming, 'They will shoot you next, sir!'" When the invaders occupied the fort, they learned that the defending soldiers had retreated before the landing had begun, leaving the civilians to be butchered by the Indian troops. Within two hours, the forts on Anunghoi were also seized with minimal effort. Elliot narrowly missed being killed by a cannonball as he reclined in a hammock on the deck of his ship. Three Chinese died in the engagements, one hundred were wounded, and more than a thousand taken prisoner. Admiral Guan's body lay among the defenders, a bayonet in his chest. The British accorded the old warrior a cannon salute from the Blenheim when his family retrieved the body and sailed off with it. With the fall of the remaining Bogue forts, the mouth of the Canton River and the gateway to Canton belonged to the British.

On February 27, 1841, Elliot made his way up the Canton River aboard the *Nemesis*. A few miles upriver, he came across the *Cambridge*, which had been captured earlier and was now surrounded by Chinese warships, all of which fled after a brief bombardment by the *Nemesis*. The *Cambridge's* Chinese crew jumped overboard as the British boarded her. Unable to tow the *Cambridge*, Elliot put the ship to the torch. The only British fatality was a marine whose musket exploded in his hands.

Elliot, now backed by more ships and soldiers, continued on toward Canton, removing barrier chains and demolishing forts. As the armada approached the city, ten thousand residents fled, including Lin's family. James Ryan, an American merchant who had remained behind, wrote that the city "never looked so desolate." The hatred of those who had not fled registered in their faces, Ryan observing that they "scowl upon every one of us in a way indicative of a greater dislike than I have ever before observed." Canton harbor was too shallow for the *Nemesis* to dock, however, so Elliot and the *Nemesis*, unaccompanied by the rest of the fleet, turned back and steamed up and down the Canton River, destroying more forts and nine Chinese warships. The Chinese had never seen a steamship before, and the sudden apparition of the *Nemesis* on the river terrified them.

The biggest loser in the British onslaught was Qishan, who was recalled to Peking. After years of service, his disgrace was total. He was not only recalled, but also arrested and put in chains. He set out from Canton en route to the capital on March 12, 1841. His entire fortune—425,000 acres of land, 135,000 ounces of gold, and £10,000,000 in cash—reverted to the master he had served so faithfully. The old mandarin's only consolation, as dubious as it was, rested on the fact that the Emperor's sentence of death was commuted to hard labor at a military encampment near China's frigid northern border with Russia.

Lin, for some reason, was not blamed for the humiliating string of naval defeats and remained in power at Canton. Perhaps the official owed his survival to the dispatches he sent the Emperor, which were outright fabrications. Lin was also deluding himself. He wrote in his diary, "Our regular troops sank two of their dinghies and shattered the mainmast of one of their warships; after which they retired." This was simply not true.

On March 13, 1841, the rest of the British fleet arrived outside Canton, and blew the Chinese ships in the harbor to pieces and knocked out the city's cannon. During the afternoon of March 19, British marines and sailors landed near the factories, and the defenders fled without firing a shot. Many refugees were cut down during the retreat. The following day, Elliot occupied the New English factory and declared peace.

Howqua now approached Elliot, begging for a truce on behalf of General Fang. Elliot agreed and used the opportunity to restore trade and at the same time deal a partial blow to the opium trade he excoriated. The trade in tea would recommence, but any opium found aboard British ships would be confiscated. However, opium importers would no longer be arrested and punished, abolishing Lin's death penalty.

The truce was just a feint on the part of the Chinese, who continued to mass troops outside Canton. Elliot daily saw Chinese ships bristling with soldiers sail past the English factories.

Chapter 12

A PRICE
ON HIS HEAD

———·——·———

"Exterminate the rebels!"

—Chinese battle cry

The truce led to a resumption of the opium trade. A single ship at this time, no longer fearing the might of the impotent Chinese navy or army, carried as many as sixteen hundred chests. The new security provided by British troops caused a rise in imports of the drug from India, and the price fell to $400 per chest. Elliot was dismayed and tried to stop the opium-laden vessels from unloading their cargo in Canton. The merchants ignored him, and Elliot did not persist, fearing their backers in Parliament.

The Superintendent of Trade had other worries besides the trade in opium. The Chinese responded to their defeat by setting a price for the capture or murder of all British citizens, with Elliot fetching top dollar at $50,000, a king's ransom in the nineteenth century.

During the battles of the Bogue, Qishan had sent a memorandum to the Emperor that was amazing for its candor and lack of courtly obfuscation. While Lin sent Peking tales of great Chinese victories that never happened, Qishan told the Emperor that the Chinese army, corrupt and out of date, was no match for the might of the barbarians and counseled strategic surrender in future battles, which seemed inevitable given the resumption of the opium trade. For his honesty, Qishan had been recalled to Peking. He was replaced by three mandarins with whom Elliot would find it impossible to negotiate, in contrast to his working relationship with Qishan, even though it too had been prickly.

One of these replacements, General Yang Fang, shared Qishan's conciliatory attitude toward the invaders and urged the Emperor to allow the opium trade to continue, because he reasoned that if the British occupied themselves with making money, they would have little time and desire to wage war against the Chinese. The Emperor dismissed Fang's advice, saying, "If trade were the solution to the problem, why would it be necessary to transfer and dispatch generals and troops?" Instead, the Emperor ordered Yang and the other two members of the triumvirate, Ishand and Longwen, to retake Hong Kong, the loss of which continued to obsess the humiliated Emperor.

Toward the end of March, 1841, Elliot and his staff decided to attack Amoy, about four hundred miles northeast of Canton, with the date set for the second week of May. Before the attack could begin, however, Elliot fell ill in Macao. Adding to his woes was intelligence that Chinese troops were massing outside Canton along warships and fireboats, while forts in the area were being repaired. Yang Fang used the presence of the troops and war machinery to urge Elliot to return to the bargaining table, by letting him know that the Chinese military forces now outnumbered the British—not much of a threat or bargaining chip considering the primitive conditions of the Chinese forces and their recent track record in battle. Elliot heeded the warning, but instead of suing for peace, he cancelled the attack on Amoy to concentrate on the armed camp that Canton had become.

On May 11, 1841, Elliot boarded the *Nemesis* with his wife and made for Canton. There he saw the newly repaired forts bristling with new cannon. He also noticed a parade of Chinese warships sail past the factories. Elliot sent the prefect of Canton a letter demanding that war preparations by the Chinese cease.

On May 21, 1841, Elliot ordered the British and urged the Americans to leave the factories. Only a few Americans ignored Elliot's recommendation; the entire British population complied. In less than twenty-four hours, the foreign quarter became a ghost town. The quiet was shattered at midnight when the Chinese attacked, shelling the factories from opposite riverbanks.

Fireboats stuffed with cotton drenched in oil were launched against the British warships, which were becalmed. The *Nemesis* was able to steam away from danger, firing on the Chinese warships, which sought cover behind the fire ships. The fire ships missed the British vessels and crashed into the shore, where they set the city ablaze. The *Nemesis* fired on the forts and silenced their artillery. By the next morning, the sea battle was over. The Chinese had failed to dislodge the British.

On May 25, 1841, the *Nemesis*, towing seventy sailing ships teeming with two thousand troops, reached Tsingpu, two miles northwest of Canton. Tsingpu had a natural harbor from which the British could launch an attack on the northern heights of Canton. The troops and artillery disembarked. As they marched toward Canton, Chinese soldiers screamed and waved their weapons at the invaders, but didn't attack and kept a safe distance.

On May 26, 1841, it was decided to assault a hill and tower that made up part of the wall that defended Canton. Once captured, the hill would make an excellent position for artillery, which would shell the city and force a quick surrender, the attackers were certain. The Chinese defended the hill briefly, inflicting only one casualty on the British, then fled.

The following day, May 27, at 10 A.M., a mandarin waving a white flag appeared on the wall of a nearby fort. With Thom translating, the mandarin begged for a cessation of hostilities. Through intermediaries, Hugh Gough told the mandarin that he would only negotiate with the commander of the Chinese forces in Canton, but agreed to an armistice while waiting for the officer. He never appeared, and Gough resumed preparations for an attack. Around seven the next morning, the British were about to begin shelling the city when Chinese on the nearby fort's walls again waved white flags, but this time also bellowed Elliot's name "as if he had been their protecting joss," according to Edward Belcher. The real reason the defenders shouted out Elliot's name was that they mistook a naval lieutenant climbing the hill for the Superintendent of Trade. The lieutenant carried instructions ordering the troops not to continue the attack because Elliot was already negotiating with the Chinese over the fate of Canton.

But on May 29, 1841, General Fang broke the truce and ordered his men to attack Canton with the battle cry, "Exterminate the rebels!" That same day, manned (!) fire rafts unsuccessfully tried to set fire to British ships docked at Whampoa, five miles west of Canton, while the fire rafts' crew threw stinkpots at the enemy vessels and attempted to board them with grappling hooks. Chinese troops also invaded the foreign factories, looting, then tearing them down. British ships sailed up the Pearl River and began to bombard the walls of Canton. Elliot decided not to invade the city because his forces, decimated by dysentery, had dwindled to twenty-two hundred men, while the occupiers of Canton numbered more than twenty thousand.

Another truce was agreed to, with the Chinese promising to pay a $6 million ransom within seven days and the British promising not to sack the city if the money was paid. The British government was at last seeing a "profit" in its war against the Chinese. Six million dollars was more than twice the amount the government earned from taxes on tea per annum. The cost in human lives was another figure that the Whig capitalists who controlled Parliament at this time did not care to take into account. Canton was also to be demilitarized, with only a skeletal garrison force remaining in the city. The Chinese would compensate the owners of the looted and demolished factories, and the Spanish were to be reimbursed for the loss of the brig *Bilbaino*, which the Chinese had burned two years earlier by mistake, thinking it was a British ship carrying opium. In return for these humiliating concessions from the Chinese, the British agreed to leave the Canton River and pull their troops out of all the forts they had occupied. The issues of the opium trade, British possession of Hong Kong, the resumption of trade, compensations for the now mythic twenty thousand chests of confiscated opium, and the exchange of ambassadors were ignored for the sake of securing an end to the hostilities, which the Chinese were clearly losing. The treaty also avoided any mention of a British victory or Chinese defeat to save the Emperor face and encourage his acceptance of the deal.

The urban residents of Canton accepted the humiliating terms of the settlement, but the peasants in the surrounding countryside were appalled and enraged by the loss of face. The peasants belonged to long-standing militia that was used from time to time by the government to quell uprisings. To the British, the militias at best were no threat and at worst a bad, anachronistic joke, armed as they were with cudgels, hoes, and a handful of matchlock rifles. Perhaps it was the contempt for the militia that led the British to engage in acts that, regardless of their morality, were also bad strategy, since the purpose of the British invasion was to pacify a population, not enflame it. But enflame it they did: one foraging expedition turned into looting, including the desecration of a tomb's riches and its corpse, a special abomination for the ancestor-worshipping Chinese. Even the *Canton Repository*, the local British newspaper and not exactly an organ of independent reportage, spoke of the British outrages as "doings of which it is a shame to speak."

The looting and desecration brought the militia to the boiling point, but an incident on May 29 made the resentment boil over at last. At Sanyuanli, a village a few miles northwest of Canton, British troops stormed a peasant hut and raped the women inside. Militia members began to mass on the hills above the village the following day. Outnumbered, the British decided to attack, and in the first skirmish, the militiamen fled. More Chinese to replace those who had retreated appeared at the top of the hill, about seven thousand, almost twice as many as in the first confrontation, and ten times the number of British. Again the British decided offense was the best defense. The Chinese turned and fled again, but before the British could pursue them, a torrential rainfall began. The British decided to make an orderly retreat, but found themselves immobilized in mud and water that reached to their knees.

The Chinese ended their retreat and counterattacked. The rain made the British flintlocks unusable and suddenly the two sides found themselves more evenly matched. During a lull in the rain, the Indian soldiers used the opportunity to dry their muskets, and renewed gunfire halted the Chinese attack, until it began to rain again, and the pursuit resumed. The Chinese militia soon surrounded the British and Indian soldiers, and a massacre seemed inevitable. Then, a band of marines armed with waterproof percussion muskets turned up, and under a flurry of gunfire, helped their comrades escape. Despite the close call, the battle represented another victory for the British, who lost only one man. The Chinese, as usual, decided to rewrite history, and hailed the British retreat as a great Chinese victory. As the story spread throughout the countryside, it inspired thousands more peasants to join the "victorious" militia.

Undeterred, the next day, May 31, more militia began to mass near the British troops. Gough, the British commander, sent word to the prefect of Canton, She Baoshun, that he would attack if the militiamen did not disperse immediately. She Baoshun was so terrified by the threat that he left Canton and visited Gough to assure him the militia was not acting under his or the Emperor's orders. Then, in what must have been a humiliating turn for the prefect, She Baoshun addressed the irregulars, informing them that a peace agreement had been reached with the barbarians, and that the militia must allow the British to depart while they themselves disarmed and returned to their villages, which the militia did.

The disbanded Chinese irregulars continued to embroider the legend of the great "victory" at Sanyuanli, in which thousands of British had fled or been killed, including a general. As the tale grew taller, it was reported that the entire British expedition would have been exterminated if She Baoshun had not intervened. News of the Chinese triumph reached the Emperor and emboldened his advisors, who urged him to build on the victory and bring an even larger army into the field against the barbarians. Inaccurate or wishful intelligence like this would have disastrous effects on Chinese policy.

For all his efforts at peacemaking, the luckless She Baoshun found himself booed when he administered a test to bureaucrats, which they needed to pass in order to ascend the government hierarchy. The bureaucrats punctuated their insults by throwing inkwells at the disgraced prefect, who resigned before Peking could fire him. Perhaps because of the language barrier or a failure of intelligence, the British did not know they had "lost" the battle, and did not realize the propaganda and military purposes to which the Chinese were putting this revisionist history.

In a letter to the Foreign Office, Elliot explained the tactical reasons for a cease-fire: "The disappearance of the municipal authorities and the police, the flight of the respectable inhabitants, the sacking of the town by the rabble, its certain desolation, its not improbable destruction by fire, and our hurried departure from the ruins." Elliot feared the operation would kill the patient. The settlement was a Band-Aid that covered a gangrenous fissure, a truce, not a peace treaty. In particular, the failure to address and solve the opium problem made another conflict inevitable. As Chinese soldiers left Canton in compliance with the settlement, civil rule broke down, and the city fell into chaos. Departing soldiers, like victors rather than losers, looted the city, mobs of civilians fought each other, and the sacked co-governor of Canton, Yishan, beheaded some coolies who had the temerity to stop his litter and demand to know his plans to stop the mayhem. He had none. Yishan was leaving with the soldiers. The $6 million was paid promptly and just as promptly shipped out of the country, half to India, the remainder to England. Having made the Canton factories safe for its residents, Elliot turned his conqueror's eye on the next prize, Amoy. Meanwhile, the genuine victors encountered a more efficient enemy, disease. In the semitropical heat, minor wounds and even scratches turned gangrenous. Dysentery, malaria, and diarrhea created so many casualties; the warships became hospitals for the decimated troops.

On July 21, 1841, Elliot was in Hong Kong preparing for the assault on Amoy when a typhoon struck the island. It died down by mid afternoon, but three days later another typhoon swept over the island. No British warships sank, but the damage to masts, rigging, and sails postponed the Amoy expedition. Elliot's cutter, the *Louisa*, was wrecked by the second typhoon, and the Superintendent of Trade swam ashore, where he narrowly escaped capture by a passing war junk. Elliot fared worse on shore. A merchantman from India, along with opium and cotton, brought with it a copy of the *Canton Press*, which reported that Elliot had been fired—four months earlier! The newspaper came in one of Jardine, Matheson's swift clippers, which scooped the formal announcement of Elliot's dismissal by Palmerston on April 30, 1841.

Chapter 13

THE SACKING OF AMOY, NINGBO, AND CHARLES ELLIOT

"...not only prison guards and common soldiers, but every official from mandarin and high military commanders down was apparently an opium smoker; capricious and neglectful of duty, sometimes cruel."

—Jack Beeching

The British press vilified Elliot for making peace with the Chinese instead of pushing for a decisive victory. Editorials pilloried him for failing to establish an exchange of ambassadors, and the $6 million in reparations was dismissed as representing only a fraction of the cost of the expedition. Palmerston added to the cavils in a letter to Elliot that didn't mince words as it explained the reasons for his dismissal. "Throughout the whole course of your proceedings, you seem to have considered that my instructions were waste paper, which you might treat with entire disregard, and that you were at full liberty to deal with the interests of your country according to your own fancy." Elliot pleaded that the unpredictable variables of disease and bad weather had tempered what he still considered a successful tour of duty. The ex-Superintendent took issue with the accusation that he had been soft on the enemy and published a pamphlet, in which he wrote, "It has been popularly objected to me that I have cared too much for the Chinese. But I submit that it has been caring more for lasting British honour and substantial British interests to protect a helpless and friendly people..."

Palmerston was also outraged that Elliot had abandoned Chusan in return for Hong Kong, a barren island without a harbor or habitable structures. The $6 million settlement was only a fraction of the cost of the twenty thousand confiscated chests of opium, a forfeiture that still rankled in Britain and wounded national pride and greed. Even Queen Victoria joined the chorus of condemnation after a consultation with her Foreign Minister. "All we wanted might have been got, if it had not been for the unaccountably strange conduct of Charles Elliot, who completely disobeyed his instructions and tried to get the lowest terms he could," she wrote her uncle, King Leopold of Belgium.

Despite the British government's displeasure with Elliot's military efforts, it deigned to keep Sir Hugh Gough in charge of the land troops in China, but replaced the ailing Sir George Elliot with Sir William Parker as commander-in-chief. Sir Henry Pottinger, a veteran of the Afghan wars and a diplomat who had worked for the East India Company, took Charles Elliot's post as Superintendent of Trade for an annual salary of £6,000—twice his predecessor's and a slap in Elliot's face.

The new British warlords assigned to China, Sir Henry Pottinger and Sir William Parker, both had an impressive résumé and both entered military service at the precocious age of twelve. Pottinger served as a cabin boy and fought in the Napoleonic Wars. Through family connections, he received a commission as a cadet in the Indian Army. Parker was even better connected, a nephew of Admiral Lord St. Vincent. At thirty-one, he retired with the rank of captain and a fortune in prize money from French ships captured during the Napoleonic Wars. Parker spent the next fifteen years on his estate in Litchfield as a gentleman farmer before being called out of retirement by a desperate and frustrated Palmerston.

Pottinger and Parker traveled together from London to Macao, arriving in the Portuguese outpost on August 9, 1841, in the steamer *Sesotris*, after a voyage of only sixty-seven days. Troops from India arrived to garrison Hong Kong at about the same time. Elliot graciously greeted the newcomers there and left the country in mid August on the *Atalanta* with his wife and son. If the British merchants in China hoped for a more amenable chief than the fractious Elliot, they were shocked when Pottinger told the residents of Canton that he "could allow no consideration connected with mercantile pursuits…to interfere with the strong measures which he might deem necessary, and if they put either themselves or their property in the power of the Chinese authorities, it must be clearly understood to be at their own risk and peril."

If Elliot was arguably a Sinophile, Pottinger was a contemptuous Sinophobe with little understanding or appreciation of rigid Chinese protocol and the all-importance of saving face. When the Prefect of Canton went to Macao to greet Pottinger on his arrival, a huge concession rarely accorded representatives of the barbarians, Pottinger snubbed the prefect and sent a subordinate to meet him.

On August 21, 1841, a new armada of thirty-two ships, including four steamers loaded with four regiments of twenty-seven thousand men aboard (1,350 had been left behind to guard Hong Kong and threaten Canton), set out from Macao en route to Amoy, which they reached four days later under favorable winds. Amoy, a barren granite island three hundred miles north of Macao, wasn't much of a prize except that it was closer to Peking and thus the British presence was more threatening to the Emperor. A treeless coastal backwater with little arable land whose food had to be imported, Amoy was favored by pirates and smugglers who carried on illegal business with Singapore. Amoy had been fortified with a new sod and granite façade one thousand yards long, bristling with ninety-six embrasures and two hundred guns to defend the city's harbor. An additional forty-two guns and ten thousand troops, including fierce Manchu contingents, defended the citadel within Amoy. On nearby Kolungsu Island, which protected the approach to Amoy, there were seventy-six guns, including rare modern artillery smuggled in from Singapore. The *Modeste*, *Blonde*, and *Druid* left the fleet for Kolungsu, where they blasted the walls from only four hundred yards away.

At a safer distance, two British ships bombarded Amoy with long-range guns. The majority of the Chinese cannons at both Amoy and Kolungsu were antiquated and fixed in position, and again failed to do any damage to the British fleet as Pottinger sailed past them aboard the steamer *Phlegethon*. The weather was hot and humid. After ninety minutes of fire from the British ships, most of the Chinese guns fell silent, and the British landed a group of Royal Irish soldiers without opposition. Sir Hugh Gough disembarked from the *Nemesis* at 3:45 P.M. The *Modeste* and the *Blonde* had neutralized five of Amoy's batteries and put out of commission twenty-six Chinese warships in the harbor, but despite three hours of shelling, the British were unable to silence all of Amoy's guns. Sir Hugh Gough personally led a bayonet charge, circling around and attacking the fortress on its south side.

The Manchu defenders discharged their matchlocks at the invaders, then fled with their wounded in tow. When he realized the battle was lost, the commander of the Manchus marched into the sea straight toward the British ships as though mounting one last personal charge, but in reality, he committed suicide by drowning himself. The Chinese put a positive spin on the commander's death, as witnesses reported to the Emperor that the Manchu chief had "rushed out to drive back the assailants as they landed, fell into the water and died," turning a suicide into an unlikely attack.

Meanwhile, the Irish troops climbed over the walls, opened the gates, and let their comrades in. Among the items left behind by the fleeing soldiers, the Irish soldiers found opium pipes lying besides the artillery pieces on the walls. The opium-impaired defenders had been defeated in part by the very drug they were fighting against. When the invaders reached the city's treasury, they found records indicating the presence of thousands of silver dollars, but the loot had vanished. Government officials had smuggled out the bullion in hollow logs, pretending to be lumber traders. While prize money like the bullion was considered legitimate spoils of victory, looting of private property was made punishable by death, and Gough had several men executed for the crime. After a week's delay due to storms, Gough left Amoy after garrisoning the city and continued north toward the ultimate prize, Peking.

When a ship belonging to Dent stopped along the way to pick up provisions in the vicinity of Keeto Point near Chusan, one of the men was kidnapped and beaten by the locals. A few days later, British troops from the *Phlegethon* landed and burned two villages in retaliation. In a letter to Lord Auckland, Sir William Parker wrote, "I sincerely hope that [the burning of the villages] may have the effect of checking similar acts of atrocity on the part of the Chinese."

By September 25, 1841, the entire fleet had assembled and it was decided to take the fort of Dinghai on the island of Chusan. Dinghai was better fortified and had more artillery than Amoy, and its defenders put up an impressive fight, but the British managed to take the fort with only one casualty. The Manchu commander, General Keo, slit his own throat when he realized that the British would prevail. The stiffness of the Chinese resistance stiffened Sir Henry Pottinger's resolve. He wrote Palmerston, "Under no circumstances will Tin-hai [Dinghai] and its dependencies be restored to the Chinese government, until the whole of the demands of England are not only complied with, but carried into full effect." Conquest and occupation became powerful bargaining chips in all future negotiations with Peking.

———·———

War fever back in England was stoked by another prisoner-of-war crisis, this time on the island of Taiwan. The British ship the *Nerbudda*, transporting British and Indian troops and support staff, went aground off Taiwan. The white soldiers fled in lifeboats, leaving the Indians behind. The Indians spent five days on the immobilized ship until dehydration and hunger forced them to go ashore on rafts. Chinese soldiers seized them, stripped them naked, put them in chains, and crammed them into small cells. In March 1841, fourteen survivors from the opium ship *Ann*, which had also gone aground on Taiwan, joined the imprisoned crew of the *Nerbudda*. Their jailers' cruelty, according to one historian, was compounded by their addiction to the drug the prisoners' ship carried. "Everyone on Formosa [Taiwan] to whose arbitrary power they became subject—not only prison guards and common soldiers, but every official from mandarin and high military commanders, down—was apparently an opium smoker; capricious and neglectful of duty, sometimes cruel," according to Jack Beeching. Desperate for victory and good news to report, the Chinese officials on Taiwan reinvented the two shipwrecks as successful naval battles in their reports to the Emperor, who rewarded them with honors and money.

———·———

After a week in Dinghai, the British left a garrison behind and proceeded to Jinhai, ten miles due east on the mainland, and began the attack on October 10, 1841. Jinhai was a more difficult target, its fort resting atop a sheer cliff. Almost four thousand Chinese troops defended the city and its citadel. But by using a flanking attack, Gough and a force of fifteen hundred men managed to take the fort in less than twenty-four hours after a vigorous pounding by the *Wellesley* and *Blenheim* to cover the ground attack. By early afternoon, the British controlled Jinhai, suffering only three fatalities and sixteen wounded. Several hundred Chinese died defending the city. After an unsuccessful attempt at drowning himself, the Chinese commander of the fort, Yukien, managed to commit suicide by overdosing on opium, a symbolic end and emblematic of one of the major causes of the conflict. Yukien's suicide took the fight out of the Chinese.

The British captured 150 guns, some antiques, others state-of-the-art, including an amazing identical Chinese replication of British cannons. Dozens of prisoners were taken, then released because Gough couldn't spare the men to guard them. But before their release, the POWs were threatened with the indignity of having their Manchu queues lopped off with jackknives by British sailors, who had promised their girlfriends and wives back home they would send the pelts as souvenirs. The victims were assembled in public for their tonsure, a ritual humiliation that the British commander—to his credit—forbade after learning of the plan.

On October 13, a flotilla of seven British ships landed troops on Ningbo, ten miles southeast of Jinhai. The city opened its gates to the invaders without a fight as a Royal Irish band played "Saint Patrick's Day in the Morning." When the invaders found the building where their countrymen had been kept in cages, they burned down the prison in rage, but kept one of the cages as a grisly souvenir, which was sent to India for public exhibition as a symbol of Chinese barbarity.

While individual reprisals by the conquerors were frowned on for tactical reasons, official punishment emanated from the top. Sir Henry Pottinger didn't bother with euphemisms when he wrote to the Foreign Secretary that he "looked forward with considerable satisfaction to plundering Ningpo [Ningbo] as a reprisal for the maltreatment there of British prisoners." And plunder the British did. The occupiers seized Ningbo's municipal funds, totaling $160,000, while the residents paid an additional ransom of 10 percent in the form of property and excise taxes. The British settled in Ningbo for the winter, but they failed to provide police protection after the local police had fled. Chinese freebooters looted what the British hadn't already expropriated and beat those who refused to give up their possessions voluntarily.

Not everyone shared Pottinger's to-the-victors-go-the-spoils philosophy. Both Sir William Parker and Sir Hugh Gough chided Pottinger that the city had surrendered after being promised its inhabitants would not be molested, physically or financially, and they complained that Pottinger's active-passive policy toward Ningbo was a breach of British honor. Pottinger's jubilant letter to Lord Palmerston describing the sack of Ningbo showed that his colleague's objections had not moved him.

But by the time Pottinger's letter reached London, the Whigs were out of office, and the new Tory Foreign Secretary, Lord Aberdeen, a High Church moralist, received Pottinger's news with a disgust he didn't bother to hide. Pottinger and Aberdeen had been schoolmates at Harrow, but old school ties didn't bind the two men, who were bitter rivals.

Sir Henry had recently been elevated to baronet, which added the honorific "Sir" to his name, but in a note Aberdeen made in the margin of Pottinger's letter, the Foreign Secretary snubbed the new baronet by referring to the plenipotentiary as "Mr." rather than "Sir Henry." "The worst proposal I have seen from Mr. Pottinger…it ought not to pass unnoticed," was scribbled on Pottinger's letter.

The easy victories in China were also pyrhhic, however. Due to illness and the garrisons left behind, Gough now found his troops reduced from the original twenty-five hundred to only seven hundred capable of fighting. They decided to winter in Ningbo, where humiliated residents demonstrated their rage at the occupiers by throwing rocks and feces at any British soldier who had the temerity or rashness to move about the city unescorted. When Sir Henry Pottinger arrived in Ningbo on January 13, 1842, besides looting the city treasury, he had also ordered the confiscation of all the Chinese ships and provisions and other property, including the main pagoda's bell, which was sent to India as another symbolic prize. Gough was horrified by this desecration, fearing the seizure would make Peking even more intransigent.

Pottinger appointed the Reverend Dr. Karl Gutzlaff, a Prussian missionary and translator, to the top post of civil magistrate in Ningbo. Although Dr. Gutzlaff had come to China to spread the faith, he became a ruthless chief executive. During his tenure, he sentenced local miscreants to hard labor in the quarries of Hong Kong, where they were kept in chains. The new magistrate appointed a former pimp, Yu Dechang, as the city's chief of police. Based on his knowledge of the residents of Ningbo, Yu drew up a list of rich citizens from whom the British could extort more "ransom." Yu also spied on the Imperial forces massing near Ningbo to retake the city by using a network of forty operatives who spied on both the military and private citizens, as sources of more extortion and intelligence.

The Emperor at last took action, sending his cousin, Yijing, to Soochow, fifty miles northwest of Ningbo, where he recruited inhabitants of the region to oust the invaders. The forty-eight-year-old general was an honored veteran of the wars against Muslim rebels in Xinjiang Province a decade earlier. Yijing was atypical of the men who fought under him. Unlike the British occupiers of Ningbo, who were career soldiers, Yijing commanded an unlikely band of literary scholars whose area of expertise lay in interpreting the teachings of Confucius, not prosecuting a war of national defense. Beeching has noted that many of these academics turned weekend warriors overcame their fears with large amounts of opium, further weakening their minimal military skills.

On March 10, 1842, Yijing's ill-trained force of five thousand intellectuals attacked Ningbo. They were met at the gate by a barbarous sight—a head impaled on a pike with a sign that said, "This is the head of the Manchu official Lu Tai-lai, who came here to obtain military information." Enraged and undeterred, the attackers scaled the walls at the southern and eastern gates and managed to make their way to the center of the city. But they were quickly repelled by a mere 150 men under Gough's command. British witnesses reported that the attackers appeared visibly impaired by opium, including the second in command, General Zhang Yingyun, whose mission was to coordinate the rearguard and bring them into the city once the gates had been breached. Bei Qingjiao, a mandarin and literary scholar who served as the expedition's unofficial historian, described Zhang's behavior during this pivotal time in the assault. Bei noticed signs of agitation or craving appear on the General's face. Then, as the troops under his command fled instead of attacking, Zhang collapsed in a narcotic daze, an opium pipe still in his mouth. As his men abandoned him, Zhang abandoned the fight by crawling to his litter and joining the exodus.

Thus, the defenders of Ningbo had the advantage of two weapons on their side: state-of-the-art technology and chemical warfare. Using a single piece of artillery, a howitzer, the British scattered the attackers and tore them to pieces. The pile of shattered corpses reached a height of fifteen feet, blocking the streets and any hope of escape. Not all the attackers were Ivory Tower academians. A ragtag volunteer force of aboriginal Chinese from the Golden River area showed up outside the gates just before the attack and were assigned to the western gate. Before scaling the walls, they abandoned the Chinese version of modern arms, discarding their government-issued matchlocks, pikes, and swords in favor of their traditional spears. Spear-throwing aborigines were even less of a match for the British than the eighteenth-century-era regulars. The defenders mowed down the aborigines with musket fire, annihilating the entire band of 150 ghosts from China's past.

Employing ill-equipped aborigines the way the French and British deployed Iroquois and Hurons in another conflict on another continent a century earlier was not the only desperate military strategy of the Chinese. One plan concocted by the attackers called for monkeys holding firecrackers to be sent against British warships and set them afire in a scene that, if it had happened (it didn't), would have seemed straight out of *The Wizard of Oz*. Another plan called for Chinese merchants to sell smallpox-contaminated meat to the British, though General Yijing vetoed this plan as unethical.

The regular Chinese army suffered five hundred casualties in the attack on Ningbo; amazingly, the British escaped unscathed. The easy victory had a demoralizing effect on the Chinese and repercussions far greater than the loss of a mere half-thousand men. During the battle, the dramatic effectiveness of Britain's technological superiority created a defeatist mind-set in the Chinese army. In all future battles, a fatalistic resignation paralyzed the military and made the contests even more uneven than they already were.

For failing to retake Ningbo, the Emperor sentenced Yijing to death, but as usual, the Emperor's imposition of the ultimate penalty was more a "death threat" than an actual sentence. His real goal was to disgrace the victim with loss of face, since the sentence was usually commuted to imprisonment, or in Yijing's case, his appointment as Peking's representative in the backwater of Yarkand, Turkestan. It was career death rather than the real thing, but in a society where face and honor were prized as highly as life itself, ritual humiliation may have been more painful than execution.

Retreating from Ningbo, the Chinese made an attempt on Jinhai by sea, but they were thwarted in a way that added humiliation to disaster, which their "instant historical revisionism" turned into a fictitious victory by the band of scholars/historians who endured defeat. Two hundred seventy Chinese vessels blockaded Jinhai, but the commander of the ships, Chen Tingchen, was too timid to disembark his troops. The vessels sailed back and forth for an entire month, at the end of which time Chen, having salvaged pieces of a British ship that had run aground, forwarded the flotsam to Peking as proof of a great Chinese naval victory over the barbarians, who remained ensconced in Jinhai despite their alleged defeat at sea.

Having failed at overt conflict, the Chinese now began a war of attrition. Barbarities multiplied on both sides. The occupiers found their food poisoned. One soldier was kidnapped and his mutilated corpse discovered in a bag. More abductions followed. The British retaliated by burning the neighborhood where the body bag had been dumped. Chinese prisoners were bound queue to queue, and many residents of Jinhai fled. The remainder continued a reign of surreptitious terror on the occupiers. Up river, the village of Tzeki was taken. The British vented their rage at the Chinese guerilla attacks by using POWs for target practice and bayoneting survivors.

Chapter 14

CHINESE MASADA

*"...foreigners have contented themselves with loot and rape,
but there has been no general slaughter."*

—A resident of Shanghai

When Sir Henry Pottinger sailed into Hong Kong Harbor aboard the *Blenheim* in February 1842, he found a city transformed since its takeover by the British. Hong Kong was undergoing a metamorphosis into a modern, Westernized city. By the time of Sir Henry's arrival, there was already a four-mile road—and two dozen brothels to entertain the conquerors and builders who swarmed over the island. While the tea trade continued in Canton, opium, under the protection of a British garrison, now passed through Hong Kong en route to the mainland. It was estimated that 25 percent of the ships that stopped at Hong Kong carried the drug.

In September 1841, Melbourne and the Whig government had fallen, in part because of dissatisfaction with the prosecution of the war in China. They were replaced by Sir Robert Peel and the Tories, who despite their objections while in opposition, did not reverse course but escalated operations. Almost one hundred more ships, including eight of the newfangled steamships and a fifth regiment, were dispatched to China. The troops under Gough swelled from three thousand to ten thousand.

Hostilities resumed on May 18, 1842, with a landing at Chapu, a town seventy-five miles northwest of Chusan. British progress up the coast to the ultimate goal, the capital, would be incremental. The invaders landed on Chapu without resistance until they reached a joss house further inland, where three hundred Chinese had barricaded themselves in and refused to surrender. Attempts to take the house were stymied by gunfire from the besieged, which killed one of the attackers and wounded several others. Finally, the British blew up part of a stone wall and set fire to the wooden portions. The valiant efforts of the defenders delayed the fall of the city for hours and enraged the attackers, members of the Royal Irish, who wanted to kill the survivors, until officers intervened. Instead, the captives were again ritually humiliated by having their queues tied end to end in groups of eight to ten, then marched in public through the captured city. Despite the efforts of officers, some POWs were bayoneted.

Taking the village itself was easier. The walls surrounding it were more decorative than defensive, low-lying and undefended by men or artillery. As the British pushed through the gates, the defenders fled to Hangzhou, fifty miles inland. The British stayed behind, and in Chapu they came upon a scene of horror in a Manchu barracks. The Manchus had a military tradition of not being taken alive, and they lived up to (and died for) their tradition. After poisoning their wives and children, as indicated by the victims' black and bloated faces, the soldiers slit their throats in a grim reprise of Masada. The Emperor's representatives in Chapu, mandarin courtiers, also committed suicide.

The next attack occurred at Wusong at the mouth of the Yangtze River on June 16, 1842. Control of the river would cut off the important city of Nanking, 175 miles inland. The British hoped that the capture of a major metropolis like Nanking would bring the Chinese to the bargaining table and obviate the much harder task of taking the capital, which as symbol and practical seat of government would be defended more strenuously than backwaters like Jinhai and Ningbo. Forts along the Huangbu River, an estuary of the Yangtze, fired at the British ships and caused three fatalities. But the superior firepower of the British managed to silence the forts' artillery, which ceased operation by mid-evening. A landing party of marines and sailors encountered some short but sharp resistance before seizing the city walls.

On June 19, Shanghai, a few miles to the south, was taken without a shot, although the British found two pieces of artillery behind the walls. As the invaders clambered over the walls before opening the city gates, the townspeople fled. Three hundred sixty guns were seized along with nine tons of gunpowder. The citizens of Shanghai bribed the British with $300,000 to prevent looting, but the British commanders lost control of their men and scattered looting occurred, compounded by even worse pillage by local Chinese thugs, whose predations the British chose to ignore, perhaps because it made their own men's malfeasance seem less objectionable.

An eyewitness account of a Chinese scholar conveys the tragedy that the entire campaign involved for local Chinese residents. A wealthy and respected government official, the scholar Cao, was living in a walled home with a courtyard in a suburb of Shanghai when British soldiers smashed through his front door with their musket butts. After seizing everything that was portable, including the old man's entire food supply, the looters wanted their host to show them where his silver lay buried on the property. Pulling his head back by its queue and sticking a knife to his throat, a soldier shouted over and over, "*Fan ping! Fan ping!*"—literally, "foreign cakes," an idiom for silver. There was no buried bullion, and the soldiers departed, but Cao and his family's suffering was not over. After three days of starvation, his wife managed to find half of a chicken, but just as she was about to prepare it for her famished family, about thirty Chinese thugs materialized and ran off with the victims' only hope against starvation.

The next day, Cao went door to door, begging for food for his wife and two young sons, but the city had already been cleaned out. In a surprisingly optimistic account, Cao wrote that the "foreigners have contented themselves with loot and rape, but as the city fell without resistance there has been no general slaughter. They are pressing the people into their service to do all their heavy work, such as shifting gun emplacements and gunpowder. They take anyone, Buddhist monks, notables, and well-known people." The barbarian at the gates had become the occupier within them.

Despite Shanghai's strategic and commercial importance, the British stayed there for only a week before moving on to Nanking. But before they could take the city they hoped would end the war, the walled city of Zhenjiang, fifty miles west of Nanking, had to be taken. Three British brigades landed outside the city walls in the early hours of July 21, 1842, a day so humid and hot that twenty British soldiers died from dehydration, the only casualties the attackers sustained. Manchus fired down from the walls, but their weapons were eighteenth-century guns called gingalls, which were so heavy and unwieldy, they had to be fired from tripods.

Grenadiers smashed through the city's main gate and bayoneted the Manchus, who had not fled their post. The twenty-eight hundred defenders barricaded themselves in the area of the city where their ethnic group was quartered. The Masada scenario played itself out again. Before taking their own lives, the soldiers strangled, poisoned, or cut the throats of family members. The Manchu commander, General Hailin, orchestrated a *suttee*-like end for himself, gathering up all his court papers, sitting on the pile, then torching them. "Worthy of a nobler and a better fate," Pottinger wrote in his diary of the general's death. Many residents of the city did not share Pottinger's gallant assessment of Hailin's self-constructed funeral pyre. Before his death, unable to vent his rage against the British, the general turned on his own side. The Manchus and Chinese considered themselves different races, and Hailin's orders have the flavor of genocide as he rounded up innocent civilians, ethnic Chinese, throughout the city and had them executed on spurious charges of treason.

The poet Zhu Shiyun, who lived on the outskirts of the captured city, deplored the terror of the Manchus and their masters, the Manchu Dynasty in Peking. His account of the depredations of government troops against their own people reflects the gradual turn in public opinion, which began to feel that the British invaders were less burdensome than their rulers. General Hailin, Chu wrote, "was in a very excited state. All over the town he arrested harmless people on the ground that they were in league with the enemy. He handed them over to the Prefect to imprison and flog. It was only at the four gates that he had a cannon pointing outwards. Inside the city his whole activity consisted in arresting passersby on suspicion of their being traitors. Whenever women or children saw Manchu soldiers, they fled in terror, upon which the soldiers ran after them and slew them, announcing to Hailin that they had disposed of traitors, for which he gave them rewards." The barbarians—different and the same—were now on both sides of the gates.

In contrast to the Manchu atrocities, public opinion regarding the occupiers improved on July 24, 1842, when a rapist and a looter from among the ranks of the invaders were hanged with placards around their necks warning others to avoid their fate, although in a telling racial footnote, the condemned men were Indian, not British soldiers. A proclamation on August 16, 1842, officially forbade looting, although it implied that it was still going on since "looters" were now ordered to pay for what they plundered instead of facing the death penalty. On September 5, 1842, another proclamation by the British not only legitimatized but encouraged the opium trade by advising distressed residents to visit Sui-shan "where opium is on sale very cheap—an opportunity not to be missed."

As they fled Zhenjiang, its residents set fire to the city while the British looted what the flames failed to consume. Leaving a small garrison behind, Gough exited Zhenjiang, but blew a huge hole in the wall in case the city had to be retaken later. With the capture of Zhenjiang, the British gained control of all military and commercial traffic on the Yangtze. The Viceroy of Nanking, Yilibu, summed up the situation for his Imperial master: "The Yangtze River is a region like a throat, at which the whole situation of the country is determined. Now they have already cut off our salt and grain transportation and stopped the communication of merchants and travelers. That is not a disease like ringworm, but a trouble in our heart and stomach." In addition, the way now lay open for the British to take the great city of Nanking—both strategically and psychologically important as the former capital of the Ming Dynasty. The fall of Zhenjiang and the threat to Nanking, which would undoubtedly be followed by an advance on Peking itself, at last roused the Emperor from his lethargy—the Son of Heaven was desperate to end the hostilities before his sacrosanct capital was endangered.

Chapter 15

"EARLY VICTORIAN VIKINGS"

*"...strongly impress upon the Chinese plenipotentiaries how much
it would be to the interest of that Government to legalize the trade."*

—Lord Palmerston to Sir Henry Pottinger

As the barbarian British advanced like the incoming tide toward Peking, in the spring of 1842, the emperor appointed Yilibu, the Viceroy of Nanking, and a high-level mandarin and intimate, Qiying, as plenipotentiaries to deal with the invaders. The appointment represented a dramatic comeback for the Viceroy, who had successfully negotiated a truce with Charles Elliot in late 1840. After the fall of Chusan, the Emperor had ordered Yilibu to retake the crucial stronghold, but lacking men and materiel, he had declined the commission, for which he was stripped of his titles and sent into internal exile and disgrace. As the Emperor's replacements in the field and at the negotiating table fared no better, however, Yilibu was restored to favor and ordered to treat with the British again. Leaving Peking on April 15, 1842, the newly appointed Imperial emissaries were under orders from the Emperor to do anything, promise everything, but halt the British advance before it reached the capital.

The urgency of Yilibu's mission increased during his journey, as the British took two more critical cities on the Yangtze River: Shanghai on the coast and Wuchang, four hundred miles inland and due east. Yangzhou, another city on the Grand Canal that guarded the approach to Nanking, saved itself from sack by scrounging up $300,000—only half the amount the British had demanded but accepted *il faut de mieux*. As the British land forces approached the walls of Nanking with the seventy-four-gun

Cornwallis and the *Blonde* threatening the city by sea, Yilibu raised a white flag before a shot was fired.

Unlike previous Imperial emissaries who felt their first duty was to tell the Emperor what he wanted to hear, Yilibu and Qiying recognized the impending disaster and wrote Daoguang, "Should we fail to ease the situation by soothing the barbarians, they will run over our country like beasts, doing anything they like." This, of course, had already happened, but the two mandarins were the first to tell the Emperor about it.

Yilibu's initial approach to the British had been a tactical mistake. Displaying the arrogance typical of the stratified hierarchy, he had first sent a low-ranking soldier to meet Sir Henry Pottinger. The Sinophobe Pottinger may have not known much about the rigid protocol and hierarchical nature of Chinese society, but the knew enough to know that he was being insulted when he was asked to negotiate with a low-status emissary. He declined to meet Yilibu's "inferior" messenger, demanding instead a meeting with Yilibu himself, whom he also insisted must negotiate as plenipotentiary so that all decisions would be final and not depend on Peking for ratification, a ruse that had invalidated previous agreements between the British and representatives of the Emperor. While Yilibu hesitated, Pottinger increased his negotiating leverage by ravaging the length of the Yangtze. The fall of Zhenjiang, however, had panicked the Emperor, who at last granted Yilibu genuine plenipotentiary power as Pottinger demanded.

But while Yilibu waited for confirmation of his authority from Peking, Pottinger strengthened his position again by having the fierce new steamship the *Queen* train her guns on the walls of Nanking. He also stationed eight-inch howitzers on the beach and aimed them at the city. Yilibu sent a subordinate, Zhang Xi, who boarded the *Queen* with orders to beg the British not to begin bombarding Nanking. While Yilibu was always gracious, his subordinate for inexplicable reasons took an aggressive, abusive position in his negotiations aboard the steamship.

Pottinger was blunt in the face of Zhang Xi's effrontery. He told Yilibu's messenger that *after* Nanking fell, the capital would be next. With bravado that tried to hide the powerlessness of his position, Zhang Xi boasted that the recent military successes of the British were due to the kindness and forbearance of the Emperor, "who cannot bear to kill or injure human creatures," but if pushed too far would arm every inhabitant of the empire, including children. Zhang Xi laced his tirade with obscene epithets describing the invaders. When the translator Thom objected, Zhang Xi exploded with, "You kill people everywhere, plunder goods, and act like rascals; that is very disgraceful; how can you say…you are not rebellious?" In Zhang Xi's memoirs, he recounted that at this point in his harangue he pounded the negotiating table with his fist and spat on the floor. Thom later wrote that Zhang Xi became so volatile that they feared a physical attack on Sir Henry was about to follow.

On August 9, 1842, Yilibu sent a document from the Emperor, which the courtier claimed proved his negotiating authority as plenipotentiary. The British did not take the bait and made threatening moves toward Nanking by bringing the *Cornwallis* within firing range of the city walls and landing, unopposed, a brigade that camped outside the walls. Still the troops did not attack.

Two days later, Yilibu responded by offering a $3 million sweetener, which Qiying would bring in person to the Queen. The offer mollified the British enough to postpone an attack on Nanking, and Pottinger agreed to compose a treaty, which Yilibu said he would read, though he could not promise agreement. The mandarin misinterpreted the British offer as a sign of weakness and resorted to the classic Chinese passive-aggressive ploy of using procrastination instead of negotiation, conceding nothing and hoping to weary the enemy rather than defeat them outright.

While Yilibu pretended to examine the treaty, the British replied by informing the Chinese that the attack on Nanking would commence on August 13, 1842. The next day, Yilibu swallowed his pride and at last made a personal appearance aboard the *Queen*. He promised to begin serious negotiations as plenipotentiary if the attack were called off, to which the British agreed. Four days of emissaries traveling back and forth from ship to shore led to Yilibu's acceptance of the treaty, but despite his claim of plenipotentiary status, he insisted on sending a copy to Peking for the Emperor's approval. The *soi-disant* plenipotentiary dared not risk another disgrace, which he suspected would be punished this time with death instead of exile.

The British accepted Yilibu's abdication of plenipotentiary power and invited him and his colleagues aboard the *Cornwallis* on August 20th, where they served them tea and cherry brandy. Underneath the mutual civility, the British remained suspicious of their guests, whose past duplicitousness and procrastination had so maddened Elliot and driven him into disgrace. In contrast to Pottinger's icy skepticism, Yilibu and Qiying exhibited the ceremonial courtesies of the polished mandarin. Spotting a painting of Queen Victoria in the ship's cabin, they bowed deeply to Her Majesty's image. Lords Macartney, Napier, and Amherst must have smiled down from heaven's Foggy Bottom.

While Yilibu waited to hear from Peking, negotiations with Pottinger continued. During one meeting in Nanking, Pottinger broached the issue that lay at the foundation of the hostilities more than any other matter—the trade in opium. At first, the Chinese refused to even discuss the subject until Pottinger agreed to keep the minutes of the meeting secret. Then, Yilibu let loose decades of resentment toward the substance that had devastated the court, the army, and the population at large. Yilibu suggested a commonsense solution. Stop production of the crop in British-controlled India. Pottinger countered that some other enterprising nation would take over cultivation and importation into China. Pottinger threw the responsibility back in China's court by arguing, "If your people are virtuous, they will desist from the evil practice; and if your officers are incorruptible, and obey their orders, no opium can enter your country." It's hard to tell if Pottinger was being naive or cynical, since he knew corruption was endemic among government officials and the craving for opium, once established, made virtue an irrelevant vice. Pottinger's suggestion was a face-saving, disingenuous argument that Latin American countries often use against the U.S. today: kill demand and you kill the trade.

The Chinese realized that the opium issue was a deal-breaker, and the Empire was desperate for a deal—any deal that would get the barbarians out of the Emperor's front yard and return to the south, so they let the matter drop. The issue of allowing more Christian missionaries to proselytize in China was such an implacable one that neither side, both intent on a treaty, ever broached it.

The unfortunate Yilibu found himself negotiating with two intransigent parties, the British and his employer. During the middle of face-to-face parleys with Pottinger, Yilibu received instructions not to meet with the British until they sailed away from Nanking. Yilibu demonstrated remarkable bravery and pragmatism by ignoring the Imperial edict and continuing to treat with Pottinger. Then orders arrived that under no circumstances was Fuzhou to be opened to the British, another missive Yilibu ignored, and he accepted the British demand for access to the port.

Slowly, what would become known as the Treaty of Nanking began to emerge from the negotiations. The terms represented an almost total diplomatic defeat for a country that had already suffered so many military defeats. The original demand for $6 million in reparations for the confiscated chests of opium and the cost of the British military expedition now ballooned to an extortionate $21 million, half of all China's yearly tax revenues. Swallowing his pride and no doubt fearing for his neck, Yilibu accepted the amount, which would be paid on an installment plan.

The British gained everything they sought except legalization of the opium business. Despite their military defeat and nonexistent negotiating power, the Emperor's representatives refused to agree to formal recognition of it. Despite written instructions from Lord Palmerston to "strongly impress upon the Chinese plenipotentiaries how much it would be to the interest of that Government to legalize the trade," Pottinger did not press the issue after receiving a message from the Emperor via Yilibu that "gain-seeking and corrupt men will for profit and sensuality defeat my wishes, but nothing will induce me to derive revenue from the vice and misery of my people."

Yilibu and Qiying expanded on their master's wishes in another letter to Pottinger that said, "Our nations have been united by friendly commercial intercourse for 200 years. How then, at this time, are our relations so suddenly changed, as to be the cause of a national quarrel from the spreading of the opium poison? Multitudes of our Chinese subjects consume it, wasting their property and destroying their lives. How is it possible for us to refrain from forbidding our people to use it?" The discussion of the opium controversy remained *sub rosa*. The Chinese did not want publicly to admit that a shocking portion of the population had become habituated to the drug. Pottinger, as Palmerston's faithful servant, brought up the topic in a secret meeting, considered "unofficial contact" so that the Chinese could deny ever having had it.

Although Pottinger had called the meeting, the Chinese began the discussion by asking why the British simply did not forbid opium production at its source, India. With their own absolutist system of government, the Chinese failed to understand Pottinger's rebuttal that the British constitution (an elusive document if ever there was one) did not grant Parliament the right to halt poppy cultivation. And if the British did somehow find a pretext to halt production, the Americans and French would fill the vacuum with opium produced in Turkey. As conservative American politicians in this century have also done, Pottinger tried to place the blame and responsibility on consumers. Although he had served in India where poppies were grown and had firsthand experience of the addictive properties of the product, he offered the Chinese a version of Mrs. Reagan's "just say no" policy: if China stopped buying the drug, British India would stop growing it. Then Pottinger suggested a solution that has the flavor of current headlines—decriminalization: "Your people will procure the drug in spite of every enactment. Would it not be better to legalize the importation?" After conferring with the Emperor, the two Chinese officials told Pottinger that Peking would agree to all the British demands except official acceptance of the opium trade.

On August 27, 1842, Peking approved what it thought was the complete text of the treaty. The draft was signed two days later aboard the *Cornwallis*. Yilibu was so ill he had to be carried on to the British ship, where the signatories, Qiying, Pottinger, Parker, and Gough, gathered in the cabin. Assistants affixed the seal of Pottinger and Yilibu to the treaty, which was so detailed that it filled four silk-bound volumes. A sumptuous lunch was followed by running both the British and Chinese flags up the *Cornwallis*'s masts. Utterly demoralized, the Emperor's representatives signed the treaty without reading its humiliating terms! Claiming it was a Manchu custom and a symbol of agreement, Qiying then insisted on stuffing Pottinger's mouth with candied plums at dessert time. An Englishman present wrote, "I shall never forget Sir Henry's face of determined resignation." Despite the strained *bonhomie*, the mandarins, no doubt fearing their master's reaction to the document they had just signed, appeared very nervous and left immediately after lunch.

Qiying's playfulness with plums masked despair over the terms of the treaty. The British agreed to return Chusan and Amoy, but only after the reparations had been paid in full. The British would gain access to and the right of permanent residence at the ports of Canton, Amoy, Fuzhou,

Ningbo, and Shanghai. Each port would house a British consular official. The cumbersome Cohong, which diluted the authority and operations of British traders, was to be abolished. The irritating pretense that the British were tribute bearers inferior to China's superior civilization now melted away in the face of superior British military might, as the treaty now codified the equal status of both nations. Hong Kong was declared a permanent colony of Britain. Nanking would remain blockaded by the British fleet until the first reparations installment—$6 million of the $21 million—was paid. Yilibu sent his master an edited version of the Treaty of Nanking, which omitted the sticking points Peking had insisted on.

The British fleet remained at Nanking for several weeks while Pottinger waited for the first installment. During this time, sailors and soldiers went sightseeing and behaved like boorish vandals, chipping away at pieces of priceless monuments like the Porcelain Tower as souvenirs. When Gough learned of the vandalism, he ordered a halt to it. This absent-minded pilfering would be replicated a decade later by a grotesque act of cultural and historical vandalism that climaxed the Second Opium War, the burning of the Emperor's Summer Palace outside Peking.

Within a few weeks, the rain and humidity had dispirited the besiegers, and illness spread across the fleet. The infamous "Hong Kong fever" decimated the island's new owners, and half the soldiers at Gulangsu on the island of Amoy had to be hospitalized. Without waiting for the reparations to arrive, Pottinger ordered the greater part of the fleet to leave the city. On October 12, 1842, with $6 million in ransom aboard at last, the rest of the British fleet departed from Nanking.

The departure of the fleet did not thoroughly ease tensions between the British and the Chinese, however. In the face of Chinese anger at their humiliation, Pottinger had to brandish British military might in China one more time. In November 1842, opium merchants decided to bring their wives along for the trip from Whampoa to Canton, which violated a *purdah*-like taboo of the Chinese against mixing the sexes. Residents of Canton seized and burned the flag that flew over the British factory there. Defenders of the American factory shot five rioters, and Chinese police managed to disperse the crowd at the factory before the riot turned into an international incident. The real victims of the riot were the luckless shipwreck survivors of the *Ann* and *Nerbudda*. Unable to vent their fury on the foreign factories, the mob plucked the *Ann* and *Nerbudda* passengers and crew from jail and beheaded all but a few, who survived to give graphic accounts of the massacre to the press back home. Pottinger threatened retaliation, and a viceroy named Yiliang rushed to Canton, where he arrested the ringleaders of the executions and sent them to Peking for punishment.

As much as the Chinese loathed their diplomatic and military humiliation, the bulk of the British press hailed the Treaty of Nanking. "It secures us a few round millions of dollars and no end of very refreshing tea. It gives an impetus to trade, cedes us one island in perpetuity, and in short puts that sort of climax to the war which satisfies our interests more than our vanity and rather gives over glory a preponderance to gain," the *Illustrated London News* crowed. Like the treaty itself, the press made no mention of the cause of all the hardship, misery, and death: the equally deadly opium trade. Indeed, now under the complete sovereignty of the British, Hong Kong fulfilled one of its most important functions as the offloading point for opium. The number of enthusiastic buyers swelled under British protection. Despite the finger pointing by both sides, Chinese demand encouraged British supply. It remained a poisonous and poisoning relationship, devastating the buyer and discrediting the seller.

Not everyone in Britain was happy with the outcome, however. *The Times of London*, which had long condemned the opium trade, did not share the general bullishness toward the Treaty of Nanking and gave the victors the derisive sobriquet, "Early Victorian Vikings," a prescient nickname considering the pillaging that the next Opium War would bring. Ironically, a change in British government brought some moral support to the official Chinese position on opium. High Church Anglican members of the new ruling Tory party continued to rail against the drug. On January 4, 1843, Lord Aberdeen, Pottinger's new boss at the Foreign Office, told the envoy, "The British opium smuggler must receive no protection or support in the prosecution of his illegal speculations." This was a 180-degree turn away from the policy that had led to all the recent bloodshed and budget-busting expense. An Order in Council gave Pottinger the power to "forbid the opium traffic in Hong Kong." Pottinger paid lip service by issuing a lukewarm threat on August 1, 1843: "Opium being an article the traffic in which is well known to be declared illegal and contraband by the laws and Imperial Edicts of China, any person who may take such a step will do so at his own risk, and will, if a British subject, meet with no support or protection from HM Consuls or other officers." Officially, at least, there would be no more gunboat diplomacy to cow the Chinese and act as bodyguards for what were, in fact, drug runners.

Despite such tardy morality, there was simply too much money to be made from the trade, not only for the *tai pans* like Jardine, Matheson, and Dent, but for the British Exchequer as well: tax revenues from opium balanced the budget. At the time of the First Opium War, the trade accounted for 10 percent of the Exchequer's budget. In a letter to a colleague in London, Matheson remained untroubled by Parliament and Pottinger's public handwringing because he knew it would come to nothing. "The Plenipotentiary [Pottinger] had published a most fiery Edict against smuggling, but I believe it is like the Chinese Edicts, meaning nothing, and only intended for the Saints [High Church Anglicans] in England. Sir Henry never means to act upon it, and no doubt privately considers it a good joke. At any rate, he allows the drug to be landed and stored at Hong Kong." The merchants ignored their home country's sanctions, and Pottinger's behavior was passive-aggressive at best, hypocritical at worst, and totally ineffective at halting or even limiting the land-office business.

As the opium trade continued to thrive in China, some British officials didn't even pay lip service to suppression, openly encouraging importation. The new Governor-General of India, Lord Ellenborough, actually scolded the Foreign Minister for his scruples. "Her Majesty's Government should do 'nothing to place in peril our Opium Revenue. As for preventing the manufacture of opium, and the sale of it in China, that is far beyond your power,'" he wrote. When the captain of the British ship the *Thalia* boarded another vessel en route to China packed with opium and tried to seize its cargo, he received an official reprimand from Ellenborough that ordered him "not to interfere in such a manner with the undertakings of British subjects," and sent him back to India in disgrace.

Unsupported even by the Prime Minister, who feared the evaporation of his shaky Parliamentary majority, Lord Aberdeen ultimately bowed to public opinion and chose *realpolitik* over morality, eventually instructing Pottinger, "I think [you] may be permitted to suspend the exclusion of opium from the waters and harbours of Hong Kong for the present, if [you] should think expedient to do so."

———•——

The end of the First Opium War was not the end of the controversy over the drug trade in either China or Britain. Just as the Treaty of Nanking continued to have serious repercussions for the Manchu dynasty, so too its reverberations echoed in the conscience and at the heart of British political life in London. While the Foreign Minister Lord Aberdeen vacillated on the opium issue, his boss, Sir Robert Peel, the Prime Minister, had no such qualms over trafficking in the drug—though he kept a delicate distance from the shabby business by using W.B. Baring, at the time a junior minister at the Board of Control (and also a member of the great banking family), as his spokesman. Speaking for both the head of the Tory Party and the Government, Baring told Parliament that there was no remedy but legalization. As so many others had done before, Peel transferred culpability to the users and their leaders, and alleged that the Emperor had done nothing to halt distribution and use. Sir George Staunton refused to acquiesce in this Chinese-like revisionist history and responded, "The Chinese government could and did stop the traffic effectually for four months previous to the seizure of the opium [chests]."

While the opium *tai pans* and cotton-mill owners of northern England who hoped to open up China to the textiles they were overproducing had bought Members of Parliament to promote their business goals, the "abolitionists" found their voice in disinterested adherents of Low Church and dissenting faiths. The main champion of the anti-opium lobby was a defector from the Tory party, Lord Ashley, a devout Evangelical, who bolted from his party, but declined to join the Whigs because of his distaste for the party's support of the pernicious trade—even though Ashley was Palmerston's own son-in-law.

In 1843, a year after the Treaty of Nanking, Ashley, backed by petitions from Quakers, Wesleyans, Congregationalists, and Baptists, delivered an excoriating indictment of the opium trade in the House of Lords, condemning it as "utterly inconsistent with the honour and duty of a Christian kingdom." A pious philanthropist who also fought child labor in coal mines and cotton mills, Ashley (later the Earl of Shaftesbury) was worldly enough to realize an appeal to economic common sense would draw more support than one to basic morality. In his speech before Parliament, the peer pointed out that ill will, not to mention war in China, would spoil legitimate imports like textiles. Unfortunately, this point seemed more like wish-fulfillment than economic reality on Ashley's part because his listeners and their rich supporters, the cotton-mill owners, et al., knew that the Chinese had a textile industry of its own sufficient enough to supply the entire nation's needs. For all Ashley's good intentions and moral outrage, opium remained the one import with which indigenous Chinese production could not compete.

William Gladstone, who had so eloquently attacked the drug traffic on behalf of his sister's suffering several years earlier, remained publicly silent in the post-mortem debate on the China war, but confessed to his diary: "I am in dread of the judgement of God upon England for our national iniquity toward China." *The Times*, too, remained an implacable foe of the opium traffic. An editorial on December 3, 1842 called for Parliament to resign itself to the loss of tax revenue from opium and take responsibility for the unjustness of the recent war. "We owe some moral compensation to China for pillaging her towns and slaughtering her citizens, in a quarrel which could never have arisen if we had not been guilty of this national crime." While Gladstone and Ashley looked toward heaven with sadness and guilt, however, their mercenary colleagues in the House of Commons set their sights much lower—on the bottom line. Opium was big business, a tax windfall, and moral qualms seemed a small price to pay for such a cornucopia of riches.

Sir Robert Peel finally trumped the opium opposition with a claim that was pure deception—but ended the debate. Again using Baring as his spokesman, he declared that the Chinese Emperor had at last agreed to the legalization of opium and British importation into China. Peel's fabrication temporarily silenced his critics in the House of Commons and the press, but no amount of deception and wishful thinking could prevent another violent eruption over the issue that the Emperor and Peel had supposedly settled.

The First Opium War left a significant mark on the lives of most of its major participants. For his service in settling the "Chinese matter," the

leader of the "Early Victorian Vikings," as *The Times* had called them, Sir
Henry Pottinger was rewarded with the lucrative post of Governor of
Madras. Yet while Parliament granted him an annual pension of £1,500, he
never received a peerage, the usual reward for a successful plenipotentiary—the old soldier had become too deeply tainted by the haggling over
opium. As for the much maligned Charles Elliot, he did penance for his
perceived failure by being appointed governor of a succession of backwaters—Bermuda, Trinidad, and finally, with symbolic richness,
Napoleon's place of exile, St. Helena.

Jardine and Matheson both left China and entered Parliament as
staunch Whig supporters of Palmerston's expansionist policies. Jardine represented the seat of Ashburton, and Matheson took over his partner's seat
in 1843 when Jardine died of an undiagnosed but painful illness. From
1847 to 1868, Matheson represented the seat of Ross and Cromarty in Parliament. Jardine's mysterious death created the myth of a curse on all who
profited from the opium trade. The myth ignored the fact that Matheson
lived to the ripe old age of ninety-one. Before his death in 1887, he married, bought the entire island of Lewis off the coast of Scotland, and built
a lavish castle there that cost half a million pounds. He also endowed the
Chair of Chinese at London University, a bequest of mordant irony.

Jardine and Matheson's Chinese counterpart, the long-suffering go-
between, Howqua, died of diarrhea a year after the Treaty of Nanking was
signed. Despite the fact that the Treaty put him out of business as liaison
between Britain and China, the shrewd merchant had continued to expand
his horizons and trading opportunities, particularly with the help of American advisors, through whom he even invested in American railways. At the
time of his death, he was probably the wealthiest man on Earth—and
achieved immortality of a sort as a popular waxwork image at Mme. Tussaud's, an honor not granted Pottinger or Elliot.

Governor-General Lin's effigy also became a cynosure at the museum,
although the plaque under his statue claimed he had destroyed £2.5 worth
of British property—without mentioning that the property was contraband opium. The Emperor eventually forgave Lin in 1845 and assigned
him a new post, but he died near Canton in 1850 before he could return
to service. The Emperor's wrath over the humiliating Treaty of Nanking fell
unevenly: Qiying remained in favor, while Yilibu was sent into exile bound

in chains reserved for common criminals. A different sort of immortality was granted to the martyred Father Perboyre when, in 1889, the Catholic Church beatified him, guaranteeing him an eternity in heaven, if not at Mme. Tussaud's.

Chapter 16

THE TRADE IN POISON AND PIGS

"...iniquities scarcely exceeded those practiced on the African coast and on the African middle passage have not been wanting...the jails of China [have been] emptied to supply 'labour' to British colonies...hundreds [of coolies] gathered together in [holding pens], stripped naked, and stamped or painted with the letter C (California), P (Peru) or S (Sandwich Islands) on their breasts, according to destination."

—John Bowring, British Consul in Canton, to Foreign Secretary Lord Malmesbury, 1852

Tragically, the Treaty of Nanking represented only a truce, not an end to hostilities between China and Britain. Amid all the terms and conditions, no mention was made of opium. Officially, the narcotic remained illegal to use and import. Unofficially, it continued to be big business and provided the tinder for the Second Opium War of 1856. During the fourteen years between the First and Second Opium Wars, an interval that was more like an armed truce than peace, the opium octopus spread its tentacles from the coastal cities, where it had been contained until the end of the First Opium War, to the interior of China through the newly opened port of Shanghai and the Yangtze River, which provided an easy highway for the drug's infiltration of the hinterland.

While the Chinese were literally and physically addicted to the drug, the British government and British businessmen who engaged in trade in China were addicted to opium financially.

The grand vision of northern England's mass-produced cotton textiles penetrating China as thoroughly as opium had done turned out to be a chimera. The Chinese continued to favor their homespun cloth and failed to buy British wares. On the other hand, the British couldn't get enough of Chinese silk and tea. Together with Britain's benign addiction to the caffeine in tea (unlike opium dens, afternoon tea didn't degenerate into weeks of intoxication and lost work suffered by opium smokers), silk contributed to a trade imbalance that resulted in the outflow of silver from Britain to China. In 1857, a year after the second war began, the British paid the Chinese £15 million for silk and tea. Despite the growing popularity of the drug, the Chinese spent only £7 million on opium, £1.5 million for cotton from India, and £2 million for British manufactures, which left Britain owing China £4.5 million. And the Chinese would only accept payment in silver bullion.

Between the two wars, the opium business came to be known as the Poison Trade, an accurate description of the drug's effects on its users. An even more odious form of commerce also began at this time, nicknamed the Pig Trade—the "pigs" being coolies hired or kidnapped for indentured servitude overseas. Despite the fact that the slave trade had been outlawed by Britain in 1807, the treatment and transport of these forced laborers did not differ much from African slavery. The term "shanghaied" comes from the fact that many coolies were drugged and put on crowded, filthy ships with such high mortality rates that on average half the passengers died en route to their destinations.

While turning a blind and amoral eye to the opium trade, representatives of the British government in China were horrified by the Pig Trade. The Chinese government also deplored the traffic in human flesh, and Britain's consular officials in China were at the time trying to improve relations with the Emperor for the sake of trade and peace. John Bowring, Britain's top official in Canton, wrote a graphic letter of complaint in January 1852 to the Foreign Secretary, Lord Malmesbury, decrying "iniquities scarcely exceeding those practiced on the African coast and on the African middle passage have not been wanting…the jails of China [have been] emptied to supply 'labour' to British colonies…hundreds [of coolies] gathered together in *barracoons*, stripped naked and stamped or painted with the letter C (California), P (Peru) or S (Sandwich Islands) on their breasts, according to destination." *Barracoons* were filthy, crowded holding pens for both volunteers and those who had been shanghaied.

The Poison Traders, as the opium merchants came to be known, detested their confreres, the Pig Traders, because the distributors of the drug needed the goodwill of the Chinese to carry on their business, and the coolie trade represented a gnawing loss of face and an assault on Chinese pride. Bowring's son, an employee of Jardine Matheson, wrote a memo to his bosses that crystallized the opposing interests of the traffic in humans and narcotics: "The irregular and fraudulent shipment of coolies [might jeopardize] the immense interests both British and Anglo-Indians involved in the opium trade, giving more than three millions sterling of revenue to India."

Ironically, back in England, the opium merchants and the faith-based opposition to their trade found a common cause to unite against the Pig Trade. The powerful lobbies briefly combined in Parliament and secured the enactment of the Chinese Passenger Act in 1855, which, while not outlawing the trade in coolies, codified and improved the conditions in which they were transported to their places of labor.

Meanwhile, the tentacles of opium continued to spread throughout China, reaching all the way to the top rungs of society. In 1850, the Daoguang Emperor died and, in his will, begged forgiveness for agreeing to the shameful Treaty of Nanking. His fourth son and successor, Xianfeng, was nineteen when he ascended to the throne. Unlike his industrious father, Xianfeng cared little for government and, although married to a Manchu princess, became obsessed with one of his concubines, Cixi, to the point where he spent most of his time in bed with her, trading puffs on an opium pipe. After bearing him his only son, Cixi was elevated to the rank of co-empress with the title Empress of the Western Palace—Xianfeng's first wife being the Empress of the Eastern Palace.

As the mother of the heir, Cixi soon wielded enormous influence in the Imperial Court. A master of intrigue, after Xianfeng's death she staged a palace coup against the regency council that initially came to power and established herself and Xianfeng's first wife as co-regents, who would rule China until her son came of age. After the death of the Empress of the Eastern Palace, Cixi ruled China alone until her own death in 1908—first as sole regent and then as Dowager Empress after her son's accession to the Dragon Throne. Cixi's control over her husband and interest in government, which contrasted with Xianfeng's indifference, was particularly noteworthy and surprising since she was also an opium addict, who nevertheless seemed to be able to function despite the drug's intoxicating effects. (Some historians suspect Cixi stuck to a maintenance dose that prevented both impairment and withdrawal.)

Meanwhile, other disasters, both man-made and natural, also afflicted both the Manchu Dynasty and the people of China. High government office, which in the past had only been obtainable by passing rigorous examinations that guaranteed the competence of the ruling class, now became available to anyone who had £800. The mediocrities (albeit rich mediocrities) who came to power as a result of this secular simony proved unequal to the responsibilities they had purchased, and the once industrious and highly educated Chinese bureaucracy decayed rapidly. Adding to China's woes during the chaotic lull between Opium Wars, in 1856 the Huang He River overflowed and destroyed thousands of acres of rice paddies. The capital began to starve. Such drastic problems invited a drastic solution for the woes of the Chinese people and the punishment of an unresponsive government and its narcotized leader.

Chapter 17

STRANGE INTERLUDE

"Plunder the rich to relieve the poor."

—Battle cry of the Taiping Rebels

As had happened before in China, the decay of the Imperial Court, combined with famine among the people, soon led to rebellion. While the British occupiers remained quiescent, an anti-Manchu native revolt almost toppled the necrotic Manchu Dynasty. The Taiping Rebellion began in the southeastern province of Guangxi in 1851 and lasted until its final suppression in 1864. Consequently, it was against this background that the Second Opium War occurred The Taiping Rebellion colored the calculations of Europeans and Manchus alike. At its zenith, the rebellion controlled seventeen provinces in south and central China. It was the most destructive civil war in the history of humanity, as the combination of military action, religio-political repression and retaliation, and famine caused by the dislocations of war claimed the lives of between twenty and thirty million people.

The leader of the movement was Hong Xiuquan, the fourth son of a hard-working rural family in Guangdong. Hong's family were Hakka, a minority people in southern China with distinctive customs and language that set them apart from the mainstream of Han Chinese society. With much sacrifice on his parents' part, Hong managed to get a decent education and to pass the first examinations that would allow him to try for a place in the scholar-gentry. After failing in his first two attempts to obtain the scholar's degree, however, Hong left home in humiliation and went to

Canton, where he continued to study in hopes of passing the civil-service examination and becoming a scholar. There he came in contact with Protestant missionaries and their converts, and apparently glanced briefly at a Christian tract of translations into Chinese from the Bible.

After failing the civil-service examination a third time, Hong suffered some sort of nervous breakdown, accompanied by delirium and a series of dreams or visions that had a profound affect on him. In these dreams, Hong found himself talking with an older, bearded man with golden hair, and a younger man whom he called "Elder Brother." The younger man gave him a sword and taught him to "slay demons." Hong was apparently a mystic—what the nineteenth century called a neurasthenic and what psychologists today might label a histrionic personality. Initially, he does not seem to have associated these dreams with the Christian doctrines he had been exposed to, and after recovering, for the next six years he worked as a village schoolteacher—still intent on passing his examinations.

In 1843, however, Hong failed the scholar's examination for the fourth and last time. It was the end of his ambition to become a member of the scholar-gentry, and his failure threw him into a full breakdown. He seems to have become catatonic for nearly a month, coming out of his stupor occasionally to scream, "Kill the demons," whom he later identified as the Chinese gods and the Emperor. As he recovered from the breakdown, Hong reread the Christian tracts he had earlier dismissed—and in a sudden realization, he decided that the men in his visions had been God and Jesus. With a logic that may explain his failure in the scholars' examination, he reasoned that since he had been addressing Jesus as "Elder Brother" in the dreams, then he too must be a Son of God. Convinced that God had sent him to Earth with a purpose, Hong began to preach his own version of Christianity and to attack Confucian shrines. Such activities angered the locals and he left his village for Guangxi, though the authorities continued to allow him to teach.

In 1847, Hong returned to Canton to study the Bible more closely with an American Southern Baptist missionary named Isaacher Roberts. Shortly thereafter, he relocated to eastern Guangxi in a rugged area known as Thistle Mountain, where he continued to preach and to develop his own new doctrine. In this isolated region, Hong began to attract converts, many from the Hakkas and from other "outsiders" in Chinese society, like the

Zhuang and Yao mountain tribesmen. He was also joined by many members of Triad organizations. The Triads had begun as secret societies in southern China who opposed the foreign Manchu Dynasty and hoped one day to restore the old Ming dynasty to the Dragon Throne. By the nineteenth century, they had become associated with common piracy and banditry, though they maintained their hatred of the Qing. Perhaps drawing on their influences, Hong's new creed began to combine his peculiar Christian doctrines with a commitment to destroying the Manchu Dynasty. For Hong Xiuquan, the Manchu Dynasty represented evil demons fighting against God the Father—and he had been sent by God and his Elder Brother, Jesus, to destroy the demons and restore China to its original path of righteousness.

By 1851, the year the rebellion officially began, Hong had recruited over twenty thousand converts, who came to be known as God-Worshippers. Hong's philosophy of opium abstinence attracted addicts who seem to have found in Hong's tenets a cure for their obsession. His most prominent disciple, a charismatic ex-opium smuggler and illiterate coal salesman, Yang Xiuqing, became the movement's military genius. The Taiping Rebellion was at once a political/military force and a proto–twelve-step program for recovering addicts—a form of liberation theology that liberated its adherents from substance abuse, and it was hoped, from an abusive central authority.

There were several other prototypical elements in the belief system of the God-Worshippers, including communalism, socialism, and an attitude that recalled Robin Hood and anticipated Marx. The Triads had long gone into battle with the cry, "Plunder the rich to relieve the poor," and Hong adopted the slogan as his own. Hong formulated his code of behavior based on the same elements of the Bible that had inspired St. Francis of Asissi, and adopted the passage from the Gospel of St. Matthew that commanded the faithful, "If thou wilt be perfect, go and sell what thou hast, and give to the poor, and thou shalt have treasure in heaven." All plunder and other funds were pooled in a common treasury and shared equally by members of the collective. Hong abolished private ownership of land and imposed the death penalty on those who tried to hold on to their wealth. The Taiping movement was also deeply puritanical, with a long list of voluptuary taboos, including alcohol, gambling, alcohol, tobacco, prostitution, concubinage, the Pig Trade, and other forms of slavery. Like

Cromwell's England, Taiping-controlled China was not a very merry place. Women were treated as equals, a shocking development in the deeply misogynistic and paternalistic Chinese society. Female adherents held prominent positions in the army and the bureaucracy.

In 1851, Hong christened the movement Taiping Tianguo ("Heavenly Kingdom of the Great Peace") and named himself its "Heavenly King," a neat promotion since his rival in Peking was merely Heaven's Son. Hong chose the royal (king—*wang* in Chinese) rather than the Imperial title and set himself up as a rival emperor because in his hierarchy God held the superior title.

The threat of land expropriation disturbed Peking (as well as the reactionary Queen Victoria who had heard of the rebellion in far-off England) more than the sect's heretical beliefs, and the Emperor ordered the Governor of Guangxi Province, Zhen Zuchen, to exterminate the rebels. Zhen, aged sixty-seven, was a devout Buddhist, and he respected the God-Worshippers, whom he did not molest, but beheaded any Triads who fell into his power as common bandits.

In 1850, China had already endured four years of famine when the Emperor decided to escalate the attack on the rebels. Dissatisfied with Zhen's selective exterminations that spared everyone except the Triads, the Emperor called Lin Zexu out of retirement and disgrace and ordered him to eradicate the God-Worshippers. However, Lin never got to enjoy a last hurrah because he died, at age sixty-seven, en route to Guangxi Province. In January 1851, government troops were repulsed from Thistle Mountain by ten thousand rebels armed only with pikes and halberds. Women fought alongside the men in another anticipation of both the Soviet and Maoist brigades, where the sexes were treated equally—at least equal in being allowed to fight and die for the cause.

New orders and tenets followed the movement's military success. Hong adapted the Ten Commandments for Chinese sensibilities, naming the Emperor as a false god in the First Commandment, and adding obedience to Hong and his officers to the Fourth. Adherence to the Commandments and the combination of temporal and spiritual authority in Hong turned the rebel community into a genuine theocracy. The movement was also puritanical and, like many such sects, past and future, the Heavenly Kingdom of the Great Peace was riddled with hypocrisy at the top. Hong ordered all men and women to be separated by sex, even married couples. Anticipating Freud, Hong seemed to understand the powerful effects of sublimation through sexual abstinence—perhaps he hoped to sublimate sexual energy into increased military prowess—because he forbade sexual intercourse for everyone except himself. His flagrant promiscuity typified the sexual hypocrisy of many cult leaders and fundamentalist ministers of our own time and the past. Long before Sun Yatsen introduced the custom as a symbol of rebellion against the Manchu Dynasty, the God-Worshippers cut off their queues or pigtails, a universal symbol of servitude to the alien Manchus.

By the fall of 1851, the God-Worshippers' ranks had swelled from the original few thousand starving peasants fleeing the famine in Guangxi to one million crack troops. The rebels repulsed several more attacks on Thistle Mountain by Imperial troops. The cult's ban on opium may explain their military success against the Emperor's army, which suffered a 90 percent rate of addiction. On September 25, 1851, Hong felt confident enough to leave his sanctuary and march to Yong'an, sixty miles northeast of his redoubt. His troops laid siege to the city, which opened its gates without a fight. The acquiescence of the defenders was aided by Hong's brilliant propaganda efforts. Printing presses churned out his religious tracts, which included the unusual admonition for the times and practices that civilians were to be spared—hence the ease with which city after city fell to Hong's forces as they cut a swath across China, marching in a northeasterly direction. Like Lenin and Mao, Hong focused on the theoretical and organizational aspects of command, and relegated the dirty job of fighting to his *generalissimo*, the reformed opium smuggler Yang.

Hong's forces had covered fifteen hundred miles when they reached the city of Wuchang on January 12, 1853, blew open the gates, and massacred every Manchu soldier they found on the grounds that they were demons. Hong also continued his custom of imposing the death penalty on moneylenders and corrupt bureaucrats, which endeared him to peasants and the embryonic proletariat and reinforced the Leveller aspect of the sect.

Hong now set his sights on the pivotal prize that had tempted the British, Nanking, defended by only seven thousand Manchus and six thousand regular troops, against the eighty thousand men and women of Hong's army, which began to lay siege to the city on February 28, 1853. Two weeks later, the rebels entered the city after blowing a hole in the city's wall.

Hong was merciless to the people in Nanking he considered demons, and the movement began to evolve into a sanguinary crusade that seemed to contradict its Christian teachings, but typified many revolutions like the French and Russian that degenerated into violence. Besides killing the usual suspects like Manchus, moneylenders, corrupt government officials, and the ostentatiously rich, their women and children were also pro-scribed. While the God-Worshippers prayed for their victims, the prisoners were herded into a building, which was then set afire. Manchus could be easily identified and killed by the distinctive flatness of their skulls, which had been ritually deformed during infancy. In all, twenty thousand people were butchered and their corpses thrown into the Yangtze River during the twelve-year revolt.

Hong entered his new capital, which he was to hold for a decade, on March 30, 1853, carried in a litter and accompanied by thirty-six women of exceptional beauty riding horses—a shocking sight in China where women generally maintained a more demure demeanor. Hong retired to the Viceroy's palace and never left it for ten years. He seems to have plunged into depression and sexual obsession. He stopped shaving and was attended by eight hundred female servants. French observers spread specious stories that Hong kidnapped and raped French virgins commandeered into his harem.

The wealth and comfort of Nanking seemed to soften Hong and his generals, who were spared his prohibition of sex. Hong paid lip service to the revolution's original goal of capturing Peking and ousting the demon who ruled there, but his commanders shared his lassitude, and only a small army was dispatched in May 1853 to take Peking. Even so, news of the approach panicked the capital. The Emperor made plans to flee, and most of his generals did. By October 1853, the rebels were one hundred miles away from the capital when the Emperor, displaying atypical energy and innovation, unleashed his secret weapon.

The Taiping's soldiers consisted of infantry and no cavalry, although they did possess cannon. The Emperor hired Mongol mercenaries, ferocious, filthy cavalrymen commanded by Senggelinqin. It was a huge gamble because the Mongols had once ruled China, and their current leader was known to have pretensions to the Manchu throne. However, it was a gamble that paid off. The rebel infantry was no match for the faster-moving Mongols, who were expert bowmen and lancers. The Mongol cavalry dispersed Hong's army before it could seriously threaten Peking, and the rebels resorted to ineffectual guerrilla actions until March 7, 1855, when their leader, Lin Fengxiang, was captured, along with his entire army, which had dwindled to five hundred. The prisoners were shipped to Peking and beheaded. The God-Worshippers, however, remained entrenched in Nanking.

As a counterforce to the dangerous Mongols, the Emperor called on a retired soldier and scholar, an ethnic Chinese from Hunan province called Zeng Guofan, who was found by the Emperor's messengers, Cincinnatus-like, tilling his fields. Zeng spurned the Emperor's feckless, opium-impaired troops and assembled a force from his home province of Hunan untainted by opium and infused with Confucian ideals as galvanizing as the rebel's Christian cocktail of borrowed ideology. Like the Imperial Court, his officers were all scholars. By October 1854, Zeng had recaptured Wuchang, and from there launched an attack on Nanking and invested its walls. Despite the overwhelming superiority of his troops, who by now numbered one hundred twenty thousand, Zeng spent the next ten years besieging the Taiping capital before capturing it in July 1864. The fate of Hong and one hundred thousand followers remains the subject of debate. Zeng claimed they all committed suicide when the city fell, but some historians believe the general had them put to death.

One of the bloodiest wars in history and certainly China's most sanguinary, the Taiping Rebellion cost twenty to thirty million lives. The Empire, already weakened by the incursions of the British, never recovered from the rebellion. The collapse of the Manchu Dynasty within a few months of the Revolution of 1911 devolved from these external and internal cataclysms. In Napoleon's phrase, the rebellion was the "thunderclap" before the revolution.

Chapter 18

OUTRAGEOUS SLINGS AND THE *ARROW'S* MISFORTUNE

———•—•———

"The English barbarians have attacked the provincial city, and wounded and injured our soldiers and people. Wherefore I herewith distinctly command you to join together to exterminate them, killing them whenever you meet them, whether on shore or in their ships."

—Ye Mingchen, Viceroy of Canton

Like the Treaty of Versailles in the next century, the *Diktat* of Nanking caused more problems than it solved. China bristled at the humiliating conditions of the pact, which surrendered symbolic and practical forms of her sovereignty to the British. The resentments simmered for a long time, however. It wasn't until 1856, fourteen years after the Nanking treaty, that Chinese anger boiled over into outright acts of aggression.

In February 1856, a French priest, the Abbé Auguste Chapdelaine, was converting Chinese in a village called Xilin in the remote province of Guangxi, which by unfortunate coincidence was also the center of the Taiping rebels' resistance and sanctuary. The priest was arrested and imprisoned in a cage set up in the village square. Like Father Preboyre, Chapdelaine was in violation of Chinese law by carrying his work into the interior. It did not help that the missionary seemed to the Chinese to share the same beliefs as the God-Worshippers, in whose province he was also working. In fact, Chapdelaine and all other Catholics were appalled by the bastardized Proto-Protestant creed of the rebels and supported the Manchu ruler in Peking. At worst, the French missionary could be accused of guilt by geographical association. On February 29, 1856, the beloved Abbé, still wearing his trademark Chinese clothes, was beheaded, dismembered, and eviscerated by his executioners, who an hysterical French press claimed then proceeded to cook and consume the Abbé's heart. Historians agree that the

Chinese killed the priest, but the grisly feast afterward is widely considered an urban legend.

The powerless French representative in Canton, the Comte de Courcy, blustered and sent furious letters to city's Viceroy, Ye Mingchen, but took no military action to avenge the death of the popular priest. Ye realized that the French had no stomach for a fight, and sent the Comte an insulting reply explaining that the atrocity was a simple case of mistaken identity: "[Chapdelaine] dressed and spoke like a Chinese; nobody thought him to be French," Ye wrote.

The British problems began at Canton, although the spark that ignited the Second Opium War might have occurred at any of the other five ports opened up by the Nanking accord. On October 8, 1856, the *Arrow*, a 127-ton lorcha, a hybrid with a British hull and a Chinese junk's sails, registered in Hong Kong as a British vessel. In reality, it was owned by a Chinese merchant and manned by a Chinese crew of fourteen. The *Arrow* had docked in Canton with a cargo of rice from Macao en route to Hong Kong. The *Arrow's* figurehead captain was a twenty-one-year-old Belfast native, Thomas Kennedy. His presence on board and the Hong Kong registration allowed the real Chinese operators to claim the privileges granted genuine British ships by the Treaty of Nanking.

Kennedy was not on his vessel when the incident occurred that would launch the Second Opium War, known as the Arrow War. He was on a lorcha captained by another figurehead chief, his friend John Leach. Also aboard was Charles Earl, captain of the *Chusan*. At eight A.M., the two friends were having breakfast when they noticed two large warships flying the Emperor's flag with mandarins and sixty marines on deck sail into Canton harbor and approach the *Arrow*. Officials from the Imperial ships boarded the *Arrow* and arrested her crew—all native Chinese—bound them, and threw them into the hold of one of the Imperial ships. Leach, Kennedy, and Earl jumped into a *sampan* and rowed toward the Chinese junk. Although the master of a Portuguese lorcha nearby later swore that he did not see the British flag flying above the lorcha, Kennedy insisted that he had seen a Chinese marine pull down the Union Jack. Relying on a smattering of Chinese, Kennedy protested the seizure, but the marines responded with curses. Kennedy softened his posture and asked that two of his crew be allowed to stay on the lorcha as caretakers. The mandarins granted his request and carried off the twelve remaining crew members.

The *Arrow* at first seemed an unlikely prize for the Chinese to seize, since it only carried rice, not opium. But the *Arrow* possessed a troubled past. The *Arrow* had been built by the Chinese as a cargo ship, but it had been captured by pirates, then recaptured by Canton's Viceroy Ye Mingchen, who sold it at auction to a comprador employed by a British firm. The comprador took advantage of the connection and registered the *Arrow* as a British ship with all the advantages that entailed. While ownership and registration had changed, the new owner(s) had failed to purge the crew, and three pirates remained among them. That was the excuse the Chinese mandarins had used to seize all but two of the crew. It later emerged that the registration had lapsed, so despite arguments to the contrary, it was technically not a British ship.

Kennedy reported the seizure to the acting British Consul, Harry Parkes, who spoke fluent Chinese and had been a consular official at four of the five ports opened by the Treaty of Nanking for fourteen years. The problems with the *Arrow's* status did not deter Parkes. The combative Parkes went to the war junk at once, where he railed about "the gross insult and violation of national rights [the Chinese] had committed." Parkes cited the Supplementary Treaty of 1843 that required the Chinese to ask the permission of the British Consul before arresting a Chinese citizen serving on a British-registered ship. Parkes demanded that the twelve crewmen be handed over to his custody at the British Consulate immediately. The Chinese commander explained that one of the sailors was the father of a notorious pirate, and the other crewmen were needed to testify about the father's guilt or innocence—hence they would all be held. When Parkes persisted in his demands, one of the mandarins slapped him.

Humiliated, Parkes returned to the British Consulate and composed a letter to Ye Mingchen, who was also the Imperial Commissioner in charge of foreign affairs and the Viceroy of Guangxi and Guangdong Provinces. Canton was the capital of Guangdong. "I hasten therefore to lay the case before Your Excellency [Ye], confident that your superior judgment will lead you at once to admit that an insult so publicly committed must be equally publicly atoned. I therefore request Your Excellency that the men who have been carried away from the *Arrow* be returned by the captain to that vessel in my presence and if accused of any crime they may then be conveyed to the British Consulate, where in conjunction with proper officers deputed by Your Excellency for the purpose, I shall be prepared to investigate the case." Perhaps Parkes had second thoughts about his complaint to Ye and decided not to inflame the already incendiary situation by lodging a second complaint against the mandarin who had slapped him.

Ye was not the kind of bureaucrat to whom sweet reason or fine points of international law could be appealed to for satisfaction. He had crushed the Taiping Rebellion within his two provinces with great brutality, pronouncing summary execution on every captured Taiping rebel along with their wives and children. The butchery in Canton sometimes rose as high as two hundred executions per day.

Parkes also complained to a more sympathetic ear, his superior, Sir John Bowring, the governor of Hong Kong, that the seized seamen, flying under a British flag (or maybe not), deserved the same rights and protection as British subjects. Bowring was delighted with the opportunity that the *Arrow* seizure provided, and in a secret letter to Parkes said, "Cannot we use the opportunity and carry the city question? If so, I will come up with the whole fleet," which consisted of sixteen men-of-war and three steamships in Hong Kong Harbor. By "carry the city," Bowring meant that the British would at last be allowed to move out of the factories and set up shop and living quarters throughout Canton, as per the English-language terms of the Treaty of Nanking. The Chinese translation justified segregating the foreigners in their factories because it was argued that the xenophobic Cantonese would slay the British if they came to live among them. Isolation was for their foreign "guests'" protection, not to limit their movement, although both concerns applied to the Chinese interpretation of the treaty. Palmerston had given orders not to push the issue of British housing in Canton because he did not think the claim was worth going to over: his representatives on the scene, however, ignored these instructions.

Two days later, Ye responded to Parkes's letter. He could free nine of the crew, but insisted on keeping the remaining three because they had been pirates. One had led an attack on a Chinese ship in September. As for possession of the *Arrow*, Ye claimed her crew had sworn an oath that Chinese had built and owned the vessel. It was not by any stretch of the imagination a British ship. As a sign of good faith, Ye sent his letter to Parkes accompanied by nine of the crew members.

More interested in making a diplomatic point than he was in the plight of the hostages, Parkes refused to accept custody of the nine sailors and wrote another letter to Bowring in Hong Kong suggesting that the British retaliate by seizing one of the Chinese junks that had commandeered the *Arrow*.

On October 14, the British followed Parkes's recommendation. The British gunboat *Coramandel* boarded a Chinese vessel without a fight and towed it to Whampoa. British intelligence was lacking in this effort because, as it turned out, the ship was a private craft, not government owned. Ye ignored the incident intended to provoke him into retaliating. In the meantime, Bowring had a chance to inspect the registration of the *Arrow*, something Parkes had not bothered to do, and discovered that the *Arrow's* registry as a British ship had expired on September 27. Technically, the Chinese had not violated British territoriality by seizing her crew.

Despite his discovery, Bowring determined to goad Ye into action and consequently had Parkes write the Viceroy on October 21. The letter was an ultimatum: Ye had twenty-four hours to free all twelve crewmen of the *Arrow* and to provide a public apology and a promise to respect all British shipping in China, including apparently "British" ships that weren't actually British. If Ye didn't comply, "Her Majesty's naval officers will have recourse to force you to compel complete satisfaction."

Ye seems to have had a failure of nerves—and a good recollection of Britain's track record for backing up threats—but he also needed to save face. He returned the entire crew, but refused to apologize and in the future offered only to consult with the foreign interlopers over criminals like the *Arrow* pirates. "Hereafter if any lawless characters conceal themselves on board foreign lorchas, you, the said Consul, shall of course be informed of the same by declaration in order that you may act with the Chinese authorities in the management of such affairs," Ye wrote Parkes on October 22, the deadline date for British retaliation. Ye offered a compromise that would avoid similar incidents in the future when he added, "Hereafter, Chinese officers will on no account without reason seize and take into custody the people belonging to foreign lorchas, but when Chinese subjects build for themselves vessels, foreigners should not sell registers to them..."

for it will occasion confusion between native and foreign ships, and render it difficult to distinguish between them."

Ye's equivocation was just what Parkes and Bowring needed as an excuse to resume hostilities. On October 23, Parkes ordered Rear-Admiral Sir Michael Seymour to seize and destroy the four Barrier Forts five miles south of Canton. Two of the forts fired back on the British fleet before surrendering, and five defenders were killed, the first deaths in the Second Opium War. Seymour blamed the Chinese for the casualties, telling Parkes the "loss of four or five killed on the part of the Chinese [was] solely arising from their ill-judged resistance to our force."

Seymour's easy victory inflamed Parkes's war fever, and the Consul decided to bring the war home to Ye: "Should Yeh [Ye] still be contumacious," Parkes wrote the Admiral, "I think that the residence of his excellency, which is not far from the waterside, should also in that case feel the effects of the bombardment."

Ye called out the city militia, which responded with less than war-like enthusiasm. Unlike the popular Commissioner Lin, Ye lacked the support of rank-and-file soldiers because of the innocent Chinese he had murdered to combat the Taiping Rebellion. And Ye's two hundred warships were antique toys compared to the British's state-of-the-art gunboats and steamers.

Parkes made one more token demand to Ye to grant British residents the right to live and work outside the factories. Ye rejected the demand, and on October 28th, the British replied by having the steamer *Encounter* shell the rooftop of the Viceregal residence. Ye gained some popularity among the disaffected populace when news circulated that the fearless Viceroy had remained in his courtyard, reading a book, as the shells missed him.

Ye added psychological and real terror to the mismatched conflict by increasing the price on British heads from $30 to $100. (The inflation of war, since the British offered £20 per Chinese enemy.) Ye's proclamation on November 28th made this blood-curdling offer: "The English barbarians have attacked the provincial city, and wounded and injured our soldiers and people. Wherefore I herewith distinctly command you to join together to exterminate them, killing them whenever you meet them, whether on shore or in their ships." Parkes seems to have particularly irritated Ye, because he offered a fortune for the times—$30,000—for killing the Consul. Other high-ranking British leaders fetched $5,000.

Within a day of the bombardment of Ye's palace, British guns had blown a hole in Canton's walls. As a force of sailors and marines poured through the hole in the wall on October 29th, Chinese guns mounted on the walls were not fired at the invaders, who entered the city in an eerie silence broken fitfully by the staccato sound of antique matchlocks, which failed to bag a single British soldier. Farcical elements undercut the British victory. While W.T. Bates, the captain of the HMS *Actaeon,* planted the British flag atop the wall, he was joined there by James Keenan, the U.S. envoy in Hong Kong, waving the Stars and Stripes. The United States had remained neutral during the conflict between Britain and China, and Keenan's solo act of "diplomacy" was apparently due to the fact that he was visibly intoxicated.

The British pulled a large cannon through the breach in the wall and began to shell Ye's palace. Seymour led a party to take Ye's residence, which was empty. The ogre of Canton had fled his lair. Seymour didn't have enough men to hold the city and soon abandoned it in favor of the greater safety of his encampment outside the walls. He also sent Ye a threat, though one that was somewhat undercut by the Admiral's retreat: "The lives and property of the entire city are at my mercy, and could be destroyed by me at any moment," he told the mandarin.

Ye sent an emissary to Parkes with an offer of truce, but the Consul rebuffed the tender and made vague threats about the British allying themselves with the Taiping rebels. This was merely bluff, however, since his superior, Bowring, feared and loathed the Jacobinsim of the God-Worshippers. He much preferred to deal with the Emperor, who also loathed the Leveller aspect of the rebellion, as one conservative to another. The bluff was transparent to both men.

As Seymour continued his siege of the city, he also gained control of all seagoing traffic in the gulf of Canton, chased away Chinese warships in the gulf, destroyed forts in the area, and continued to shell Canton. He estimated it would take five thousand troops to invest the city, and Bowring turned down his requests for reinforcements from Hong Kong because his own forces were spread thin controlling the new British possession.

Ye now threw himself into the saber-rattling with a proclamation ordering the residents of the Canton to remain calm. "Preserve quiet minds, guard your property, [do not] give way to alarm," he said from the safety of his hiding place. Chinese, as well as the few remaining European residents of the factories, began to desert Canton as Seymour's bombardment made them run for their lives. The exodus of foreigners increased in proportion to the desertion of their servants, the "help problem" causing more hardship and distress than the cannonades of their compatriots outside the walls. Snipers inside the city returned the fire of the British with antiquated matchlocks, a token and worthless resistance that was more psychological than strategic. Back in England, pious opinion was mollified by the strange intelligence from Seymour that he refrained from shelling the city on Sundays. God and guns both rested on the Seventh Day.

By the end of October 1856, Ye finally agreed to parley with the British, but still refused to meet them in person, sending one of his subordinates instead—a face-saving insult to the British. In fact, Ye remained defiant. On October 30, he reiterated the bounty on foreigners dead or alive, turned down Bowring's request for in-person negotiations, and sent Seymour a letter of reproach that contained an oxymoronic amalgam of divine right and populism:

> In the administration of all matters in China the rule adhered to is that which heaven shows is the right one to pursue: the chief consideration is the people. It is said in *The Book of History*, 'Heaven sees as my people see; Heaven hears as my people hear.' Is this not an additional reason why I should be unable to constrain the people? I must add that as it is the habit of Your Excellency's nation to adore the spirit of Heaven, it behooves you in my opinion so much the more to conform in your actions to the principle given us by heaven. Let Your Excellency maturely consider this.

Trade evaporated during the siege, and Howqua and other members of the Cohong faced ruin. On November 12, 1856, the Hong merchants paid a call on Parkes at his residence. Howqua explained their impossible position. They agreed in principle with the British demand to live and do business outside the factories, but they also conceded their lack of power to bring this about. Parkes summed up the Cohong's impotence by saying, "Their weight as a class both with [the] authorities and people is far less than we suppose. The people, particularly the rural population, were opposed to our admission." By placing the blame on the faceless masses in the famine-devastated countryside, the wily Hong merchants apparently hoped to deflect culpability from Britain's real adversaries, Ye and his master, the Emperor. The British refused to participate in this diplomatic and military fantasy.

The Canton stalemate dragged on until November 17th, when Bowring left Hong Kong for Canton, where he was again rebuffed in his attempts to meet with Ye. In a letter to the Foreign Minister, Lord Clarendon, Bowring reported, "I have exhausted all the means with which I could influence either the hopes or fears of this incarnation of ancient Chinese pride, ignorance and unteachableness."

The British mistrust of the Taiping rebels kept them from accepting military assistance at this critical time. Toward the end of November, an armada of rebel ships with fifteen hundred fighting men aboard tried to sail into Canton harbor, hoping to coordinate their attack with the expected British assault, but the rebels were stopped by the British at the Bogue by a fleet under the command of Captain Keith Stewart.

Harry Parkes used the offer of help from the Taiping rebels to intimidate and threaten Ye, telling one of Ye's assistants that "partisans of the revolutionary factions had intimated their wish to cooperate in an attack on the city, but that the Admiral had declined all connection with their proceedings." Parkes implied that this decision could change depending on Ye's intransigence. In the same xenophobic vein, Bowring rejected two hundred coolies who had volunteered to fight for the British. The invaders hated the Emperor, but were even more appalled by the property-hating God-Worshippers.

Ye mistook the British lack of manpower for a lack of resolve, and in mid December, he felt emboldened enough to order the destruction of the factories while officially denying any involvement in it. Shortly before midnight on December 14th, a torch-bearing procession of Chinese provocateurs burned the factories to the ground. The British water-pump system failed because its source was Canton harbor, and low tides couldn't provide enough pressure for the pumps. An impromptu bucket brigade proved ineffective against the inferno. All that remained of the foreign establishment were the British chapel and boathouse. Parkes was in Hong Kong on December 15th, but a member of his staff, Henry Lane, perished in the flames.

Ye's generous bounty on Europeans may have prompted an atrocity on December 29th. The Chinese crew of the steamship *Thistle*, which carried mail from Hong Kong to Canton, mutinied en route and beheaded all eleven European passengers, with the help of Chinese soldiers who had disguised themselves as passengers. The *Thistle* was set ablaze and found drifting in Canton harbor with the headless victims in the hold. The heads had been taken so the crew could collect Ye's bounty, which had risen to $100 per head. It is not known if Ye specifically ordered the massacre, but the seamen did have the insignia of his troops on their shirts.

The Chinese found fire a primitive but effective tool against the superior technology of the British. In January 1857, they launched a flotilla of fire ships containing eight thousand pounds of gunpowder against Seymour's ships in the harbor. They failed to do any damage, but the incident, coming on the heels of the factories' fiery obliteration, seems to have unnerved the Admiral, who didn't retaliate with a more vigorous bombardment as might have been expected. Two weeks after the destruction of the factories, Seymour, fearing another attack—this time by sea—sailed out of Canton harbor with two ships, the *Niger* and the *Encounter*, and made for the relative safety of Macao. Thanks to the invention of the telegraph and the deployment of steamships, communications between Britain and her far-flung colonies and foreign markets like China became much quicker. An incident in Hong Kong was reported in England fast enough to influence the Parliamentary debate and elections in the early months of 1857.

On January 15, 1857, four hundred foreign residents of Hong Kong who had eaten bread from a local bakery became violently ill. The doctor's verdict was arsenic poisoning. The culprit, if he had fatal intentions, was incompetent because he put so much arsenic in his dough that the victims vomited up the poison so there were no fatalities. Bowring, his wife, and his children were among the victims, and Lady Bowring almost died. In a letter to the Colonial Secretary Labouchere, a frazzled Bowring wrote, "I beg to apologize if anything should have been forgotten at this last moment. I am shaken by the effects of poison, every member of my family being at this moment suffering from this new attempt upon our lives." The owner of the bakery went on trial despite the fact that his own family had eaten the poisoned bread, and he was acquitted. But the public demanded a culprit, and the all-purpose villain Ye became the chief suspect. Ye maintained a cynical innocence, telling Napoleon III's representative, the Comte de Courcy, "Doubtless there are many Chinese whose hatred against the English has been much increased, but to poison people in this underhand manner is an act worthy of detestation."

In any case, there was little he could do: "Whoever he is, the author of this poisoning is an abominable creature, but since he is in [British-controlled] Hong Kong, I find it difficult to proceed against him."

The British authorities in Hong Kong had no such qualms and arrested fifty-two of the bakery's employees after Bowring prevented a mob from lynching the suspects, who were all jammed into a single room only fifteen feet square for nineteen days, their jailers pleading lack of space. In a reference to the 1756 incident in Calcutta, the incarceration was dubbed "The Black Hole of China" by the press. The prisoners were moved to more spacious quarters after the prison doctor warned that the crowded conditions would lead to plague.

Hysteria over the poisoning generated a witch hunt and a huge dragnet of five hundred arrests, including some charged only with being "suspicious looking." The possibility of more poisonings and false arrests panicked the native population of Hong Kong. In 1857, nearly half of the Chinese residents of the island fled to Australia or California.

The *Arrow* incident and the *Thistle* massacre had already provided a pretext for Bowring's military ambitions toward Canton, which he revealed in a letter to Lord Canning, the Governor-General of India, on January 10th, before the poisoning incident. But it was not than arsenic that fueled the Governor of Hong Kong's military goals. Bowring asked Canning to send reinforcements from India because Seymour's timid patrol in the gulf of Canton was clearly not working. Bowring wanted to occupy the city. "The gate of China is Canton, and unless we can force an entrance there, I believe the difficulties of obtaining any improved position in China will be almost invincible. The valor of H.M. naval forces [is] not able to take the city." Bowring told Canning that he had discussed the military impasse with Admiral Seymour, and both men agreed on the necessity of "military aid to the extent of 5,000 men, with a small body of artillery." The British cabinet had anticipated Bowring's requests, and on January 31, 1857, before learning of his request to Canning for more troops, the government told the Governor-General of India to dispatch a regiment and artillery to Canton. On February 9, 1857, the Foreign Minister ordered Seymour to seize the entrance to the Grand Canal and thus cut off the capital's rice supply. Peking would be starved into submission since military victories alone had failed to move the Emperor and his court to comply with Britain's demand for commercial and missionary access to China. Bowring received orders to obtain new concessions: a permanent British ambassadorial presence at the Imperial Court and more ports and rivers opened to British ships.

Back home in England, money worries more than the lurid arsenic incident galvanized the public discussion both inside and outside Parliament. *The Times* estimated that the conflict in China had already cost £10,000,000 in lost trade and tax revenues. A strange-bedfellows alliance arose in both houses of Parliament that combined greed and moral anguish.

In early 1857, the Earl of Derby, leader of the Tory opposition in the House of Lords, brought a motion of no-confidence against the Whig Government and Palmerston's management of the conflict in China. On February 24, 1857, Derby denounced Bowring and Palmerston's designs on China as a bald-faced and illegal land grab and usurpation of an independent nation's sovereign powers: "I am an advocate for the feeble defenselessness of China against the overpowering might of Great Britain. I am an advocate for weakness against power, for perplexed and bewildered barbarism against the arrogant demands of over-weaning self-styled civilization." Calling the *Arrow* issue "the most despicable cause of war that has ever occurred," the Earl argued that the ship was not really a British vessel and had no right to be registered as such. Hence, the seizure of her crew, while regrettable, was not an attack on British sovereignty. Bowring and Parkes were inflaming the situation by mistreating the alleged villain, Viceroy Ye. "I must say that the language of the Chinese officials is throughout forbearing, courteous and gentlemanlike, while the language of the British officials is with hardly an exception menacing, disrespectful and arrogant."

Derby called on the conscience of the bishops in the House of Lords whose "position peculiarly qualifies them to impart and inculcate the adoption of those high and holy maxims by which we are commanded not to defraud our neighbors and to live peaceably with all men." He also appealed to his secular colleagues "to declare that they will not sanction the usurpation of that most awful prerogative of the Crown, the declaring of war; that they will not tolerate the destruction of the forts of a friendly county; that they will not tolerate the bombardment and the shelling of a commercial and open city." Derby's speech received a standing ovation—but it did not translate into action against the government's intention to escalate the war in China. Lord Clarendon's assistant, Edmund Hammond, wrote a cynical note to his boss that the Archbishop of Canterbury's seat would soon be vacant and suggested that dangling the possibility of replacing him in front of the opposition bishops in the House of Lords would stop them from joining the Derby backlash. "A report judiciously circulated as to the declining health of the Archbishop of Canterbury would probably neutralize the effect of Lord Derby's wordy peroration as regards the Bench of Bishops," Hammond said. The promise of a coveted Garter knighthood would also take the fight out of the secular peers inclined to support Derby's pacifist plank: "A similar report…as to the contemplated appropriation of vacant Garters might not be without its effect."

Palmerston's cynical distribution of power successfully co-opted the influential Lord Shaftesbury. Shaftesbury, a philanthropist who had also been one of the most vociferous critics of the opium trade, sided with Palmerston because the Prime Minister had bribed the peer by allowing him to control the appointment of bishops, appointments which brought with them a cathedral, extensive lands, and a salary from rents that allowed bishops to live like lords. But Shaftesbury's conscience was troubled even as he enjoyed the dispensation of lucrative favors. In his diary, he equivocated over his course of action: "A sad result. Right or wrong, the government must be supported to bring these matters to a satisfactory close. Hope and believe that God, having employed [the Prime Minister] as an instrument of good, would maintain him. But his ways are inscrutable." Nevertheless, Shaftesbury confided to his journal while maintaining a public silence on the issue that "opium and Christianity could not enter China together."

Lord Clarendon had the difficult job of rebutting Derby's arguments. When he stood up to give his speech after Derby, the cheers for Derby still rang out in the House. The Foreign Secretary insisted that the *Arrow* was a British vessel and condemned the Chinese seizure of it. He also lambasted the Emperor's refusal to live up to the terms of the Treaty of Nanking. Finally, Clarendon made the case for military rather than the diplomatic action Derby sought. "I fear that we must come to the conclusion that in dealing with a nation like the Chinese, if we intend to preserve any amicable or useful relations with them, we must make them sensible of the law of force, and must appeal to them in the manner which they alone can appreciate."

Members in the Lords also attacked the man on the scene, Bowring. The Tory Lord Malmesbury denounced the Governor of Hong Kong as a duplicitous warmonger who lied to both the enemy, Ye, and his own colleague, Admiral Seymour. Despite his bullishness toward the opium trade, Lord Ellenborough, a former Governor-General of India, complained that Bowring had "disregarded the instructions of four successive Secretaries of State, supported, as I suppose he is by an influence with the government which I cannot comprehend." While Shaftesbury focused on the moral issues, Ellenborough condemned the government's activities in China for pragmatic economic reasons. After two more days of debate, Derby's motion of censure was put to a vote. The government won the division with 146 in favor of its China policy and 110 against. Apparently hoping for the pinnacle of the episcopacy, Canterbury, all but three of the bishops in Parliament voted for the government. Despite his victory, the debate had enervated and unnerved the infirm, seventy-three-year-old Prime Minister.

On the same day the Whigs persevered in the House of Lords, the Commons took up the debate over the *Arrow's* registry and Bowring's request for reinforcements to invade Canton. Richard Cobden, a radical MP from Manchester and a zealous pacifist who had also denounced the popular Crimean War, brought a similar motion of no confidence/censure. Cobden justified the seizure of the *Arrow's* crew as a legitimate exercise of Chinese sovereignty and condemned Bowring's and Seymour's response to it. Cobden tried to appeal to the greed rather than the conscience of his colleagues when he pointed out that war was bad for trade and that Bowring's posturing in Canton had killed British commerce there. Cobden, like Derby, pleaded for negotiations rather than force. "Is not so venerable an empire as that deserving of some sympathy—at least of some justice—at the hands of conservative England?"

In his speech supporting censure, Gladstone refused to leave the embarrassing issue of the opium trade out of the debate, especially after Samuel Gregson, the eccentric MP for Lancaster and chairman of the East India and China Association, read into the record a letter from British merchants in China claiming that there was no traffic in opium there! Gladstone shouted his response: "Your greatest and most valuable trade in China is in opium. It is a smuggling trade. It is in the worst, the most pernicious, demoralizing and destructive of all the contraband trades that are carried upon the surface of the globe." Disraeli lent his predictable eloquence to the Opposition by calling for "negotiations and treaties" instead of blockades and bombardment. The future Conservative Prime Minister taunted the Whigs by daring them to call new elections and run on their true platform: "No Reform! New Taxes! Canton Blazing!"

The Whig rebuttal to Tory claims on conscience was delivered by several MPs, with the Prime Minister giving the final speech before the vote. When the Chinese had seized the *Arrow's* crew, they had pulled down the Union Jack, a symbolic act that seemed to enrage Parliamentary fire-breathers more than the graver offense of detaining the crew, who were arguably under the protection of the flag that had been lowered. Robert Lowe, an MP and the military's Paymaster, wrapped himself rhetorically in "this very flag brave men had held to their breast and glued there with their best heart's blood rather than surrender it on the field of battle even to a gallant enemy." Sir James Matheson, the "Member for Opium," as the press sneeringly referred to the MP representing the boroughs of Ross and Cromarty, did not dare to defend his bread and butter—opium—in Parliament because he feared being turned into a combination whipping and poster boy for opium's legion of critics in and out of the House of Commons.

In contrast to the opium MP's reticence on the subject, Palmerston's speech rambled on about the drug business and was studded with inappropriate jokes and filled with contradictory assertions that may have reflected more his age and a debilitating case of gout and the flu instead of intentional deception. Befuddlement rather than facts seemed to drive his claim that the British government opposed the opium trade, which he insisted had nothing to do with the present conflict. Then he gutted his own argument by attributing the war to an imbalance in trade that could only be rectified by the sale of opium. "The existing restrictions on our commerce are one cause of that trade in opium to which [Cobden and Derby et al.] so dexterously alluded to...We can pay for our purchases only partly in goods, the rest we must pay in opium and silver."

In a dramatic rebuff to the House of Lords, an unlikely coalition of Radicals and Tories (Conservatives) carried the vote of censure 263 to 247.

Gladstone wrote in his diary that the outcome of the vote did "more honour to the House of Commons than any I remember." The Queen, however, with whom he would later have a tortured relationship, did not share the moral certitude of her future Prime Minister. Her Low Church leanings apparently threw up no moral qualms over the opium issue. Although she remained, as usual, above the fray publicly, Victoria, thirty-eight and pregnant with her eighth child, confided in her husband Prince Albert that she was "grieved at the success of evil party motives, spite, and total lack of patriotism."

With the fall of his government, Palmerston dissolved Parliament and adopted Disraeli's ironic advice, using the *Arrow* incident as his rallying cry and confirming the government's commitment to stay the sanguine course in China. "There will be no change, and there can be no change, in the policy of the government with respect to China," he said in his stump speech. Palmerston continued to argue that the *Arrow* was a British ship, but saved his venom for the moral turpitude of Britain's new bogeyman, Viceroy Ye. Palmerston demonized Ye as the Lucrezia Borgia of Canton, and found the tactic an effective vote-getter. "An insolent barbarian wielding authority at Canton has violated the British flag, broken the engagements of treaties, offered rewards for the heads of British subjects in that part of China, and planned their destruction by murder, assassination and poisons." The Prime Minister called the Viceroy "one of the most savage barbarians that ever disgraced a nation. Yeh [Ye] has been guilty of every crime which can degrade and debase human nature." Palmerston also tried to seize the moral high ground from the Radical-Tory alliance by insinuating that his opponents' true motive was to force the Whig ministry to fall, not save China from Britain's just claims against her. The Prime Minister predicted wholesale massacre of the European residents of Canton if the House did not back the war party.

———•••———

The British voting public was already floating on a jingoistic cloud of self-congratulation over the victorious conclusion of the Crimean War, and Palmerston's histrionic appeal to patriotism nourished the popular blood-lust. Equally histrionic, the Tory opposition ridiculed Palmerston's arguments as pious hypocrisies and reminded voters of the underlying economic considerations that literally and figuratively were poisoning the people of China and relations with their uninvited British guests. The Tory MP Sir James Graham melodramatically declared on the hustings, "The real object [of the war] is to drug the people of China with opium, and the effect of it here is to enhance the price of tea." Manchester's MP, Richard Cobden, made similar appeals to his constituents, who were unmoved and elected his Whig challenger instead.

Although Palmerston had praised Bowring during the Parliamentary debate and the subsequent general election, the Governor of Hong Kong's war-mongering in China had so alienated other members of Parliament, including those of Palmerston's own party, that the Prime Minister decided to appoint a plenipotentiary above the Hong Kong chief to carry out the tortuous negotiations with the Imperial Court. The Duke of Newcastle was Palmerston's first choice, but the peer rejected the thankless job that would be second-guessed and dissected by Parliament and public opinion back home. On March 13th, in the middle of the general election, Palmerston announced the appointment of a new envoy to China, the popular Scottish peer, the former Governor of Jamaica (1842–46) and Governor-General of British North America (1847–54), James Bruce, the eighth Earl of Elgin and twelfth Earl of Kincardine, an aristocrat of ancient lineage and a direct descendant of Robert the Bruce.

Lord Elgin was the son of the famous antiquarian who preserved or vandalized—depending on whether you're British or Greek—the friezes on the crumbling Parthenon by stripping them from the ancient edifice and sending them to England for safekeeping from wartorn Athens or personal gain. Lord Byron, a champion of the Greek *risorgimento*, denounced the seventh earl as a "rapacious vandal," and Elgin's sale of the friezes to the

British Museum for £35,000 in 1816 seemed to confirm his reputation as a mercenary rather than a preservationist, although he sold the marbles at a loss that led to his bankruptcy and exile from England to escape creditors in an era when unpaid bills landed you in debtor's prison until you paid up. The eighth Lord Elgin would follow in his father's footsteps, although unlike the debate about whether the seventh earl was a thief or connoisseur, his son would go down in history as an unequivocal vandal of priceless antiquities.

Queen Victoria followed the Parliamentary campaign closely, but made no public comment. In a letter to Uncle Leopold, however, she revealed herself as partisan as any Whig backbencher from a rotten borough. With her trademark mangled syntax and Byzantine illogic, she wrote the King of Belgium:

> My dearest Uncle, the Opposition have played their game most foolishly and the result is that *all* the old Tories say they certainly will *not* support them; they very truly say Lord Derby's party—that is those who want to get into office *coute que coute* [at all costs]—whether the country suffers for it or not, wanted to get in under *false colours*, and that they won't support or abide—which they are *quite* right in. There is reason to hope that a better class of men will be returned to support the Government, not a particular cry of this or that. [original emphasis]

Palmerston's jingoistic attack must have surprised even him with its effectiveness. During the three-day voting period that began on March 28, 1857, the Whigs returned to office with the biggest landslide since the election of 1832, when the revolutionary Reform Bill was passed. Palmerston enjoyed the confidence of the people, their Queen, and Parliament. He would have been surprised to learn that he lacked the confidence of the man to whom he had entrusted the prosecution of his China policy, a world-famous diplomat who took up his new post with grave moral and tactical reservations.

Chapter 19

PEER PRESSURE

———————

"There is here an idée fixe *that nothing ought to be done till there has been a general massacre at Canton."*

—Britain's plenipotentiary to China,
the Earl of Elgin, 1857

The day before Palmerston named him plenipotentiary to China, Lord Elgin wrote to his wife in Scotland describing the doubts that made him reluctant to accept the job. Although Elgin had not spoken out publicly because of his recent diplomatic positions, he had not supported the Whig policy toward China:

> My Dearest, I have had a note from [Palmerston] followed by an interview. The proposal is to undertake a special mission of a few months' duration to settle the important and difficult question now embarrassing us in the East and concentrating the attention of all the world. On what grounds can I decline? Not on political grounds for however opposed I might be to the Govt. that would be a reason to prevent them from making the offer, but not me from accepting it. The very mission of a Plenipotentiary is an admission that there are errors of policy to be repaired.

The Countess of Elgin wrote back, "Dearest, it was unexpected but if your conscience and feelings tell you to say yes I would not for the world dissuade you. God bless you my own darling. I promise you to do my best not to distress you. Forgive me if I can't write more today. Your own ever Mary."

Elgin brought to his new post an impressive résumé (Governor of Jamaica at thirty, Governor-General of British North America at thirty-five), an impeccable pedigree tinctured with royal blood (one ancestor had been King of Scotland, Robert the Bruce, who also gave Elgin his last name)—and a mountain of debts inherited from his improvident Mr. Micawber of a father, the controversial plunderer-preserver of Greek sculpture. (The seventh Earl, Thomas Bruce, hadn't sold all the marbles to the British Museum. The eighth used leftover pieces as paperweights at Broomhall, his stately home in Fife, Scotland.)

Unlike many men of his birth and time, Elgin was not a xenophobe. His education had been continental by default, growing up in Paris where his father had fled in 1820 to escape creditors after ruining himself by buying the Parthenon friezes from the Ottoman Sultan. The Earl hacked off the temple's *bas-reliefs* and bundled them off to England, where the British Museum bought the priceless sculptures for the firesale price of £35,000—one-third the amount the Earl had paid the Turk. Vandal or preservationist, Elgin was no businessmen. Although he died in 1841, his debts were not finally paid off by his hard-pressed son until thirty years later.

From his father's improvident behavior, the eighth Earl learned thrift and became fluent in French while in Parisian exile. His facility with the language helped charm the insurrectionary French Canadians during his tenure as Governor-General of British North America. In his ambassadorial posts, he tended to stay above partisan politics, and his lack of xenophobia and genuine interest in other cultures and people allowed him to reach out to opposing sides, as when he created a scandal in Canada by inviting the radical leader of the Quebecois revolt, Papineau, to dine at the Governor-General's residence in Canada. The aristocrat did not share the prevalent racist estimate of people of color, including most significantly, the people of China.

The day before he left England, Elgin received detailed instructions for his tasks in China from the Foreign Minister, Lord Clarendon. Elgin's brief from the Foreign Office was the antithesis of what the war party in China, Bowring and Seymour in particular, wanted and expected. Clarendon ordered Elgin that under no circumstances was he to try to retake Canton, Seymour's and Bowring's fixation. The British government remained obsessed, instead, with acquiring the right to send a permanent ambassador to Peking to conduct and direct negotiations with the Imperial court officials instead of using provincial governors as inefficient go-betweens. Epitomizing the fact that British policy was fueled by the profit motive, Elgin was ordered to demand the opening of new ports to British ships and trade. His superiors also wanted him to force the Chinese to comply with the provisions of the Treaty of Nanking. He was to use military force only as a last resort if the Emperor balked at these concessions—in which case, Elgin was urged to contain his military actions to naval attacks in order to spare British lives.

The Earl made his own demands on his handlers: he wanted the British military forces in China to be under his sole command. Also, preferring to deal from a position of strength, he did not want to begin negotiating with the Chinese until British troops had arrived to back up his demands. The Foreign Secretary and the Commander-in-Chief, the Duke of Cambridge, agreed that Elgin might wait for reinforcements to arrive before negotiations began. However, the military contingent was to be under the joint command of Lieutenant-Generals Ashburnham and Seymour, who would decide when and where to attack.

Despite his ancient lineage, Elgin was thoroughly modern, and he made record time in his journey to China by riding on the newly constructed railroad that cut across the Isthmus of Suez and united the Mediterranean and Red Seas. From Suez he took ship for China. As he rounded the coast of India in late May, Elgin came across troops who had been summoned from Bombay to Calcutta. From them he first heard of the dramatic events in the subcontinent that would delay his own business in China for nearly a year.

In May, sepoys, Indian troops of the East India Company Army, stationed in Meerut had refused to accept orders from their British officers. On the 10th of May, the entire garrison mutinied, killing the officers, their families, and as many other Europeans as they could find. As word spread, similar outbreaks occurred among other sepoy units of the Army. Within days, the mutiny had become a widespread rebellion when the soldiers were joined by disgruntled Indian princes tired of the British Raj. As bloodshed engulfed much of northern India, the British were in serious danger of losing complete control of their greatest Imperial possession— the foundation of their strength as a world power.

Although the initial news was so sketchy that Elgin only thought to hurry his China mission, when he arrived in Singapore on June 3rd, he found two letters waiting for him from an old Oxford classmate—Lord Canning, the Governor-General of India. They contained dire news and begged Elgin to divert troops assigned to his China mission to India. Canning's letters conveyed the urgency and desperation of the situation to his old classmate—along with a rather plaintive promise: "If you send me troops they shall not be kept one hour more than is absolutely needed."

Elgin couldn't consult with his superiors, Palmerston and Clarendon, because the telegraph line ended at Alexandria, and it would have taken two months for a query to London for instructions. Nevertheless, without hesitation, he diverted seventeen hundred troops of the 90th Regiment from Mauritius, already in Singapore waiting to accompany him to China, and sent the soldiers to help quash the rebellion in India. Clarendon's biographer credited the Earl with saving the British Raj, which, although an overstatement, perhaps, makes the decision a fascinating historical "what if...?"

While waiting for the troops to leave India for China, Elgin's intellectual curiosity led him to examine the phenomenon that underpinned his foreign mission. In Singapore, he stopped off at an opium den to witness the evil effects of the drug firsthand. "They are wretched, dark places with little lamps. The opium looks like treacle, and the smokers are haggard and stupefied, except at the moment of inhaling, when an unnatural brightness sparkles from their eyes," he wrote his wife on June 8, 1857.

The practical effect of Elgin's compliance with Canning's request for men was that the Earl continued on to China with only one ship, the *Shannon*, and no troops. He arrived in Hong Kong on July 2, 1857, where the Chinese gave him a warm reception, allegedly because they considered the shape of his ears a sign of good luck. Admiral Seymour gave the new plenipotentiary a much less enthusiastic welcome because the Earl arrived solo, with none of the troops the Admiral longed for to satisfy his monomania of taking Canton by force.

Seymour continued to press his new boss for an attack on Canton, which was backed by a petition to Elgin from eighty-five British opium merchants who believed that if Canton fell to the British, the Emperor would capitulate to their demands to comply with the Treaty of Nanking and grant new concessions. Their unvarnished petition made no pretense to higher motives and called for "the complete humiliation of the Cantonese." Elgin was more amused than pressured by the bloodlust of these wannabe Masters of the Universe when he wrote in his diary, "There is here an *idée fixe* that nothing ought to be done till there has been a general massacre at Canton." Regardless of his own inclinations, Elgin could not satisfy the armchair warriors because the troops were still stuck in India suppressing sepoys.

While his relationship with Seymour was equivocal, there was outright disagreement between Elgin and Harry Parkes. Parkes thought the plenipotentiary wasn't tough enough for the job. "He may be a man that suits the government well, very cautious, having ever before him [placating] Parliament, the world, the public, etc." Parkes began a campaign against the Earl almost as soon as he arrived in China with a flood of letters to Hammond, Permanent Under-Secretary at the Foreign Office, in which he criticized Elgin's generous treatment of the Chinese. Parkes told Hammond that Elgin's leniency was certain to be interpreted as weakness by the enemy.

If Seymour and Parkes were hawks when it came to settling the "China Problem," Sir John Bowring was a vulture. Regardless of Elgin's behavior in China, his very presence there was an affront to Bowring, who had been in charge until Parliamentary denunciations during the vote of censure and subsequent General Election prompted the appointment of a plenipotentiary who outranked him. Bowring felt he had been demoted, and he had. A Chinese official in his position would have committed suicide after this loss of face. Instead, Bowring worked behind the scenes to bring his new boss down. In a letter to Clarendon that combined compliance and self-pity, Bowring seemed to accept the new pecking order when he wrote, "A great success attends [Elgin], I doubt not. For this and more will I labour whoever shall reap the glory. I am getting old now, and there has been much trampling on my bald bare head, but I trust before I die to see the great purpose accomplished for which I wish to live, and for which I hope Providence may have spared me through many, many troubles."

In contrast to his whining deference to the Foreign Minister, Bowring presented a more prickly face to the new plenipotentiary. Bowring lectured and hectored Elgin on the imperative of full-scale military action against

Canton in particular and the morass of the mandarins and Emperor in Peking in general.

"There is quite an explosion of public opinion as to the fatal mistake which would be committed by any movement upon Peking until the Cantonese question is settled," Bowring wrote Elgin. "Many think such a movement might imperil the whole trade of China. I am quite of the opinion that any action which refers the Canton question to the Emperor would be a most injurious and embarrassing step."

Elgin ignored Bowring's unsolicited advice and continued to push for negotiations—or failing that, a surgical strike that would result in the least loss of lives (British and Chinese, the latter a concern his fellow China hands did not share). Above all, Elgin, like his employers at Whitehall, did not want to create a major military conflict that could topple the Manchu Dynasty and lead to a chaotic Balkanization of China, which would be even harder for the British to negotiate with and control than the current regime. Plus the prospect of the mad "King" of the Taiping rebels, with his ban on private property, stepping into the vacuum created by an ousted Emperor terrified the propertied classes who had hired Elgin. Despite their huge cultural and political differences, the Chinese and British were both imperialists who shared the same horror of anarchy or worse—the Jacobean populism of the God-Worshippers. Elgin, however, revealed himself in his diary to be a reluctant imperialist and a benevolent racist: "Can I do anything to prevent England from calling down on herself God's curse for brutalities committed on another feeble Oriental race? Or are all my exertions to result only in an extension of the area over which Englishmen are to exhibit how hollow and superficial are both their civilization and their Christianity?" A crystal ball would have told him the latter alternative would prevail, and the good-natured peer would have been horrified to hear that he would be its main perpetrator, immortalized and demonized by posterity more vividly than his evil coeval, the butcher Ye, or the anti-opium zealot Lin.

———————

After assessing the situation on the ground, the industrious but impatient Elgin decided not to wait for reinforcements from India, but to go there himself to coax troops away from the Governor-General, Lord Canning.

Elgin managed to gather a small force of four hundred marines and sailors on the fifty-gun *Shannon* and sailed for Calcutta, where he landed on June 14, 1857. He found a city abandoned by its European residents after a false scare that the sepoys were marching on the city to slaughter all its white inhabitants.

Elgin was horrified by what he found in India. He was particulary shocked by stories that British troops had gone on an orgy of hangings in reprisal for sexual atrocities attributed to the Indians that apparently were total fabrications. A Major Renard ordered the execution of twelve Indians for turning their faces the wrong way as Renard's troops marched past them. The Major also burned down every Indian village he passed, and hanged another forty-two villagers along the way.

The reprisals shocked the devout Elgin. In a letter to his wife, he lamented, "I have seldom from man or woman since I came to the East heard a sentence that was reconcilable with the hypothesis that Christianity had come into the world. Detestation, contempt, ferocity, vengeance, whether Chinamen or Indians be the object." Contempt for people of a different color and the brutality that accompanies it are like a virus. The pious Earl would have been shocked had he known then that in less than three years' time he would be infected by the same corrupting pathogen.

After a disillusioning stay in India, where he wrote his wife, "It is a terrible business this living among inferior races," Elgin returned to China aboard the steamship *Ava* on September 20, 1857. Something—whether it was the cruelty of the British Raj he had just witnessed or a premonition of the cruelty he would have to exercise at his new posting—troubled the Earl, who according to a report filed by one of Ye's spies, was seen "stamping his foot and sighing." Or maybe it was his mounting frustration with Bowring's insubordination. By now, relations between the two men had become so strained that Elgin refused Bowring's offer of hospitality at his consular residence and remained aboard the cramped *Ava* during the sweltering summer.

Bowring had taken advantage of Elgin's India trip by making overtures to Ye in strict violation of his instructions from London that all communications should be between the Chinese Viceroy and the plenipotentiary. When Elgin confronted Bowring with his insubordination, the latter denied it, but his demeanor betrayed the truth and soured an already distasteful relationship. "The way he dodged and insinuated revealed to me more than I had before seen of the man's character. It is impossible to put the slightest trust in him," Elgin wrote in his diary.

Baron Gros, Elgin's French counterpart in China, arrived a month later. After a condescending lecture by Bowring on the need for massive reprisals against the Chinese, the elegant aristocrat found himself sharing Elgin's opinion of the Hong Kong consul, and the two men agreed to disagree with Bowring. France and Britain's response to the arsenic imbroglio and Father Chapedelaine's martyrdom would be coordinated, measured, and hopefully light on atrocities. Gros wanted an attack on the capital, while Elgin still hoped for negotiations. But the Foreign Minister, Clarendon, chose a third option. In a letter the Earl received on October 14th, the Foreign Minister sided with Bowring. Winter was approaching, and the Bei He River, the gateway to Peking, would be frozen before an allied army arrived at the city gates. Instead, Clarendon ordered Elgin to take Canton. Elgin had been trumped and Bowring vindicated. The Earl found himself in the excruciating position of being forced to side with Bowring against Gros, who still wanted to march on Peking. "I stated to him [Gros] some facts which I think moved him a little," then Elgin let Bowring take over, which the Hong Kong consul did with relish. Bowring's obnoxiousness moved Gros more than his eloquence. Elgin described the meeting his diary: "The next day Bowring gave it to [Gros] for four hours, two on shore and two on board the *Audacieuse*. When I visited him in the evening I found him somewhat exhausted and ready to make almost any concession rather than entertain another assault of rhetoric."

In November 1857, William Reed, the new American Minister appointed by President James Buchanan, arrived aboard the huge steamship *Minnesota*, an inappropriate leviathan too large to navigate the Canton River. The fifty-gun, one thousand–horsepower behemoth was an impressive-looking but useless engine of war that may have terrified the Chinese, but that was its only use since the vessel was so large that its hull couldn't pass through the shallow rivers of China. Reed, a close friend of President Buchanan and a professor emeritus of history at the University of Pennsylvania, carried a much different brief from his Commander in Chief, which would make his relations with Elgin and Gros uncomfortable despite a veneer of cordiality (this was also part of Buchanan's instructions to his plenipotentiary). America would remain neutral in the inevitable coming conflict. Reed shared his boss's repugnance for the opium trade, and he had orders not to get sucked into a war that could be interpreted as promoting or even countenancing the commerce in contraband. In a best of all possible diplomatic worlds, Buchanan wanted to act as mediator between the warring parties and avoid a war altogether.

Ye didn't recognize the American diplomat for the friend he was to China and refused Reed's request for an audience. The former scholar, perhaps with an eye on his area of expertise, history, accepted the rebuff—and several others—without becoming embittered or a hawk on China.

Also in November, Count Euphemius Putiatin, Russia's emissary, arrived in Hong Kong aboard the *Amerika*, a paddleboat with only six guns, after spending a few days steaming around the coast near Peking in the hope that the Emperor, after rejecting every other nation on Earth, would deign to see the Tsar's envoy. Besides his minimal firepower, Count Putiatin, a hero of his country's disastrous performance in the Crimean War, brought with him to China a proposal— if the emperor would give Manchuria to the Russians, the Tsar would help his Imperial brother stamp out the Taiping rebels once and for all. The Manchu court refused to see Putiatin by citing the long precedent that Russian emissaries could only travel to China through Manchuria, and Putiatin had showed up by sea.

Dealing with ambassadorial egos and a subordinate's insubordination began to wear on Elgin, who wrote Clarendon in mid November, "It is necessary to pass a gentle hand over all these palpating strings if we would produce from them none but accordant tones. We are all more or less insane, but some are certainly more so than others." Elgin didn't identify Bowring as one of the more insane, since Clarendon shared Bowring's "insanity"—the obsession with seizing Canton.

In December 1857, three ships carrying two thousand British soldiers from Calcutta sailed into Canton's harbor, followed by a French fleet under Admiral Rigault de Genouilly. Gros and Elgin now sent Ye separate ultimata. France wanted the murderer(s) of Father Chapedelaine brought to justice, reparations, and permission to operate unrestricted anywhere in Canton. Although the *Arrow* incident had helped stir up British public

202 The Opium Wars

opinion and win the General Election, Elgin chose not to bring up the incident in his ultimatum to Ye. Instead, he demanded compliance with the terms of the Treaty of Nanking, which Peking with its trademark passive-aggressiveness ignored more and more; a permanent British ambassador in the capital; and unspecified reparations for loss of life and property arising from the (unnamed) *Arrow* incident and other hostile acts by China. With no sense of irony, Elgin shared his optimism with Ye about the mutual benefits of peaceful relations between the two powers: "Commerce has presented itself with all its accustomed attendants, national wealth and international goodwill." Elgin felt his demands were reasonable while realizing they were unpalatable to Ye and outrageous to his Emperor. In a letter to General Charles Grey, Elgin revealed the relief he got from Ye's intransigence. "I made mild proposals to Yeh [Ye] with the conviction that if they had been accepted I should have been torn in pieces by all [the British] who were ravening for vengeance or loot. But Yeh [Ye] was my fast friend…nothing would induce him to be saved."

The foreign powers' demands on Ye were more posturing rather than a genuine threat. All three of the foreign envoys knew that Ye did not have the authority to satisfy the French and British ultimata. For that reason, Ye equivocated. In the meantime, he seems to have let off steam by ordering four hundred God-Worshippers beheaded and their heads impaled on spikes atop the city walls. With no credible army or fleet to back him up, Ye may have hoped terror and threats alone would intimidate or dissuade his opponents. His brutality backfired. The British enlisted almost seven hundred enraged Hakkas, a persecuted ethnic minority in Guangxi province, some of whom participated in the Taiping Rebellion and all of whom hated the foreign Manchu Dynasty that had tried to stamp out their culture and language, to man artillery at Dutch Folly, an anchorage on the Pearl River across from the factories at Canton. Meanwhile, eight British and four French steamships arrived to add muscle and credibility to their masters' diplomacy.

Ye replied to the British and French in separate letters. To Elgin's demand for access to Canton, he claimed that one of Elgin's predecessors, Sir George Bonham, had agreed to give up access in 1850 to avoid a fight with the Chinese. And for his pacific efforts, Ye noted, demonstrating a sophisticated knowledge of Britain's class system, Bonham had received a knighthood in Britain's most prestigious knighthood, the Order of the Bath. (Ye was almost right. The Bath was second in prestige and exclusivity to the Order of the Garter.) Then the Viceroy hinted that similar restraint by Elgin would garner him admission to the Bath, unaware that the title of Earl trumped "Sir." As for revisions in the Treaty of Nanking, the Emperor had declared its terms would be held inviolate for ten millennium, Ye insisted. It would be political suicide for any courtier to broach revisions after the Emperor's sacred promise of immutability. Like a medieval baron scolding King John or Edward II, Ye speculated that Elgin's wrong thinking was the fault of his advisors, taking the onus and culpability away from the Earl. The Butcher of Canton could be as delicate as he was brutal for the sake of getting what he wanted. Ye made similar arguments in his response to the French demands.

While the Viceroy engaged in a war of words with his enemies, he displayed listlessness and apathy for the genuine war that was coming. He may have been distracted by the greater threat of the Taiping insurgents, who had overrun his province. Or as historian Douglas Hurd has suggested in his unlikely explanation of Ye's passivity, the Viceroy's sloth and inaction may have been due to the fact that "Yeh [Ye] was fat, and it was hot."

The practical effect of Ye's strategy, or lack thereof, showed itself when the British and French warships landed on Henan Island opposite Canton on December 15, 1857. The invaders disembarked without resistance and found the strategic island undefended and with no fortifications! More than two hundred Chinese warships and *sampans* (floating homes) near Henan Island fled as soon as the British landed.

On December 21, 1857, Elgin, Putiatin, and Gros parleyed aboard the Baron's flagship, *Audacieuse*. They agreed to give Ye one more chance, however symbolic, and informed him that they would postpone shelling the city if he complied with their demands. They gave Ye a two-day deadline. Their united public front hid Elgin's private misgivings, which he committed to his diary. Canton was a "great city doomed I fear to destruction by the folly of its own rulers and the vanity and levity of ours." The Earl's fear was prophetic.

During their parley, Gros and Elgin ceded command of the sea forces to Admirals Seymour and Rigault and the land troops to General Sir Thomas Ashburnham. Gros then sailed away to safety, while Elgin remained on the scene in the wan hope of preventing atrocities by the men nominally under his command. Elgin also feared huge British casualties because of the city's fortifications and the unevenness of forces that favored the Chinese. On paper, the invaders' task seemed daunting. An imposing wall twenty-five feet high and twenty feet wide defended Canton's six-mile circumference. The core of defenders, Manchurians, were expected to put up a formidable resistance because of racial loyalty to their Manchu Emperor, whose divine status made the conflict both secular and religious. The Chinese troops in Canton outnumbered the attackers five to one, thirty thousand against less than six thousand British marines, sepoys, and French seamen. But the Europeans had one tactical advantage that trumped the Chinese's numerical superiority. Their shipboard artillery enjoyed superior range and firepower compared to the defenders' guns. The lackadaisical Ye never should have allowed the enemy to take up their positions on Henan Island within easy shelling distance of Canton.

On December 22nd, Ye's deadline ran out, but the Europeans hesitated. Perhaps in the sprit of the season, on December 24th, they gave the Viceroy another three days to accept their terms. Ye didn't respond, and on December 27th, the assault on Canton began.

In the evening of the 27th, a reconnaissance team came ashore a mile from the city's walls. The next morning, British and French ships began to shell the city and its fortified towers. The bombardment went on for more than a day, and included incendiary rockets. During this time, the Chinese responded with only two shells! Once again, there were no British casualties, while the Chinese loss was estimated at two hundred during the twenty-four-hour period. The incendiaries did their job, and Canton was burning. The anti-war party in London condemned the cannonade, which they attributed to revenge rather than tactical necessity, and second-guessed the men on the scene by insisting that a three-hour bombardment would have sufficed to soften the enemy for the coming invasion. As soon as the shelling began, providing excellent cover for the invaders, five hundred French and British soldiers landed and slowly made their way through rice paddies and past a cemetery reserved for criminals. Chinese soldiers hid behind tombstones in the cemetery and responded to enemy fire by waving red and yellow flags, the Chinese colors of defiance, shooting arrows against British rifles, and firing eighteenth-century muskets called gingalls, which were so cumbersome they required two men to fire them, after which the force of the shot knocked them to the ground. The Europeans laughed at the sight of this lethal slapstick. Voltaire's description of history repeating itself in tragic followed by farcical forms applied in military engagements here. European aggression had tragic consequences for China, but battle after battle during the Opium Wars in which the European armies suffered no casualties seems farcical—except, no doubt, to the Chinese casualties.

The invaders took a page from the defenders and set up camp on the first night of the assault at the Criminals' Cemetery, where they used the tombstones for cover. The British command lodged in a temple on the cemetery grounds and did nothing when their soldiers ransacked the sacred site and smashed all the statuary, which were falsely believed to have gems and gold hidden inside.

At dawn on the 29th, the European allies woke up to a startling sight on the hills behind Canton. Fifteen hundred Chinese soldiers, half the army, had fled to the hills. They didn't fire on the invaders. They stared at the enemy as though they were at a sporting event with great seats to see the action. Ye's cruelty toward the local population contributed to their lack of martial ardor, and regardless of the moral issues, his actions turned out to be a tactical mistake as well. At mid morning, the French, led by Admiral Rigault himself, ran toward the walls carrying scaling ladders. The defenders on the walls put up little resistance, although a great deal of shelling of the attackers came from Chinese artillery on the nearby hills. By 10 A.M., British and French flags flew from the Five-Story Pagoda near the walls.

Seymour and Rigault gave orders to resume shelling the city, which had temporarily stopped in order not to hit the invading troops. Elgin had seen the devastating effects of the previous shelling and countermanded the order after a personal tour of the walls, during which time his party was not fired on. The Earl feared that the French and British Admirals' motives were punitive rather than tactical.

As usual, the death toll was lopsided. The French lost only three men with thirty wounded, while the British suffered one hundred killed and injured. Chinese casualties totaled close to four hundred fifty.

Ye was missing, but British intelligence believed he was still in the city, hiding. The Viceroy's second in command, Pih-kwei, put out a proclamation disassociating himself and his colleagues from his superior's disastrous policies.

On New Year's Day 1858, Elgin decided to assess the military position firsthand and made a tour of Canton. The absence of resistance confirmed the wisdom and humanity of Elgin's decision to veto renewed shelling. But Elgin was alarmed by the looting he saw, perhaps more as a sign of breakdown in discipline than as theft of property, although his private secretary, Laurence Oliphant, noted that the French preferred cash while the British liked souvenirs of dubious financial value. And the French were more discreet about their looting. "While honest Jack was flourishing down the street with a broad grin of triumph on his face, a bowl of goldfish under one arm and a cage of canary-birds under the other, honest Jean, with a demure countenance and no external display, was conveying his well-lined pockets to the waterside." Elgin feared losing control of the troops and ordered a halt to the looting, but he was unable to control the French connoisseurs. After some discipline was imposed, the British soldiers relapsed and joined the French in stripping the city. Elgin fretted in his diary, "My difficulty has been to prevent the wretched Cantonese from being plundered and bullied. There is a [Hindi] word called 'loot' which gives unfortunately a venial character to what would, in common English, be styled robbery. Add to this that there is no flogging in the French Army, so that it is impossible to punish men committing this class of offences." Echoing Elgin's concerns, Howqua's son and other members of the Cohong petitioned the Earl to restore order and stop the destruction of their city and trade. Within days of the invasion, 90 percent of the population had fled the once-thriving commercial center of foreign trade. Elgin rebuffed the pleas of Sir John Davis, the former governor of Hong Kong, to turn Canton into a "heap of blazing ruins." Elgin described his objections in a letter to Lady Elgin, promising, "No human power shall induce me to accept the office of oppressor of the feeble."

Elgin had no qualms, however, about official expropriations, and sent a Col. Lemon and a detail of Royal Marines to the city treasury, where they seized fifty-two boxes of silver, sixty-eight boxes of gold ingots, and the equivalent in taels of nearly a million dollars in cash. This legal plunder was put aboard the HMS *Calcutta* and dispatched to India post-haste. The war had to be paid for, and until official reparations had been wrung from Peking, freelance booty would have to suffice.

On January 5, 1858, eight thousand French and British troops marched through the gates of Canton unopposed. Harry Parkes at last got his revenge on his long-time nemesis, Viceroy Ye. Parkes led a squad of one hundred Royal Marines to Ye's palace armed with a miniature of the Viceroy to identify him. It was a clever precaution because one of Ye's subordinates tried to pass himself off as the Viceroy to save his master. Parkes was not duped, and one of his men caught Ye trying to climb over the rear wall of his palace. A marine seized Ye by his pigtail and dragged the humiliated leader to a sedan chair enclosed with bars. As his portable prison was carried off to the steamship with the symbolic name of *Inflexible*, Hakka God-Worshippers among the European troops, victims of Ye's persecutions, taunted the disgraced Viceroy and made slashing gestures across the neck, hoping their tormentor would suffer the same fate he had meted out to their brothers-in-arms. The marines found something even more valuable than their prisoner in his palace: his correspondence with the Manchu court. The allies now had a window into the Byzantine machinations of the mandarins.

Also on January 5th, Gros and Elgin agreed to name Ye's No. 2, Pih-kwei, the governor of Canton, but he would be "advised" by a triumvirate of Parkes, a Captain Martineau, and a Royal Marine, Col. Holloway, in case the new governor proved unmalleable. Because of Parkes's fluent Chinese, Elgin overcame his hesitation to appoint a man he loathed and blamed for mishandling the *Arrow* incident. The Earl's diary damned Parkes with faint praise as "clever but exceedingly overbearing in his manner to the Chinese."

The three powers behind Pih-kwei's shaky throne, Parkes, Holloway and Martineau, were granted control of the judiciary and the power to vet all of Pih-kwei's edicts prior to promulgation. Among all the allied forces, there were only three men who spoke Chinese, and in a report to Clarendon, Elgin explained why he had nominated a former enemy to the top job. "If Pih-kwei was removed or harshly dealt with we should be called upon to govern a city containing many hundred thousand inhabitants with hardly any means of communicating with the people."

In a ceremony filled with irony, Pih-kwei was let out of prison to be installed as the new governor on January 9, 1858. The pliable mandarin kept Elgin waiting because his jailers had not been informed of his "promotion" from prisoner to potentate and had delayed his release. In another attempt to co-opt the local power structure, the allies also created a combined police force of Europeans and Cantonese to stop the looting and restore the confidence of the merchant classes, who were needed to resume trade with Britain and France. Howqua and his Cohong colleagues found their nominal oppressors a source of order and relief, especially against the anti-trade zealots of the Taiping. It would soon be business as usual and as lucrative.

Despite the relief and joy of the local bourgeoisie, Pih-kwei found himself in an equivocal position as a Cantonese quisling. The fate of his former boss Ye must have been on his mind as he served his new masters. On January 27, 1858, the new Viceroy received secret instructions from Peking to organize an army of civilians to roust the occupiers. At the same time, he complied with orders from Admiral Seymour to hand over seventeen Chinese warships to fight the Taiping fleet obstructing the Pearl River. The next day, artillery on two French warships, the *Mitraille* and *Fusée*, razed Ye's palace. Ye's punishment did not end with his imprisonment aboard the *Inflexible* and the destruction of his home.

After several abortive attempts to free him from his floating prison, Elgin dispatched Ye to exile in Calcutta aboard the *Inflexible* on February 20, 1858 and justified the deportation with, "The presence of Yeh [Ye] tends to disquiet the public mind, and to render the task of restoring peace and confidence in the neighbourhood more difficult." Wingrove Cooke, a reporter for *The Times of London*, sailed with the ousted Viceroy and sent home lurid accounts, which mentioned that in addition to having executed one hundred thousand God-Worshippers, Ye had terrible personal hygiene. Readers of *The Times* were informed that the prisoner had dirty fingernails, didn't bathe or brush his teeth, and used his sleeve instead of a handkerchief to wipe his nose. The Butcher of Canton literally was reduced to a dirty old man in the eyes of Victorian England, where ungodliness was next to uncleanliness. Indeed, when an Anglican bishop sent Ye a Bible, he refused the gift, explaining that he had already read it.

In Calcuta, Ye lived under house arrest next door to another British deposee, the King of Oudh in India. Despite or perhaps because of it, Ye's record of barbarity (and bad grooming) turned him into a cynosure of the British elite in Calcutta, where he was treated more like an aging roué than a mass murderer. When Calcutta's Lieutenant General invited him to a gala, Ye spurned the invitation because he found abhorrent the European custom of close embrace while dancing. In Victorian China and India, the waltz was still risqué. When Ye died in 1859, the local Chinese refused him burial in their cemetery.

Back in Canton, the 70th Sepoy Regiment arrived in Canton in March 1858 to reinforce the British garrison, and were delighted to be assigned two hundred Chinese servants. In India, sepoys were called "niggers" by the British, and despite their new status in the pecking order, racism followed them from their home country. Within a day of their arrival, French soldiers shot three sepoys accused of looting. No Europeans ever received the death penalty for doing the same thing.

That same month, Elgin left Seymour behind in Canton and, with only two British and two French gunboats, sailed north, arriving at the mouth of the Bei He River on April 14, 1858. Gros appeared on April 20th, and was joined four days later by Seymour who, to Elgin's extreme distress, had brought with him only two more warships. Relations between the two men deteriorated to the point where Elgin vented in his diary, "I have a perfect driveller for an admiral…I am like a person in a bad dream." On April 24, 1858, the French, British, and Russian plenipotentiaries sent a joint communique to Tan, the Governor of Chihli Province. The pacifist Elgin tried one last time to negotiate his way out of the coming bloodshed. The Earl wrote Tan requesting a "minister duly authorized by the Emperor of China" to meet with the European representatives. Tan stalled by claiming—correctly—that he didn't have the power to negotiate with the foreigners. He also infuriated the British because in his letter he used larger letters for the Emperor's name and smaller ones for Queen Victoria's, even though the Treaty of Nanking stipulated Peking and London would henceforth be considered equal partners. This kind of stubborn insistence by the British on protocol and hierarchical status was almost as deep-rooted as the Chinese's, and belonged to the misguided mind-set that had also refused to kowtow.

Tan sent a second letter that adjusted the Chinese position to allow some level of negotiation by volunteering to open more ports, grant religious freedom to Christians, and most importantly, pay reparations for the Cantonese factories razed at the end of 1856. Reparations had been the stalking horse of British and Chinese negotiations for years. As for the establishment of permanent foreign embassies in the capital, Tan said he had passed the request on to the Emperor, but neglected to mention that his boss had rejected it out of hand. The Russian plenipotentiary, Count Putiatin, displaying a humanitarianism sadly lacking in his peers, begged the Chinese to comply and avoid further bloodshed. Tan, according to files found at the Quai d'Orsay, the French Foreign Office, replied to Putiatin's plea with a smirk and said, "They are only Chinese lives."

For unfathomable reasons, the Archimandrite (deacon) Palladius, the spiritual leader of the tiny Russian community in Peking, was granted permission by the Emperor to visit the European fleet toward the end of May, but had to travel in a sealed litter. Putiatin ordered the cleric to gather intelligence along the way. Palladius managed to peer through a crack in the shutters and bring with him detailed intelligence on the position of the Chinese fleet and some encouraging news. Peking was starving, the ailing Emperor's debauched life had caught up with him before reaching the age of thirty, and the terrified ruler was entertaining the idea of leaving the country.

Elgin's anxiety eased a bit as more warships, one by one, arrived during the rest of the month. By late May, a combined Anglo-French fleet of twenty-six gunboats prepared to attack the five mud Dagu Forts that guarded the mouth of the Bei He. D-Day was May 20, 1858. The barbarians were less than one hundred miles from the capital. It is no wonder that the Emperor was ill and about to run away.

Chapter 20

SCOTTISH CONQUISTADOR

*"Twenty-four determined men with revolvers, and
a sufficient number of cartridges, might walk through
China from one end to another."*

—Lord Elgin

A t high tide, the Dagu Forts (named after the village on the left bank
of the Bei He) were surrounded by water, the Bei He providing a natural moat, a fitting symbol of the medieval Chinese defenses. The entrance
to the Bei He was a scant two hundred yards in width, but the French and
British warships managed to squeeze through the bottleneck, which was a
gauntlet allegedly protected on both shores by 137 pieces of antiquated
artillery. While the foreign gunboats waited to attack, the Chinese defenders put in a Herculean effort to surround the artillery and parapets on the
earthwork walls with sandbags. The strategy of the defenders was as ineffective as their guns. The Chinese inaccurately presumed that the deep-
hulled foreign gunboats would not risk entering the river except during
high tide to avoid going aground. Seymour and Rigault were gamblers and
decided to mount a surprise attack at 10 A.M. on May 20, 1858 while Elgin
made one last attempt to have the defenders surrender peacefully. Tan
didn't even bother to respond to Elgin's peace tender.

The immobile Chinese artillery had been aimed to hit the foreign ships
at high tide, but the vessels entered at low tide without going aground. The
misaimed Chinese guns fired over the ships and didn't hit any of them. The
next obstacle to the invaders was another primitive defense system, a seven-
inch-thick boom made of bamboo. It proved as ineffective as the guns. The
British willingly sacrificed one of their ships, the *Coromandel*, which

rammed and broke the boom with ease, although in the process, the ship tore a gash in its hull. As the pieces of the severed boom floated away, the rest of the armada steamed through the gap while missiles flew over their masts and plummeted out into the river. The French *Mitraille* and *Fusée* and the British *Cormorant* fired at two of the Dagu Forts on the left bank of the river, while the British *Nimrod* and the French *Avalance* and *Dragonne* bombarded the three forts on the right.

The Chinese had more luck with their primitive gingalls, the eighteenth-century muskets that required to men to operate and knocked down their operators after each volley, which the attackers found endlessly amusing even though they were lethal in a desultory fashion. The gingalls, which unlike the earthenwork artillery could be aimed, managed to kill five British and six French, and wound sixty-one others. Even so, most of the casualties suffered by the attackers were caused not by Chinese force of arms, but by a gunpowder cache in one of the Dagu Forts that accidentally exploded as the foreigners passed by. The Chinese lost one hundred men.

The defenders were so discombobulated by the impotence of their guns that they panicked, and before the British and French contingents even landed on the riverbank, the Chinese began to desert the earthen parapet en masse. As the troops fled, the Manchu commander launched fifty fireboats stuffed with straw at the foreign ships, but the assault was as ill-fated as the gingalls. The fireships crashed into the bank at a bend in the river, and none managed to do any damage to the opposing fleet. With his last option a dramatic failure, the commander of the Dagu Forts committed suicide at the Temple of the Sea God by slashing his jugular vein and carotid artery. The Viceroy of Chihli, the province the forts were located in, received a gentler sentence, banishment to the Chinese equivalent of Siberia, the desolate border territory that abutted Russia. As the viceroy packed his bags, the Emperor condemned the Viceroy's defense of the Dagu Forts as "without plan or resource."

In his diary, Elgin described his contempt for the routed Chinese after the Dagu encounter. "Twenty-four determined men with revolvers, and a sufficient number of cartridges, might walk through China from one end to another." The Earl's newfound hubris, which contrasted with his previous pacifism, resembled that of the similarly outnumbered Spanish conquistadors, who also conquered a less technologically advanced civilization.

Elgin's success strengthened his position back home and rewarded him with carte blanche on all further military actions and negotiations. He was gradually becoming plenipotentiary in deed as well as title. After the Dagu victory, the new Prime Minister, the Tory Lord Derby, who had recently come to power after the Whig government fell for failing to pass a bill that would have imprisoned aliens suspected of spying or anarchist beliefs, abandoned his anti-war position and responded to the news with Whig-like enthusiasm.

The Prime Minister sent Elgin a congratulatory dispatch, which the envoy described as "giving me latitude to do anything I choose, if only I will finish the affair." The dovish Derby, who had eloquently condemned British imperialism in the House of Lords less than a year before, had become as hawkish as his Whig counterpart, Palmerston. Lord Malmesbury became the new Foreign Minister, but his ousted predecessor, Lord Clarendon, continued his correspondence with his intimate, Elgin. An embittered Clarendon, engaging in a serious case of sour grapes, claimed relief that he had been tossed out of office and accused the incoming Tories of being warmongers, a projection of the Whig's own platform that the Tories now adopted. "I have not the remotest idea how our successors mean to deal with the China question upon which they have committed themselves so violently and with so little foresight." Clarendon might have been describing the Whig's conduct of the war. In a parting shot that satirized the cheap political ends to which the bestowal of honors had been placed, Clarendon added, "Now that they have got Yeh [Ye] on board the *Inflexible* they will be able to apologize to him more conveniently for our rudeness, and they might send him one of the vacant Garters with a letter explanatory of it not being necessary for him to hang himself with it."

In a voyage that was more triumphal procession than attack, the foreign flotilla of a mere eight gunboats, with Seymour and Rigault aboard, made its way up the Bei He toward the next critical stronghold, Tianjin, a scant thirty miles from the end of the Europeans' rainbow, Peking. The plenipotentiaries stayed behind in the safety of Dagu Forts and sat out the *faux* hostilities, which as it turned out, was an unnecessary precaution.

As they steamed up the Bei He, both the *Cormorant* and *Fusée* ran aground numerous times, but the invaders found unlikely allies to help—local Chinese who hated the alien dynasty in the capital and volunteered their tugboats to free the ships whenever they came aground.

Their enthusiasm for the "liberators" was so great that they refused payment for their assistance, although the starving boatmen gladly accepted ship's rations of moldy biscuits.

On June 4, 1858, the little armada, whose steam power seemed to give the ships a supernatural speed compared to the fuel-challenged Chinese's, arrived at Tianjin and again met no resistance. The defenders had been disheartened to the point of surrender by the groundless rumor that the Emperor had been overthrown and replaced by a new dynasty willing to treat with the foreigners. Elgin, who decided to ignore Seymour's and Rigault's advice to stay away for security reasons, joined the war party at Tianjin on May 26, 1858. In his diary, which Elgin seemed to use like a psychotherapist, he described his continuing doubts about the justness of their cause, his pangs of conscience soothed somewhat by his contempt for the civilization this dubious cause was about to bring to heel, and perhaps obliterate. As his ship made its way up the river, he wrote:

> Through the night watches, when no Chinaman moves, when the junks cast anchor, we laboured on, cutting ruthlessly and recklessly through that glancing and startled river which, until the last few weeks, no stranger keel had ever furrowed. Whose work are we engaged in, when we burst thus with hideous violence and brutal energy into these darkest and most mysterious recesses of the traditions of the past? I wish I could answer that question in a manner satisfactory to myself. At the same time there is certainly not much to regret in the old civilisation which we are thus scattering to the winds. A dense population, timorous and pauperised, such would seem to be its chief product.

An idealist and crypto-pacifist in England, Elgin like many of his stripe past and future, found that direct involvement in a war of colonial aspirations had polarized him to the point of dismissing a two thousand–year-old civilization with a subordinate clause, "thus scattering to the winds."

Outside Tianjin, the plenipotentiaries were shocked to be met by a contingent of delighted local government officials and merchants, who believed Elgin's ships carried opium. They had turned out expecting the usual bribes to grease the sale and a lucrative role as middlemen in the distribution of opium.

The rumors that had demoralized Tianjin's defenders turned out to be fabrications. The Emperor hadn't been overthrown, but he was now willing to negotiate with the invaders and quickly sent commissioners to Tianjin in the hope of stopping the allied advance from reaching the capital. Elgin crowed in his diary about his bloodless victory at Tianjin and revealed his Whiggish loyalty to British commerce. "[I have] complete military command of the capital of China, without having broken off relations with the neutral powers, and without having interrupted, for a single day, our trade at the different ports of the Empire."

The foreigners were treated with the fearful respect due conquerors, which they were, however bloodless at this particular point. The Tianjin mandarins turned over a lavish temple called the Supreme Felicity for the invaders' headquarters. The Europeans' transformation of the temple symbolized the cultural vandalism that would soon take place on a more grotesque scale in Peking. The temple courtyard was turned into a bowling alley, the myriad altars used as washbasins, and vanity mirrors placed in front of statues of the gods.

The Emperor at last demonstrated his seriousness about negotiating with the high status of the two emissaries he dispatched to the Europeans at Tianjin. The Imperial representatives, called commissioners, were top courtiers; the seventy-four-year-old Guiliang was a senior military officer and an enthusiastic dove in the war. Observers commented on the old man's trembling hands without knowing if his shaking was caused by infirmity or fear. Hua Shan, fifty-three, a Mongol and another senior military official whom some said resembled Oliver Cromwell, in drive if not looks, accompanied Guiliang to the meeting place, the Temple of Oceanic Influences on the southwest outskirts of Tianjin. Elgin arrived at the temple on June 4, 1858, with a retinue of fifty marines and a band from the warship *Calcutta*, to add muscle and a not-so-veiled threat to the Emperor's negotiators.

The first meeting did not go well. The commissioners had more power and authority to negotiate than any other previous emissaries, but they lacked carte blanche to finalize any deal they cut with the Europeans. Elgin stormed out of the meeting, ignoring a lavish buffet the Chinese had set up for a party to celebrate a peace treaty that didn't happen that day. Elgin's snit was insincere. The courtly peer was famous for his courtesy, but after six months in China, he had realized the Chinese only responded to vigorous rebuffs and challenges. Elgin confessed his tactical bravado to his wife: "I have made up my mind, disgusting as the part is to me, to act the role of the 'uncontrollably fierce barbarian.'" The Earl's political polarization continued. As he exited in a fake huff, he bluffed and threatened to march on Peking even though he didn't have nearly enough manpower to make good on the threat. The Earl shrewdly left behind his younger brother, Lord Frederick Bruce, to continue negotiations. Elgin would not see the Emperor's men again until the signing of the treaty. One of Lord Frederick's interpreters, Horatio Lay, overstepped his role and borrowed a page from Lord Elgin's strategic *Sturm und Drang,* when he literally screamed at the Emperor's commissioners when they stuck at various clauses in the new treaty. At one point, Lay threatened to lay waste to Peking and browbeat the Emperor himself in the same manner Lay was savaging his commissioners. Eyewitnesses said the mandarins displayed visible terror at the thought of this abuse of their divine ruler.

Lay's abuse of the commissioners grew so virulent that they felt compelled to go over his head and seek help from Putiatin and the American envoy, William Reed. Reed sent a letter to Elgin asking him to rein in Lay, but Elgin ignored the request and didn't bother to reply. A clever psychologist, Putiatin asked Gros, a close friend of the Earl's, to intercede, but the Baron declined because he feared alienating a friend and losing a friendship he had assiduously cultivated. The desperate Chinese resorted to bribery, which proved to be just as ineffective, and gave Lay a horse and a saddle. The venal interpreter accepted the gifts, but didn't soften his harangues.

During the drawn-out negotiations by his proxies, Elgin grew bored, then anxious, and finally irritated, not only by the procrastinations of the Chinese, but by what he considered the unnecessary interference by Reed and Putiatin. (Gros had been wise not to interject himself into this no-win lobbying of the Earl.) Elgin's resentment against his long-time ally, Admiral Seymour, also boiled over in the heat and humidity of Tianjin, and soon his depressive anxiety earned the entire British population of Hong Kong the troubled peer's wrath. He lashed out at Reed and Putiatin in his diary, which revealed an increasing fragility of mind and a temper frayed to tatters: "These sneaking scoundrels do what they can to thwart me and then while affecting to support the Chinese act as their own worst enemies." He continued to find Seymour's contribution lacking. "The one piece of strategy to which my admiral is competent is making arrangements for the dispatch of letters. To this everything is sacrificed." Elgin referred to letters Seymour sent back to London to undercut the plenipotentiary's authority and second-guess his decisions. The Earl also found the British colony at Hong Kong objectionable for unexplained reasons. "I did not know what brutes, lying, sanguinary, cheating, oppressive to the weak and crouching before the strong—I did not know I say what they are those smooth-faced countrymen of ours who look at home as if butter would not melt in their mouths."

Elgin's resentment covered both the previous Whig and present Tory governments' handling of China affairs, and he blamed them for their lack of loyalty and support for the man on the scene. "Anything more blackguard than the conduct to me of the last Government considering the circumstances under which I consented to come here it would be difficult to imagine." A letter he received from the new Foreign Minister, Lord Malmesbury, on April 9, 1858, berated him for not concluding the peace treaty fast enough. The Tories had bowed to the popular will and supported the war for political gain. But privately, they tried to bring the expensive military operations to a rapid end. Lord Malmesbury sent Elgin a Cabinet report and orders to wrap things up: "A Cabinet has been held today and it is our anxious wish to see this Chinese business settled if it can be done without loss of honour and commercial interests as at present enjoyed. Our reputation is sufficiently vindicated at Canton and we do not look at the chance of a war with the Chinese Empire without much apprehension. I trust therefore that you will not engage us in a contest of this sort if you can possibly avoid it."

The dickering over the terms of the treaty stretched on for three weeks, with the Chinese rejecting out of hand two clauses most dear to the British and to a lesser extent the proselytizing French: free passage throughout China for foreigners and permanent British and French ambassadors at the Imperial Court. The Chinese commissioners offered a compelling reason for their intransigence and told Lord Frederick that if they accepted these two terms, it would cost the commissioners their lives. Gros and Putiatin at this point defected from the alliance and suggested that a permanent ambassador in Peking was not critical to a pact as long as the minister had access to the capital at his discretion. After much browbeating, the commissioners conceded the two points. The Treaty of Tianjin had other clauses that showed the Europeans could be as petty and obsessive about protocol as the mandarins, when they insisted that henceforth they would no longer be referred to as "barbarians" in official communications and treaties, despite the fact that in Chinese barbarian literally meant "not speaking Chinese." In a dramatic demonstration of how minor issues can underpin a major war, the clause promised that official Chinese documents and proclamations would stop referring to the British as "barbarians."

The treaty also opened up Hangzhou, Tianjin, and Nanking as trading ports. The commissioners may have welcomed this clause because Nanking remained in the control of the Taiping rebels, and if it were opened to foreigners, especially the well-armed British, they would restore order by ousting the troublemakers and do the job the Emperor had failed to. Elgin expressed satisfaction that only five British lives had been spent to secure the new treaty. Baron Gros did not share his colleague's enthusiasm and warned Elgin that "the concessions demanded are exorbitant, and perhaps even dangerous for England," while enforcing the treaty's provisions would oblige them "to use force to secure the execution of concessions obtained by force alone." Gros was a better student of Chinese political science than the Earl and quoted the Confucian principle that promises made under duress did not need to be kept. Another item in the treaty awarded the British two million taels of silver (£650,000) for "losses at Canton" and another two million in general reparations to pay Britain's military outlays in China. Despite Gros's warning, he couldn't resist the cornucopia of riches extracted from the Chinese, and the French collected reparations of two million taels (sixteen million francs). Gros's casuistry on reparations recalled Frederick the Great's description of Maria Theresa's double-think when they and the Tsar carved up Poland in the previous century: "She wept and she took."

Gros's original concerns about the concessions demanded by the treaty were contagious, and Elgin began to have second thoughts about extracting such exorbitant reparations from a tapped-out nation. In a letter to the Foreign Minister, he wrote, "Everything we saw around us indicated the penury of the Treasury," and he worried that the real cost of the extortionate demands would be the possible toppling of the unpopular Manchu regime. The stiff monetary penalty would lead the Chinese government "to despair, by putting forward pecuniary claims which it could satisfy only by measures that would increase its unpopularity and extend the area of rebellion." The humiliating treaty would also be a godsend to the God-Worshippers, Elgin warned.

Either pangs of conscience or delusional hypocrisy prompted Elgin to write in his diary that he was a friend of the Chinese people. In some ways, Elgin's claim of friendship was accurate since he refused to bring up the issue of legalizing the importation of opium despite the fact that he had specific and unequivocal orders from the Prime Minister to do so. William Reed, the American plenipotentiary, believed his colleague held "a strong if not invincible repugnance to introduce the subject of opium." Elgin pointed out the hypocrisy of the American position, which urged the British to "stop the growth and export of opium from India" when the Earl noted in a letter to the Foreign Minister, "Until recently, U.S. Consuls in both Canton and Shanghai had been partners in a merchant house trading very largely in opium."

Reed eventually did an about face and recommended legalization, which would make the trade taxable because he hoped high taxes would make the drug too expensive for all but the rich—although cynical observers felt that money rather than morality prompted Reed's turnaround on the issue. "The only remaining chance of restraint is making the drug dutiable," Reed wrote the American Secretary of State. The Chinese shared Reed's hope of taxing the drug out of business and tried to secure a tariff on opium imports of sixty taels per chest. The British wanted a tariff of only thirty taels in order not to strangle the business. The opium tax would be less than the tariff on Chinese silk and tea levied in Britain. Not surprisingly, the *tai pans* who stood to make even more money from the regularization of the opium trade did not share Elgin's moral high ground. The firm of Jardine, Matheson & Co. released a statement insisting, "The use of opium is not a curse, but a comfort and benefit to the hard-working Chinese." The opium *tai pans* exerted power through their powerful lobby in Parliament and got their thirty pieces of silver per chest.

The French, meanwhile, demonstrated a knowledge of substance abuse in China that sounds like a modern pharmacological report. An *aide de camp* to Baron Gros found that users who smoked eight pipes per day had a life expectancy of only six years. Casual consumers could expect to live twenty years after their first puff, although both the regular and casual victims would be dead on average by age fifty. Opium addicts spent two-thirds of their income on their addiction, Gros's aide reported. The Russians and Americans shared the French ambassadors' distaste for the opium trade, and in their treaties with China referred to the drug as "contraband." The French did not have the same qualms, however, about another pernicious form of trade in China, the enslavement of coolies, and inserted a clause in their treaty that legalized de facto the kidnappings and indentured servitude forced on this human chattel.

Symbolic of the devastation wrought by opium was the sad fact that it took longer to compose the Chinese translation of the Treaty of Tianjin than it did to agree on its terms. According to author Jack Beeching, the copyists and translators of the treaty, like so many in the Chinese court and army, were all addicted to opium; their drug-induced stupor slowed the translation.

The Russians came to terms first. On June 18, 1858, Putiatin accepted terms that were unacceptable to Elgin and increased the Earl's sense of betrayal and abandonment by his allies. Most important to Russia, the border between China and Siberia, the site of so much fighting, was determined to the satisfaction of both sides. Russia settled for a visiting ambassador to Peking with no permanent status, a major goal of the British and French. Christianity received formal toleration and proselytization was now permitted. The Russians also received access to two more ports, on Taiwan and Hainan. Five days later, the Americans signed a treaty almost identical to the Russians, but spelled out the terms of religious toleration in more detail.

Both the Russians and Americans included a most-favored-nations clause in their treaties, which meant that whatever further concessions the French and British received, they would also automatically enjoy. The two neutral powers in effect reaped the same benefits as the war parties but without having to go to war for them. Putiatin sent Gros and Elgin a copy of Russia's treaty with a note urging them not cause the overthrow of the Emperor with too many humiliating concessions. Reed made a similar appeal, but we only have an echo of it in the diary of Reed's secretary. "It is a difficult point to attain by foreign envoys not to destroy the prestige of the Emperor's supremacy, when it is almost all the real influence he has over his own subjects and dependencies, and at the same time teach him to say no more about it towards foreign nations."

Gros reached an agreement with the commissioners on June 23, 1858, but he hesitated to sign the treaty because he didn't want to undercut Elgin's negotiators, preferring to wait for them to finish the job. Gros concluded negotiations earlier than the British because the French sought much less from the Chinese. Indeed, the French treaty was almost identical to the two neutral powers' and did not seek a full-time ambassadorial presence in the capital. Perhaps as a face-saving gesture, Gros did demand and got approval to sign the actual treaty in Peking. When another week elapsed with no British agreement, the French ambassador became impatient and sent Elgin a letter with the implied threat that if the matter weren't concluded soon, Gros—and his military forces—would sail away. In a letter to the Quai D'Orsay, Gros revealed a bit of guilt over his treatment of his ally when he justified his actions by saying he doubted if Elgin would have waited for him if the tables had been turned.

———

Negotiations continued to stick at two concessions that obsessed the British: a permanent ambassador in Peking and freedom to travel anywhere in China. In desperation, the Chinese commissioners sought help from Gros and Putiatin, and showed them written instructions from the Emperor threatening them with death if they agreed to the two concessions. They begged Gros to intercede with his friend Elgin, who remained unmoved by the commissioners' fate (which may have been a bluff; some historians believe the Emperor's missive was a forgery). The Earl threatened to march on Peking if his terms were not met. In fact, Elgin was bluffing; he did not have the men to take the capital, but the Chinese had been so disheartened by the seemingly preternatural successes of the modern European armies and navies that the commissioners gave in.

After six weeks of toil by opium-impaired scribes, the British Treaty of Tianjin was ratified on June 26, 1858. The treaty turned out to be less negotiation and more *diktat*. By the terms of the agreement, a large portion of China would be opened to British trade. The Chinese would pay $5 million in war reparations, Christian missionaries would be allowed to proselytize unhindered throughout the country, and eleven more ports would be opened to foreign ships. Elgin ordered the Emperor's ambassadors to accept the treaty's articles with no modifications, and British gunboats backed up the demand. Taxes on imported goods were set during follow-up negotiations at Shanghai, where they agreed to a 5 percent tax. Listed among the taxable goods, which included silk and brocades, was opium. The tax agreement represented de facto legalization of opium without explicitly bringing the subject up. The legalization infuriated a growing movement in England that had been petitioning Parliament to outlaw the trade, which was had already bee made illegal in the British Isles, except in the watered-down (actually diluted with red wine) patent medicine, laudanum.

The Imperial representatives signed the document, but when they returned to court, the Emperor again rejected the humiliating terms. His decision was not hard to understand. The Chinese negotiators had given in on every British demand, including a single tariff of 5 percent on European imports, which had been taxed repeatedly by local authorities as the goods passed through China. British merchants felt that the local tax collectors were making up the "tax code" as they went along, and that the "taxes" were more like a form of freelance extortion by the venal provincials.

Elgin was so intent on wrapping up negotiations that the normally obedient plenipotentiary ignored Clarendon's instructions to bring up the issue of opium importation and legalization. Clarendon's waffling on the issue demonstrated his own repugnance for the trade, but his orderly mind felt an equal revulsion about allowing a major source of British revenue (one-third of the Exchequer's budget at the time of the First Opium War) to go unregulated and, more important, uncollected. If the reluctant Clarendon was willing to do business with the devil, he wanted him to pay his due. Elgin didn't want even to broach the subject, despite this order from the Foreign Minister in April 1857:

It will be for your Excellency when discussing commercial arrangements with any Chinese plenipotentiaries, to ascertain whether the Government of China would revoke its prohibition of the opium trade, which the high officers of the Chinese Government never practically enforce. Whether the legalisation of the trade would tend to augment that trade may be doubtful, as it seems now to be carried on to the full extent of the demand in China, with the sanction and connivance of the local authorities. But there would be obvious advantages in placing the trade upon a legal footing by the imposition of a duty, instead of its being carried on in the present irregular manner.

Elgin continued to ignore the issue during the June negotiations, possibly because Clarendon was no longer his boss, having been replaced as Foreign Secretary in February by Lord Malmesbury, who had not given the Earl similar instructions about the possibility of legalizing opium. Ironically, at this time, the American ambassador Reed received orders from the Secretary of State to negotiate an effective treaty that would formally make importing opium illegal, despite the fact that American merchants were second only to the British as the biggest drug lords in China.

Like Elgin, Reed ignored his superior because, although he found the trade morally repugnant, the ambassador despaired of practical efforts to suppress such a seductive, if devastating, pastime enjoyed by millions of Chinese unlikely to give up their habit because of orders from faraway America. Like any enterprising Yankee, Reed hoped to at least profit from an enterprise that could not be eradicated and wrote his superior in Washington, "Most honest men concur that nominal prohibition is in point of fact encouragement, and that the only remaining chance of restraint is making the drug dutiable and placing it under direct custom house control." As usual, order and venality trumped moral misgivings.

On the evening of July 3, 1858, with four hundred men and a navy band serenading them, Elgin signed the Treaty of Tianjin at the Temple of Oceanic Influences under the eerie light of paper lanterns. Despite the fear that their acquiescence would cost them their heads, the commissioners gamely invited Elgin to a lavish dinner at the temple after the signing. One of the commissioners, Hua Shan, gave the Earl several volumes of poetry.

The next day, Gros signed the French treaty, but added new demands including the release of all Chinese Christians imprisoned for their faith, which the pressured Chinese commissioners agreed to. The Baron sent a triumphant report of the signing to the Quai D'Orsay, *"Je suis heureux de pouvoir annoncer aujord-hui à Votre Excellence que la Chine s'ouvre enfin au Christianisme, source réelle de toute civilisation, et au commerce et à l'indus-trie des nations occidentales."* ("I am happy to be able to announce today to Your Excellence that China has at last opened itself to Christianity, the real source of all civilization, and to trade and the manufactures of the nations of the West.)" Gros's elation—not to mention that of the Americans and Russians—sprang from the fact that the most-favored-nations clauses in their treaties meant that all the hard work by the British negotiators to secure a permanent ambassador and unrestricted travel would also accrue to their nations, even though not explicitly spelled out in the treaties.

Back home, Elgin's efforts received mixed reviews, although most were favorable, in particular British public opinion. The Earl's private secretary, Laurence Oliphant, noted the impressive cost/benefit ratio of the casualties and reflected the bullish consensus on the war's conclusion in his 1860 account of the campaign, *Narrative of the Earl of Elgin's Mission to China and Japan*: "Hostilities with the Empire of China had terminated with a loss to the British arms of about twenty men killed in action...and a treaty had been signed far more intensive in its scope, and more subversive of imperial prejudices than that concluded fifteen years before, after a bloody and expensive war, which had been protracted over a period of two years." With only twenty casualties on the British side, the war had only been "bloody" for the Chinese. *The Times of London*, often the Earl's harshest critic, praised Elgin's work as "manly and consistent." One journalist didn't share the general *bonhomie*. Karl Marx, the European correspondent for the the *New York Tribune* at the time, wrote a letter to his writing partner, Friedrich Engels, which contained his usual paranoid take on capitalism and its duplicity: "The present Anglo-Chinese Treaty which in my opinion was worked out by Palmerston in conjunction with the Petersburg Cabinet and given to Lord Elgin to take with him on his journey is a mockery from beginning to end." Elgin's eternal gadfly, Harry Parkes, complained that the Earl had failed to ratify the treaty in Peking to ensure the Emperor's agreement.

The depressive Elgin failed to share the general elation about the ratification of the treaty. He had been thoroughly disillusioned with the Byzantine machinations of the Chinese commissioners and their Emperor. The British had not bullied the Chinese into submission, Elgin believed, but had led them to terms advantageous to both nations. The happy conclusion (for Britain at least) to the conflict did not diminish Elgin's disenchantment with the "irrational" mandarins whom Lay and Elgin's brother, Frederick Bruce, had haggled with during the negotiations. He wrote the Foreign Minister on July 6, 1858, "[Frederick] Bruce felt very sensibly the painfulness of the position of a negotiator who has to treat with persons who yield nothing to reason and everything to fear, and who are moreover profoundly ignorant both of the subjects under discussion and of their own real interests." In his diary, the Earl revealed his frustrations over his dealings with the Chinese and his bizarre belief that the subjugation of China had been for the nation's own good. "I have an instinct in me which loves righteousness and hates iniquity and all this keeps me in a perpetual boil. Though I have been forced to act almost brutally I am China's friend in almost all this."

Chapter 21

HOSTILITIES RENEWED

"[We] shall teach such a lesson to these perfidious hordes
that the name of European will hereafter be a passport of fear,
if it cannot be of love, throughout their land."

—*The Times of London*

Despite his black mood, Elgin decided to take a triumphal trip up the Yangtze River with five ships, which was meant not only as a celebration, but also as a demonstration of British naval power to discourage the Chinese from reneging on the terms of the treaty. But news of guerilla raids on Canton forced Elgin to cut short his trip. The new Viceroy of Canton, Huang, had incited rebellion by ordering the inhabitants of the city to, "Go forth in your myriads, then, and take vengeance on the enemies of your Sovereign, imbued with public spirit and fertile in expedients." The Cantonese accepted the call to arms. In July, a group of irregulars secured artillery and lobbed shells at the official British residence at Whampoa. At midnight on July 21, 1858, the irregulars made a quick raid on Canton after receiving news of the humiliating terms of the Treaty of Tianjin. During a conference with the Chinese commissioners in Shanghai in October 1858, Elgin demanded Viceroy Huang's removal, since he had been the chief instigator of the irregulars' actions.

The Shanghai conference also hammered out an agreement on tariffs, including a tax on opium—an act that, for the first time in the history of Anglo-Chinese relations, seemed officially to legalize the opium trade. Unlike the previous tortuous negotiations, the Chinese commissioners, tempted by a revenue windfall, quickly agreed to a generous tariff of 8 percent, three points higher than the tax on all other imports. The deal was sweetened by the British agreement to allow the additional taxes levied by local revenue agents as the opium made its destructive way inland, which the Treaty of Tianjin had prohibited as extortionate.

But other snags impeded ratification of this coda to the Treaty of Tianjin. Guiliang and Hua Shan, the senior Chinese commissioners, reneged on the Treaty's clause that allowed a permanent British ambassador in Peking. In a letter to Elgin on October 22, 1858, the commissioners claimed—correctly—that the clause had been agreed to under duress, and suggested instead that the British ambassador visit the capital from time to time as diplomatic business warranted. The commissioners explained that xenophobia was so profoundly rooted in Peking they feared for the lives of British residents there. Four days later, the commissioners brought up a more compelling reason when they wrote Elgin, "The permanent residence of foreign ministers at the capital would be an injury to China in many more ways than we can find words to express. In the present critical and troubled state of our country this incident would generate, we fear, a loss of respect for their government in the eyes of her people." The subtext of the letter was that the humiliation might topple the Manchu Dynasty and aid the Taiping rebels, whom the British loathed more than the duplicitous mandarin court in Peking.

The commissioners' polite threat of rebellion and anarchy swayed Elgin, and he wrote to them on October 30, 1858 that he would forward their request to the Foreign Office and "humbly submit it as his opinion that if Her Majesty's Ambassador be properly received at Peking when the ratifications are exchanged next year, and full effect given in all other particulars to the treaty negotiated at Tianjin, it would certainly be expedient that Her Majesty's representative in China should be instructed to choose a place of residence elsewhere than at Peking, and to make his visits to the capital either periodical or only as frequent as the exigencies of the public service may require. Her Majesty's treaty-right will of course in any case remain intact."

Elgin's startling volte-face on this issue, over which, among others, the Second Opium War had been fought, may have reflected a desire for self-preservation as much as a tender conscience about lodging a loathed alien in the sacred capital. Regardless of the Emperor's decision, as the guerilla raids on Canton demonstrated, it would be impossible to guarantee the safety of a British legation in Peking against a mob intent on rousting the barbarians in their midst. The Boxer Rebellion forty years later would show Elgin's concern to be prophetic. The French also came out against a permanent legation in the capital, and Elgin's boss, Lord Malmesbury, supported his plenipotentiary's concession, observing "Peking would be a rat trap for the envoy if the Chinese meant mischief." Elgin was unaware that in October at the time of his conference with the commissioners over tariffs and an ambassadorial presence in Peking, the government in London had already agreed three months earlier to lodge its representative in Shanghai.

After wrapping up the negotiations in Shanghai, to demonstrate Britain's new right to travel throughout China, Elgin decided to take a two-month tour of the Yangtze River with a survey boat and two gunboats for protection in case the local Chinese did not obey the terms of the treaty agreed to by their masters in Peking and Tianjin. The Taiping controlled much of the area Elgin toured, and when Elgin's ships sailed passed the rebels' capital, Nanking, a cannon perched on its wall fired at the British. Elgin's distaste for the rebellion was confirmed by the fact that the rebels had not accepted the terms of the treaty their archenemy, the Emperor, had signed with the invaders guaranteeing free passage throughout China. Elgin's gunboat knocked out the rebel cannon with one volley. To punish the defenders of Nanking, Elgin ordered a ninety-minute bombardment of the city before sailing on. A deserter informed Elgin that despite the movement's official ban on opium, a third of the God-Worshippers were addicted to it. This statistic may explain the ever-declining fortunes of the Taiping. Elgin wanted to climax his trip up the Yangtze with a dramatic appearance in the capital, where he would exercise another treaty concession, dealing directly with the Emperor via the symbolic act of presenting a letter from Queen Victoria to her peer. But the worsening situation in Canton brought him back to the south.

The British conquest of Canton had proved ephemeral. In February 1859, guerillas ambushed and massacred seven hundred British marines in the countryside surrounding Canton. In retaliation, General van Strauben-zee, the military commander of Canton's three thousand troops, marched on the guerillas' headquarters at Shektsing a few miles south of the city, annihilated them, and razed Shektsing. The destruction of the rebels' camp was a prophetic warning of the far greater damage the British would do to the capital. The show of military resolve proved effective. A proclamation by the Emperor soon followed and met all of Elgin's demands, removed Huang from power, and ordered the guerillas to disarm.

While Elgin continued to deal with the Chinese, in the summer of 1858 his brother, Frederick Bruce, returned to London with the Treaty of Tianjin. Lord Malmesbury rewarded Bruce by naming him the first ambassador to China, a job to which his elder brother was entitled in the wake of his military and diplomatic successes—but Elgin was exhausted and despondent and did not want the post. Malmesbury warned Bruce not to trust the Chinese.

Elgin left China in March 1859, meeting his brother in Sri Lanka in April as Bruce was returning to China to take up his new post. Although generally considered a faithful mediocrity who owed his position to his more talented brother, Bruce was just as dogged as the Earl. The new ambassador had been Lieutenant-Governor of Newfoundland during his brother's tenure as Governor-General of British North America. His most recent appointment as Colonial Secretary at Hong Kong in 1844 had given him a working knowledge of Chinese customs and eccentricities, and thus qualified him for the ambassadorial post.

Bruce arrived at the mouth of the Bei He River on June 18, 1859, with an impressive force of sixteen warships to facilitate compliance with the Treaty of Tianjin and the later concessions at Shanghai. To the great relief of both Bruce brothers, the fractious Admiral Seymour had returned to London. His replacement, Rear-Admiral James Hope, who had accompanied Bruce back to China, had an even pricklier personality than his predecessor and, if possible, despised the Chinese even more. Three days after the British arrived, John E. Ward, the new American ambassador, turned up with only a small steamer, the *Powhatan*. Anton de Bourbelon, the French representative, brought only two ships with him, but the rest of the French fleet remained nearby in Indo-China.

The Emperor still sought to keep the barbarians out of his capital, and suggested ratifying the treaty in Shanghai, which all three foreign powers declined. The Emperor's representative in Shanghai summed up the untenable military position of the Chinese in a memo to his master, which also revealed that the Chinese had no intention of honoring the treaty terms:

"While the barbarians [remain hostile] it is very difficult to get a handhold for managing them. Only when China's army is efficient, supplies adequate, artillery effective and ships strong can we do as we please and repudiate anything. Speaking for the present we can only eliminate the worst, and call it a day." The frank estimate seems to have worked somewhat, for on June 18, 1859, the Emperor's Grand Council assigned three buildings to the new ambassadors. Tellingly, the new embassies were all outside the city gates.

Some of the Emperor's advisors still resisted the foreigners' presence in the capital, while delusional courtiers hoped to get the ambassadors to kowtow! These Imperial malcontents gave orders to lay down three bamboo booms, three feet thick, across the Bei He to block the "enemies'" advance. In the vain hope of avoiding another war, Bruce wrote to Peking asking that the booms be removed. There was no reply to his letter. Admiral Hope asked Bruce's permission to destroy the booms, and on June 21, 1859, a steamer under the command of Captain G.O. Willes managed to break through the first boom, but the remaining two were unbreakable, despite the use of gunpowder. Under cover of night, the Chinese repaired the first boom.

On June 25th, eight miles from the capital, Bruce received a letter from Heng Fu, the Viceroy of Chihli, suggesting that the ambassadors lodge at Beitang, eight miles north of Peking. It was a face-saving compromise, but the British, armed to the teeth with an armada of gunships and after three years of battles and maddening negotiations, had no interest in mollifying Chinese pride. As a douceur, the Viceroy sent the British fresh food. Bruce ignored the culinary bribe and told Hope to try breaking through the booms again.

In mid afternoon on the 25th, Hope ordered the guns on his flagship, the *Plover*, to begin bombarding forty Chinese cannon mounted on the shore behind the first boom. The fleet consisted of four British steamers and one French. Wearing gold braid that identified his rank, Hope unwisely stood on the deck, and a Chinese sharpshooter rewarded his bravery by hitting him in the thigh. As he fell to the deck, Hope suffered even worse injuries than those caused by the bullet. Hope remained on deck vulnerable to another attack while the ship's surgeon bound his excruciating wound. For a change, the Chinese cannon were better aimed this time, although still immobile, and Hope's second in command and eight sailors were blown to pieces. Twenty-two others suffered serious wounds.

Hope's bravery now bordered on the suicidal. He rowed over to the *Opossum*, and again stood in plain sight on the deck. Because of his leg wound, he had to hold on to the railing, which was hit by another Chinese volley. As the railing collapsed, the Admiral fell to the deck and broke several ribs. He turned over command to Captain Shadwell. The enemy artillery disabled all five of the attackers' gunships. Bruce ordered seven more warships, which had been held back eight miles away, to replace the damaged vessels. By early evening, five British ships had been immobilized by the Chinese guns and another vessel had gone aground, a sitting duck for the fort's cannon.

Although the Americans were officially neutral, when Commodore Josiah Tattnall learned that Hope had been wounded and that the disabled British ship, stranded and defenseless just past the first boom, was being battered by Chinese guns on both sides of the river, Tattnall's military camaraderie and racial solidarity overruled neutrality. After getting the approval of the American envoy, John E. Ward, the Commodore steamed over to rescue his fallen comrade. His ship, *Toeywhan,* arrived towing another vessel bristling with two hundred marines, and he shouted over to Hope, "Blood is thicker than water. I'll be damned if I'll stand by and see white men butchered before my eyes." Camaraderie wasn't the only thing fueling the American marines' assault. After months of enduring taunts from angry Cantonese, military action allowed the marines to vent their suppressed rage at the xenophobic Chinese. The racism in the Commodore's rousing cheer probably prevented it from joining the list of other great American military ripostes like, "I have just begun to fight" and the bowdlerized, "Nuts."

Around 7 P.M., as Chinese fireworks illuminated the assault and gave the carnage a festive flavor, Captain Shadwell with fifty Royal Marines and French seamen led by a French Commander Tricault landed on the mud flats outside one of the Dagu Forts. As the attackers waded through mud up to their knees, the primitive gingalls manned by the fort's defenders demonstrated their effectiveness at short range as the European troops found themselves literally stuck in the mud, unable to advance after the bridges and ladders they had brought with them to scale the fort's walls were destroyed by the Chinese. Shadwell sent word to his superiors that his men were pinned down and requested reinforcements to storm the walls. But there were no more fighting men available, and the request was denied. He was ordered to retreat with his wounded to the safety of their ships.

The British and French suffered atypically high casualties. Shadwell was wounded, Tricault was killed, and of the more than one thousand men who participated in the attack, almost half were killed or wounded. The gunboats *Lee, Plover,* and *Cormorant* were disabled, and the *Kestrel* went to the bottom of the shallow river. Some of the defeated men, who had fought in the Crimea, lamented that Balaclava had been a picnic compared to the failed assault on the Dagu Forts. On July 1, Hope informed Bruce that another assault on the forts without reinforcements would be impossible and probably suicidal.

In a dispatch to the Admiralty, Hope expressed amazement at the sudden military competence of the Chinese, which had been grimly laughable until now. "Had the opposition they expected been that as usual in Chinese warfare, there is little doubt that the place would have been successfully carried at the point of the bayonet." To save face, Bruce reported to London that the sudden military prowess demonstrated by the Dagu defenders had been made possible by the secret participation of the Russians, their nominal ally. Attributing the allegations to eyewitnesses—sailors who had participated in the assault—Bruce claimed that men in fur hats and European dress had been observed directing operations atop the fort walls. Palmerston accepted Bruce's story, perhaps for the same reason Bruce had made it up—to excuse an embarrassing defeat by a supposedly feckless enemy.

Prince Senggelinqin, who had once crushed an army of Taiping rebels, commanded the Mongol cavalry and headed the war party at the Imperial Court, had led the successful defense of the Dagu Forts, but warned against unbridled optimism by members of his own cabal. On July 5, 1859, he described the European position in a letter to the Emperor: "Their resentment must be deep. Most of the barbarian warships which came up the river were damaged. They are sure to go to Canton and Shanghai, collect [more] warships and plan revenge." The popular Prince was incensed by the collusion of the "neutral" Americans in the assault on the forts. "Although the starting of hostilities was by the English barbarians, France and America's cooperation in the melee is also inescapable."

Seng based his complaint on intelligence extracted from a Canadian POW, John Powers, who, hoping to escape imprisonment, had claimed he was a neutral American soldier. The Chinese did not free him, but accepted his claim as proof that America had abandoned its neutrality. Like many ethnocentric Chinese, Seng was weak on Western geography and history, and believed Canada was part of the United States. When an American missionary who spoke Chinese tried to explain the difference between British Canada, French Canada, the United States of America, and the North American continent, Seng described his incredulity in another letter to the court. "[The missionary] stated that America contained Englishmen and Frenchmen, and when there was fighting, the flag was the only criterion." Nevertheless, Powers's ruse worked, and he was freed a month after his capture. The gesture may have reflected Seng's desire to appease the British and not antagonize the Americans into further military action, however; at the same time he also freed an English POW who had not denied his nationality.

When news of the heavy casualties reached Britain, Lord Derby's government fell on June 10, 1859. The unrepentant hawk, Lord Palmerston, who felt his aggressive policies had been vindicated by the Dagu disaster, returned to power at the advanced but still vigorous age of seventy-five. With a rationalization that would have been amusing had it not been so uninformed, Palmerston confided to a secretary that he suspected the Dagu Forts had indeed been manned by the Russians—though that still wouldn't explain the successful defense of the forts, since three years earlier the Russians had proved as incompetent as the Chinese with their disastrous execution of the Crimean War. Frederick Bruce's tall tale had turned into a useful legend.

Despite the fantasy of Russian intervention (the Russians had not been on the Dagu parapets), Palmerston saved his full-blown anger for the Chinese and decided to abandon the incremental approach to treating with Peking, which had been advocated by both Derby and Elgin. Palmerston wrote the Foreign Office, "We must in some way or other make the Chinese repent of the outrage. We might send a military-naval force to attack and occupy Peking." *The Times of London* shared the Prime Minister's bloodlust and editorialized: "[We] shall teach such a lesson to these perfidious hordes that the name of European will hereafter be a passport of fear, if it cannot be of love, throughout their land." During a cabinet meeting in mid September 1859, only Gladstone remained a dove, and as Chancellor of the Exchequer he decided to appeal to Palmerston's fiduciary responsibilities—rather than his flexible conscience—by emphasizing the prohibitive cost of continuing the war, especially a financially ruinous assault on Peking.

Elgin sat in on this cabinet meeting because Palmerston had appointed him Postmaster-General in the new Whig government. The popular Earl seemed to be a nonpartisan cynosure pursued by both Whigs and Tories. Indeed, shortly before the Tories fell, in the wake of the Dagu disaster, Disraeli, then Chancellor of the Exchequer, had pushed to fire Lord Malmesbury and replace him with Elgin as Foreign Secretary. The demise of the Tory government precluded the appointment, but the new Prime Minister, Palmerston, retained the Earl, who longed to retire to his Scottish estate Broomhall. Elgin's sense of duty and *noblesse oblige* prevented his return to private life. But the Earl took up his new job with a heavy heart and serious misgivings, even though his duties as Postmaster-General had nothing to do with the mess in China his brother seemed to be mismanaging. On September 13, 1859, while a guest of the Queen at Balmoral, he described his overwrought state of mind to the Countess of Elgin: "Dearest, you see the dreadful news from China. I am quite overcome by it: I never closed my eyes last night."

During cabinet meetings, Elgin remained silent as Gladstone condemned his brother's desire to march on the capital and end the current conflict once and for all. Palmerston and the Foreign Office sided with Bruce, however—Peking must be taken. Even so, Elgin counseled moderation, fearing an occupation of the capital would topple the unstable Manchu Dynasty and make the Taiping rebels with their anticapitalist platform the new masters of China—a disastrous scenario for the British and their mercantilist goals. As he explained to a fellow cabinet member, Sir Charles Wood, "If you humiliate the Emperor beyond measure you imperil the most lucrative trade you have in the world. The general notion is that if we use the bludgeon freely enough we can do anything in China. I hold the opposite view."

British doves who pushed for diplomacy rather than arms in further dealings with Peking had only to look at the shabby treatment of the American ambassador John Ward by the Imperial Court in July 1859 to realize that after the upset victory at Dagu, the Chinese were in no mood for temporizing. At this high point in their fortunes, the Chinese preferred the gingall to the diplomatic note. Ambassador Ward's recent stab at diplomacy seemed to prove the intransigence of the Chinese. Ward had agreed to make a detour to Beitang, 160 miles north of Peking, and from there travel to the capital. Instead of traveling by sedan chair, like any respectable senior mandarin, Ward accepted the Chinese's humiliating offer of a wooden cart without springs or even a cushioned seat. The Chinese slyly told the Ambassador it was the Russians' preferred means of travel in China, although it was actually a typical conveyance for tribute-bearing, inferior barbarians. As the cart bumped over the potholed roads from Peitang to Peking, Ward suffered such severe joint pain from the ride that he chose to walk the last few miles. The Chinese enjoyed the spectacle of a representative of one of the great powers of the West entering Peking on July 27, 1859, on foot like a peasant. Humbled, the barbarians had returned to their proper station.

Like so many Europeans before him, Ward immediately butted up against the same old bugaboo, the kowtow. The mandarins tried to cut a deal. Instead of the required obeisance that included bumping his head against the floor nine times, they offered to accept three. A courtly old southern gentleman from Georgia, Ward said he was willing to bow, but he was "accustomed to kneel only to God and Woman." A mandarin responded, "But the Emperor *is* God."

While his British counterparts, Lord Elgin and his brother, were used to kneeling on one leg in the Queen's presence, the American refused to kneel before a not-so-benevolent despot. He volunteered to bow, but that was not nearly humbling enough for the protocol-obsessed courtiers. In a letter to the court, Ward suggested an alternative to the kowtow: "I would enter the presence of his Majesty with head uncovered and bowing low; I would stand and not sit; I would not speak unless addressed, and retire by walking backwards, never turning my back until out of his presence." Unimpressed with royalty, the ambassador didn't bother to capitalize the "his" before "Majesty" in the letter to the Emperor's advisors. The Chinese made a counter offer: would the Ambassador be willing to bow so low that he could touch the floor with his fingertips?—a major concession for the mandarins, which Ward refused.

After many letters back and forth, a risible stage musician's compromise was reached in which the American would hide his legs behind the curtain of a table so the Emperor could presume he was kneeling when in fact he would not be. But at the last moment, the Son of Heaven, galvanized by the Dagu triumph, came out of his opiate stupor, retracted the fingertip compromise, and demanded all nine head butts from the plenipotentiary. In his defense, the Emperor mentioned that since the Americans had fought at Dagu, their ambassador needed to show contrition by kowtowing.

Haggling over the kowtow dragged on for an amazing fourteen days. Finally, the Emperor ordered Ward and his entourage expelled from the city. Although it soured American-Chinese relations and cost China the support of America as a buffer and voice of moderation against the French and British, the issue of the kowtow turned out to be irrelevant. Ward returned to Peitang, where without the interference of the Emperor, he signed a treaty with Chinese officials on August 15, 1859. He also managed to accomplish his other major task, getting the Emperor to accept a letter from President Buchanan. Ward's successful resolution of the treaty impasse was helped by the fact that unlike the obsessed British and French, the American did not insist on signing the treaty in the capital. Peace was peace, whether in Peitang or Peking, Ward said.

Bruce was embarrassed by his American colleague's finesse and success, which contrasted with his own failures in China. On September 3, 1859, the British Ambassador lashed out at the Imperial court in a letter to the new Foreign Minister, Lord John Russell, "The Chinese Government are still far from recognising the rights of foreign Envoys; that whatever they may have conceded on paper, they practically refuse to admit diplomatic intercourse on a footing of national equality, and that a visit to the capital is only acceptable if it can be converted into a means of flattering the pride, and acknowledging the superiority of the Emperor of China."

By now, a weary Palmerston had tired of the protocol morass, the kowtow, and whose sovereign was superior to whose. He stuck to practical rather than polemical issues in China in a letter to Edmund Hammond, Permanent Under-Secretary at the Foreign Office, on September 12, 1859:

This is very unpleasant news from China, and I fear that
our people must have allowed themselves to be much over-
reached by the Chinese and not to have taken proper pre-
cautions for reconnoitering the ground before they
advanced up the river. But there is no use in criticising the
past. The question is what is to be done now. We must I
think resent this outrage in some way or other. To make an
attack on Peking would be an operation of great magni-
tude, but we might blockade the Grand Canal at its
mouth in the Yangtze, or we might take possession of
Chusan; but the objection to that latter operation would
be that we would be obliged to occupy it jointly with the
French."

While Palmerston proceeded with caution, the press, in a bloodthirsty
descent into yellow journalism and purple prose, smelled blood and
wanted more of it. On the same day that Palmerston confided his hesitation to Hammond, *The Times of London* called for a muscular mission
creep: since the Chinese had failed to honor the Treaty of Tianjin "by an
act faithless, barbarous and treacherous, England and France, or England
without France if necessary, [must] teach such a lesson to these perfidious
hordes that the name of European will hereafter be a passport of fear, if it
cannot be of love, throughout their land." In a similar bloody vein, the
Daily Telegraph on September 14, 1859, demanded, "There must be no fal-
tering while the blood of our murdered soldiers remains unavenged."

Unmoved by these editorials, Gladstone stuck to his pacifist beliefs
when he addressed a Cabinet meeting on September 17, 1859. The Chancellor of the Exchequer rejected out of hand Bruce's and the press's call for
full-scale war to avenge the Dagu debacle. In fact, he didn't even bring up
Dagu when he told his fellow ministers that while Britain must send more
troops to stabilize the situation and Bruce's wobbly position, the ambassador's new orders should be to force the Chinese to honor the terms of the
Treaty of Tianjin, not prosecute the secular war Bruce wanted.

As Postmaster-General, Elgin participated in the Cabinet meetings and
found himself in the excruciating position of disagreeing with his brother's
call for an invasion of the capital. He kept silent and didn't criticize his

sibling during the Cabinet sessions, but he confided his fears in a letter to Sir Charles Wood, First Lord of the Admiralty. Elgin's fear of the Taiping insurgency obviated any sense of honor he may have felt to avenge Dagu. A successful occupation of Peking could topple the Emperor, and the British would be forced to deal with something they loathed more than national disgrace, the antiproperty, antitrade rebels in control of China. To Wood, he wrote, "If you humiliate the Emperor beyond measure, if you seriously impair his influence over his own subjects, you kill the goose that lays the golden eggs," as well as 10 percent of Britain's tax revenue from opium. "[You] throw the country into confusion and imperil the most lucrative trade you have in the world. I know that these opinions are not popular. The general notion is that if we use the bludgeon freely enough we can do anything in China. I hold the opposite view so strongly that I must give expression to it at whatever cost to myself."

Moderation receded before events on the Continent when Napoleon invaded Italy and seized Austrian-controlled Lombardy. Rumors circulated that a French assault on England would follow, and another expansionist venture in China. Depending on which hysterical report one heard, the French Emperor was massing twelve thousand infantry, two squadrons of cavalry, six batteries of artillery, and twenty small gunboats to march on London...or was it Peking? If the British didn't take care of the diplomatic and military crisis in China, the French would—and to this solo victor would go the spoils, the vast market that was China...or so the hawks in Britain claimed.

Elgin remained unmoved by the hysteria over France's dark designs on either country and came up with a counterplan to his brother's. In a Cabinet memo, he suggested that rather than invading Peking and helping the God-Worshippers to power, a British fleet might blockade the Bei He River, prevent tribute in the form of rice-bearing Chinese junks from reaching Peking, and thus starve—but not topple—the Manchu regime into submission. In fact, the noble Earl was playing fast and loose with the facts, though none of his colleagues in the Cabinet knew enough about the Chinese economy to realize it: rice was not a staple, but more of a garnish in northern China. If their rice supply were cut off, the residents of the capital would eat corn and beans, which were plentiful; they were unlikely to starve. Nor was the Emperor likely to come to terms over lack of a side dish. The Cabinet swallowed Elgin's fictitious diet, however, and on October 29, 1859, the Foreign Secretary instructed Bruce to demand an apology for the casualties at Dagu, unspecified reparations, and an agreement to honor the terms of the Treaty of Tianjin. The Chinese were to be given only thirty days to respond—no more tactical delays by wily mandarins—if they failed to meet the deadline, Bruce was to follow his brother's plan and block the Bei He, *not* march on Peking.

Russell's letter to Bruce arrived in January 1860 with instructions to issue the thirty-day ultimatum at once. But Elgin's idea of a rice blockade had more problems than the Cabinet's ignorance of the Emperor's diet. The Earl had also failed to tell his colleagues that the rice armada did not sail to Peking until the spring. A blockade in January would be fruitless and ludicrous. More to the point, Admiral Hope would not be able to furnish warships for the blockade until April 1860. With London's permission, Bruce put off delivering the ultimatum until March. Meanwhile, rejecting Elgin's advice to drop the demand for a resident British ambassador in Peking, the hawkish Whig government instructed his brother to add that demand to the ultimatum. According to the new British military chief in China, General James Hope Grant, the Chinese reply to the new demand—a flat-out rejection—was "cheeky in the extreme."

Chapter 22

LORD ELGIN'S RETURN

---

*"If I had been anything but the greatest fool that the world
ever saw I should never have been where I now am.
I deserve to suffer for it, and no doubt I shall do so."*

—Lord Elgin on his return to China
to enforce the Treaty of Tianjin, 1860

By the spring of 1860, the British public and its Parliamentary representatives seemed to have grown tired of the conflict and the minutiae of the diplomatic haggling between Britain and China. The story had become old news. The issues were debated in both houses of Parliament in a desultory fashion. Only MPs on opposite ends of the political spectrum still retained any passion about the issue, with one reactionary Parliamentarian in a paroxysm of uninformed grandiosity declaring it would only take one gunboat to pacify Peking, while the Radical MP John Bright believed in calling a spade an immoral spade and said of the conflict, "Nothing more vicious can be found in our history; no page of our annals is more full of humiliation because more full of crime." A Whig MP who represented the merchant classes found his way to morality through the back door of economic practicality by insisting that alienating the Chinese further would only hurt trade—not facilitate it: "[Are we] to blow up their forts and bombard their towns and then say, 'Good people, we are a trading community. We have come here to extend your commerce and ours.'" In the Lords, Malmesbury, the ousted Foreign Secretary, warned against xenophobia after so much Parliamentary rhetoric about "barbarians": "The Chinese government is anything but a barbarian government. They are very clever and very well-educated people, and I believe they have very nearly as much knowledge of what is going on as we have ourselves."

Elgin also joined the doves. A new assault on China, the Earl said, would "carry destruction and devastation among the peoples of China, and entail ruin and distress on large bodies of British and other merchants in the China trade." Ironically, Lord Ellenborough, back from his post as Governor-General of India, where he had happily encouraged the cultivation and exportation of opium to China, now condemned Britain's "continual succession of wars," lamenting that there was not one "to which the misconduct of our own people and their own disgraceful avarice has not materially contributed." Eloquently, he continued, "It is not, my Lords, lawful to make war for the purpose of making money. To do so is to commit a crime. It is based on wrong, and wrong will not continually be protected by Providence." This may have been a unique phenomenon and fusion of opposites—Tory Radicalism.

———·——

In contrast to their usual glacial speed, Chinese officials responded quickly to Bruce's ultimatum on April 5, 1860, with a curt no. Peking remained the major stumbling block as the Holy of Holies that would be sacrilege for barbarians to penetrate. Instead, the mandarins invited Bruce to negotiate with an Imperial commissioner—not the Emperor—at Beitang, a scant fifty miles north of Peking, but near the humiliating events of the Dagu Forts and symbolically light-years away from the Emperor's hermetic city. Emboldened by the Dagu victory and lulled by British inaction during the past nine months, the Chinese also scolded Bruce for the insolence of his ultimatum and let it be known that further communications from the barbarian representative should be more respectful.

Bruce was by now completely out of his depth, but he retained the confidence of his sovereign. Through the Foreign Secretary, Lord John Russell, Queen Victoria informed Bruce that she looked forward to *his* persuading the Chinese to honor the Tianjin agreement. The Queen's implication was that Bruce, despite his series of diplomatic and military failures, would not be replaced. In the event, she was right—Bruce was not replaced, merely superceded as the top British emissary in China...by his brother. In April, Lord Elgin was ordered to return to China and take charge of the negotiations or prosecute the war, whichever was required to accomplish Britain's goals. Bruce was to remain in China to help his sibling, though in a rather inept effort to soothe his ego, the Foreign Secretary indelicately explained his brother's appointment by suggesting that the Chinese might prefer to deal with a plenipotentiary who had not been humiliated in a prior set-to, namely the Dagu mess.

Elgin by now was a reluctant diplomat who dreaded dealing once more with the maddening, passive-aggressive style of the Chinese court. Nevertheless, he felt obliged to return to the scene in order to defend his 1858 settlement, which had been excoriated by the press and the general public, and eviscerated in both houses of Parliament. His new orders had the irritating ring of familiarity to the point of government obsession, reiterating the demand for negotiations in the capital, an apology, reparations for Dagu and other British losses, and compliance with the Treaty of Tianjin. Elgin must have breathed a sigh of relief when the Foreign Office informed him that the demand for a permanent representative in Peking was off the table again—though if negotiations went well he might resubmit the issue. The new flexibility of the British government reflected its fear of toppling the Manchus and enthroning the Taipings. Also on the Foreign Office's wish list, though it was not mandatory, was the subject of annexing the Kowloon peninsula…but only if the French did not object. (British paranoia toward Napoleon's military expansionism had lessened when he made no further incursions into Italy after seizing Lombardy and giving it to his ally, the King of Sardinia and future king of *risorgimento* Italy.)

En route to China, the Earl had an audience in Paris at the Tuilleries with the genial emperor of the French, who confided that France had no territorial ambitions in China. The real reason for Napoleon III's forbearance, however, was that he planned a major move on Indo-China and was happy to leave the nation to the north embroiled with the British. A weakened China would facilitate France's intended conquests to the south. Napoleon's ambitions would reverberate into the mid twentieth century and the Vietnam War. Elgin also met with Baron Gros, who had also been called back to service in China, and the two men commiserated on their reluctance to resume the Sisyphean ordeal that was the Middle Kingdom. In Egypt, Elgin made a quick trip to the Sphinx, whose inscrutable mien reminded him of the impenetrability of the mandarin mind. The closer the Earl came to his destination, the greater became his dread of the Gethsemane cup, which he surely would have preferred, like Jesus, to pass on.

During his trip east, Elgin learned of the brutal British reaction to atrocities committed by Indians during the Sepoy Mutiny, which included British soldiers shooting hundreds of Indian mutineers from cannons. The vengeful repression of the rebellion by his fellow countrymen sent the Earl into a paralyzing depression, one of many episodes his journal entries and other personal papers suggest plagued the peer. Elgin tried to escape his depression and anxiety by immersing himself in the fantasy world of Tennyson's *Idylls of the King.* However, he perhaps worsened his mental state by also reading Lord John Russell's letters to *The Times* condemning British atrocities, even in reaction to Indian atrocities, during the Mutiny. Once again, the tender conscience of Elgin's diary contrasted with his subsequent act of vandalism in Peking.

Gros caught up with Elgin en route to China, and as the two envoys steamed out of Sri Lanka on the *Malabar,* the ship crashed into a rock during a violent storm. When a passenger asked the captain if their trip would be delayed, he responded, "Going to sea? Why, we are going to the bottom!" Although not very consoling, the captain turned out to be prophetic when the ship sank, taking with it Gros' uninsured plate and Elgin's top secret instructions from London. The Earl's dismay over his loss of paper made Gros suspicious, especially after Elgin confided to the Baron that he would be willing to replace the Manchu Emperor with a Taiping King if it would prevent the coming conflict. Gros was certain—but wrong—that Elgin's lost papers contained instructions from the British government to do just that.

The travelers were delayed for two weeks while divers retrieved luggage, Gros's tableware, and Elgin's papers, which contained the instructions concerning the annexation of Kowloon. There were no orders to serve as kingmaker in China. The Kowloon annexation might have distressed Gros more than his anxiety about a God-Worshipping anticapitalist atop the Imperial throne. However, Gros's concern about the Taiping issue marked the beginning of the two friends' estrangement.

A staggering international force of arms was assembling in China, belying Lord John Russell's secret instructions to General Grant to minimize aggression and maximize negotiation there. "Our object in going to China is to trade. An early termination of our Chinese difficulty is therefore most desirable," the Foreign Minister wrote Grant. The number of troops sent by Britain was so impressive that Elgin thought the buildup was likely to antagonize the French and scare China into a military response. The French sent a fraction of their promised contingent—seven thousand men, and the British feared that their superior numbers would alienate their ally.

In March 1860, an unfounded rumor arose in London that Napoleon III planned to seize Kowloon. The Foreign Office ordered Hong Kong's Consul, Harry Parkes, to negotiate a treaty with the city's Chinese Viceroy for a permanent lease of Kowloon in return for an annual fee of five hundred taels of silver—an insulting £160, a real estate bargain considering the economic leviathan Hong Kong would become and on a par with the twenty-four dollars worth of costume jewelry paid for another island, Manhattan. An agreement to cede Kowloon was promptly reached on March 18, 1860—its peaceful conclusion all the more amazing because the British were planning an offensive on the capital at the same time conducting amicable negotiations for Kowloon. The Chinese Viceroy of Canton acquiesced with such alacrity because he was desperately bankrupt, despite the paltry amount he received.

Chinese compliance in Hong Kong may also have been encouraged by the terrifying presence of Sikh cavalry in Kowloon, where they performed military exercises on outsized Arabian horses. The Sikhs and British in Kowloon also tested the brand-new Armstrong field gun, which would prove itself in the upcoming campaign in the north. In these war games, the giant twenty-five-pound Armstrong combined the accuracy of a rifle and the destructive power of a cannon. Designed for scattering large armies by shattering into dozens of bits of metal, the Armstrong would devastate the eighteenth-century-armed Chinese horsemen.

Although the French were armed with the outdated "Napoleon gun," they also had the consolation of a state-of-the-art seventy-five-ton gunboat, the first prefabricated warship, which was shipped to China in three sections and assembled there into a leviathan whose sixty-pound guns could, and did, blow antiquated Chinese junks out of the water and raze cities. An ingenious piece of technology, the monster of a ship had a miniscule hull that drew only five feet of water, which allowed it to steam along China's shallow rivers, including the one that led to Peking.

Because of the previous defeat, the Chinese felt certain that the Dagu Forts would again stymie the British advance. Optimistic members of the

Chinese Cotton Guild laid a $50,000 wager, deposited in the Oriental Bank of Hong Kong, that the Chinese would continue to prevail. British merchants tried to match the bet, more out of patriotism than conviction, but the fact they were only able to raise $10,000 against the Chinese $50,000 revealed the merchants' pessimism.

Despite the fact that their brothers continued to be sold into quasi-slavery on British plantations in the Caribbean and anywhere else free labor was needed by the colonial empires of Western Europe, twenty-five hundred coolies volunteered to serve in the British army, their generous $9 per month military pay, rations, and two uniforms per volunteer overcoming any nationalist or racial guilt. The British feared these quisling volunteers and refused to give them rifles, arming them instead with bamboo staves that made the Emperor's medieval men seem like futuristic killing machines by comparison. Another reason that the British refused to give the recruits proper arms was that despite the generous $9 bounty, upstanding Chinese declined the honor of betraying their nation, and those who did volunteer came from the bottom of society—thieves and drifters who drifted into the British ranks. The generous salary also scared away law-abiding Chinese because they feared the wages had been inflated to compensate them for being placed in the front lines in the future and used for cannon fodder. As an indication of just how riddled with riff-raff the coolie brigade was, crime in Hong Kong declined after the coolies left for the north. The lumpen position of the coolies as society's outcasts may explain why they were even more brutal toward their countrymen than their Sikh comrades. Lt. Col. G. J. Wolseley admired their *esprit de corps* with the kind of enthusiasm usually reserved for pets or beasts of burden: "Lawless and cruel, [but] a single coolie was actually of more general value than any three baggage animals; they were easily fed, and when properly treated, most manageable."

Commanding this hodge-podge of religious and ethnic groups was the popular General Sir James Hope Grant, who commanded special loyalty from the Sikhs because they had served under his fair leadership during the Indian revolt. Not the brightest of fellows, Hope Grant owed his promotion and command in China to his proximity to the war theater and the lack of any other commander of superior skills. Rumor had it that Sir James had risen through the ranks because of a different skill, a deft touch with the cello, which prompted his violin-playing superior to promote him. Unlike his testy relations with another military commander, the prima donna Admiral Seymour, Lord Elgin admired Hope Grant's temperament: "There is a great simplicity and kindliness about his manner which in a man so highly placed must be most winning." Elgin liked another replacement even more. The obnoxious Sir John Bowring had been replaced by Sir Hercules Robinson as Governor of Hong Kong. Elgin called the new appointee "a gentlemanlike person, and the tone of the community has undergone a great change for the better." Robinson's socialite wife increased her husband's popularity by hosting much-attended balls for military officers and diplomats in Hong Kong.

An allied force of two thousand British and five hundred French were sent to occupy the pivotal island of Chusan, which would give them control of the Yangtze and its critical role as Peking's supply road. Brutalized and terrified by past invasions, the residents of Chusan surrendered without a fight to the allies in April 1860. The French and British got into a ludicrous competition over whose flag would fly higher. When the French ran up their pennant on a higher pole than the British's, the British commandeered a taller mast from a ship to use as a flagpole, then the French found an even taller mast.

Fifty miles to the north of Chusan, across the Zangzhou and Yupan Bays, Shanghai welcomed the allies without a fight because its mayor needed reinforcements against the encroaching Taiping rebels, who had taken the city of Fuzhou, ninety miles away, on May 24, 1860. From their base of Fuzhou, it would be easy for the Taiping to take the great prize of Shanghai—if the Europeans didn't intervene. The Taiping also hoped that European operations in the north would draw the Imperial army away from the Taiping capital, Nanking.

Shanghai's mayor begged the Westerners to help him despite the fact that his putative allies constituted an invasion force in other parts of the country. The mayor had managed to stay in the good graces of the invaders while reporting their every movement to Peking. The French commander, General Cousin de Montauban, as temperamental as his counterpart Rear-Admiral James Hope Grant was charismatic, hated the Chinese in general and the Taiping rebels in particular because of their quasi-Protestantism. The general wanted to attack and annihilate the rebels once and for all.

Bruce vetoed this plan, agreeing to defend Shanghai against an invasion, but refused to take offensive action in keeping with his instructions from the Foreign Office to observe neutrality in all Chinese internal affairs. When Gros reached Shanghai, he sided with Bruce against his own military leader.

The British concept of neutrality turned out to be flexible in the extreme as Royal Marines patrolled the approaches to the city, while the French protected the city gates. The brick walls around the city were repaired and its moat deepened by the "neutral" occupiers. In contrast to the old Chinese guns, which were anchored in place and therefore impossible to aim properly, the British placed swivel cannons on the walls, which could be fired at the enemy or turned inward and used against the residents of the city, should they waver in their support of their invader-allies. The mayor of Shanghai welcomed the artillery threat on the city walls, since he feared that the poorest citizens might rise up in sympathy when the Taiping rebels attacked. To preempt such an internal revolt, the mayor festooned the walls of Shanghai with baskets packed with the heads of captured God-Worshippers.

———————

As he approached Shanghai, Elgin continued to spiral into depression and existential despair. "If I had been anything but the greatest fool that the world ever saw I should never have been where I now am. I deserve to suffer for it, and no doubt I shall do so." Elgin's later vandalism in Peking would give the Earl plenty to suffer for, although his victims' suffering would be much greater. Despite his humiliating demotion to No. 2, Frederick Bruce welcomed the return of his brother with relief as the younger man realized he was out of his depth, while his more talented sibling was in his element, however reluctantly Elgin operated in it.

Where others saw an encouraging military superiority that would check the primitive Chinese defense, the gloomy Elgin's glass was perpetually half empty rather than half full. While Lt. Col. Wolseley crowed about the expeditionary force, "England has never before opened a campaign with such a well organized or a more efficient force," Elgin fretted about the cost of the campaign and who would pay for it, concerns that the Exchequer, not the British plenipotentiary, needed to concern itself with. "What will the House of Commons say when the bill which has to be paid for this war has to be presented?" Elgin asked his diary. On a less negative note, although still tinged with misgivings, Elgin added, "[Admiral Hope] is doing things excellently well if money be not object." Word from back home exacerbated Elgin's worries. Gladstone sent him a secret note warning that if the war in China were not concluded by the next meeting of Parliament, the government might fall—the implication being that the collapse would be Elgin's fault. Rumors in London claimed that the war dragged on because Elgin was too much of an appeaser of the Chinese.

Chapter 23

TO THE GATES
OF PEKING

————·∘·————

"Here we are with our base established in the heart of the country,
in a capital climate, with abundance around us, our army
in excellent health, and these stupid people give me a snub
which obliges me to break with them."

—Lord Elgin

On July 26, 1860, 150 British ships steamed up the northern coast and landed near Beitang, eight miles north of the Dagu Forts on the Gulf of Chihli, where the French under Montauban joined the fleet commanded by Hope Grant. For the next five days, they unloaded troops from more than two hundred warships in torrential rains that turned the muddy flats into a kind of quicksand that embarrassed the soldiers by sucking their trousers off. Guns on the walls of the Beitang fort did not fire on the invaders. When the allies reached the gates of Beitang they found out why. The garrison had fled, leaving the city undefended. The wall-mounted artillery turned out to be fakes made of wood.

The twenty thousand inhabitants of the city welcomed the invaders as liberators and showed their guests where the fleeing forces of Prince Seng had buried mines inside the courtyard outside his official residence.

The people's welcome and aid were repaid with rape and looting by the allied troops. The women of Beitang escaped sexual assault by poisoning themselves with opium, strangling themselves, or drowning. The rest of the city sought refuge in the fetid marshes outside Beitang.

General Hope Grant blamed the depredations on the coolies who had allied themselves with the foreigners. The coolies were "for the most part atrocious villains...the robberies and crimes they committed in the town were fearful." Hope Grant theorized that the coolies' rampage was caused by the fact that most of them were opium addicts. The general planned to seize their drugs in order to reinstall discipline and end the rape and looting. But a Chinese advisor warned "habitual smokers would have pined away and eventually died." The experiment in zero tolerance was dropped as the coolies were needed to fight more than achieve sobriety. The Punjabi Sikhs tapped old habits from the Sepoy Mutiny and surpassed the brutality of the coolies. The British and French could not resist all the plunder they were missing out on and soon joined the Sikh and coolie savagery against the people of Beitang. The British Provost-Marshal, Captain Con, ordered thirty soldiers flogged for looting or worse, and military discipline was restored over the next week, aided by an immobilizing downpour that made rapine and plunder too much work for all but the most committed and concupiscent of the troops.

While mud made most travel impossible, an unimpeded stone causeway stretched from Beitang all the way to Tianjin. On August 3, 1860, a combined force of one thousand British and one thousand French crawled along the stone causeway for four miles, at which point they spotted Tianjin in the distance—and Prince Seng's cavalry blocking the way.

As the allies drew closer, hundreds of Manchus, Chinese, and Mongol cavalry became visible. The numbers of the defenders may have unnerved the allies at first, until they saw the primitive arms of Seng's mounted soldiers: spears, bow and arrows, eighteenth-century flintlocks, and the pratfall-causing gingalls—a veritable Keystone Kavalry. The allies lacked cavalry to fight even such primitive opponents and pulled back. The Chinese leader on the causeway sent a letter to Peking proclaiming a great victory over the invaders. It wasn't until August 12, 1860, that Hope Grant managed to assemble eight hundred cavalry with orders to march around the Chinese blockading the causeway and take them from behind. The main allied force would attack the defenders head on, using three of the new Armstrong guns. When the allies were within a mile of the Chinese, they began firing the Armstrongs, whose exploding shells scattered and tore apart the Chinese cavalry.

But the defenders were fearless. As their comrades on either side of them were blown apart by the Armstrongs, the remaining cavalry continued to approach the invaders until they got to within 450 yards, when the effectiveness of the guns at such close range finally halted the advance after twenty-five minutes of terror. The suicidal valor of the defenders impressed their opponents. Major-General Sir Robert Napier, commander of the Second Division under Hope Grant, wrote, "They bore unflinchingly for a considerable time such a fire as would have tried any troops in the world." The Chinese had been stopped but not turned back. As Sikhs gunned them down with carbines and pistols from a safe distance, the Chinese responded with spears and arrows. Lt. Col. G.J. Wolseley said that he "never saw men come on so pluckily." Although outnumbered, the better-armed Sikhs finally forced the Chinese to flee, but the Punjabis' horses got stuck in the mud, and the terrain prevented what would have been an inevitable bloodbath if the Sikhs had been able to pursue the Chinese cavalry, who fled to the safety of the Dagu Forts.

On August 12, 1860, the same day Grant Hope attacked the Chinese cavalry on the causeway leading to Tianjin, an atrocity that occurred nearby stirred British hearts back home and provided an example of what they were all fighting for—the right not to kowtow. An inebriated Irish sergeant who had helped himself to too much of the rum he was supposed to be delivering to the troops got lost and stumbled on what he thought were friendly Sikhs. They turned out to be Manchu horseman. The cavalrymen captured the sergeant and his party. They ordered the prisoners to kowtow and all complied except a Scottish Private Moyse, who was beheaded on the spot. The drunken sergeant and his men were allowed to return to their camp a week later to tell their tale, which made its way back to London, where *The Times* published a poem to honor the victim who refused to bow to the enemy, although the newspaper got his nationality wrong. "Let dusky Indians whine and kneel,/An English lad must die./And thus with eyes that would not shrink,/With knee to man unbent,/Unfaltering on its dreadful brink,/To his red grave he went." The poet who composed the elegy, Sir Francis Doyle, had been best man at Gladstone's wedding and must have alienated his pacifist friend. Doyle neglected to mention that Private Moyse's courage may have been rum-fueled and his refusal to kowtow was in keeping with his long record of insubordination. On the other hand, his commander, the Irish sergeant, was also under the influence, and that didn't prevent him from saving himself with a bit of strategic self-humiliation.

Two days after the kowtow incident, as the allies continued up the causeway, they came upon the village of Sin-ho and found the defenders had fled. Further along, the Europeans reached the mud-walled cavalry outpost, Danggu, which unlike Sin-ho was defended by Chinese troops, although their leader, Prince Seng, had abandoned the town, leaving behind only his standard. The French General de Montauban wanted to attack the town immediately, but Hope Grant felt that the troops needed a rest and refused. De Montauban decided to attack without British help, but the French were quickly repulsed by fire from forty-five guns atop the mud walls. The setback humiliated de Montauban who had led the assault himself, but it didn't lessen his pursuit of *la gloire*. He came up with a mad plan to attack next all four Dagu Forts at the same time. Hope Grant insisted on singling out one fort, the northernmost and most vulnerable. De Montauban made an equivocal entry in his diary on August 20, 1860, about his collaboration with Hope Grant. "I shall nevertheless send a French land force to work conjointly with our allies. The object of my observations is, above all, to free myself from military responsibility with reference to my own government."

The next day, the allies seized Danggu, which provided a great position from which to attack the Dagu Fort that Hope Grant had singled out and that was less than a mile from Danggu across the Bei He River. Elgin wanted to watch the fighting from atop a temple inside Danggu, but Hope Grant overruled his nominal superior because the guns of the Dagu Fort were within range of the temple that served as Elgin's headquarters. Hope Grant's insubordination probably saved the increasingly depressed Earl. On the other hand, Elgin may have just wanted a press opportunity because he had asked *The Times'* China correspondent to join him at the temple to observe the coming assault on the fort.

At dawn on August 21, 1860, eight French and British gunships began to shell the northern Dagu Fort while Armstrongs and other artillery, dragged through the muddy flats by teams of six horses per gun, got within six hundred feet of the walls and lobbed shells inside. The bombardment quickly knocked out the Chinese guns on the fort walls, and the defenders were reduced to firing gingalls and matchlocks at the thirty-two-pounders of the Europeans. At 6:30 A.M., a lucky shell from an eight-inch gun hit a gunpowder depot inside the fort. Observers said the explosion resembled the force of an earthquake and so rattled the Chinese that within half an hour even the gingalls and matchlocks stopped returning fire. Now only thirty yards from the fort, a French force under General Collineau decided to scale the walls, but there was a moat in their way, so the general forced a detachment of coolies to stand in the moat up to their necks while supporting scaling ladders on their shoulders for the French to climb up, a frightening form of "coolie labor." Hope Grant felt so guilty about the shabby treatment of the coolies that he gave them all an extra month's salary as a bonus.

Once atop the wall, the French launched a bayonet charge that scattered the few remaining defenders. Meanwhile, the British blew a small hole in the fort's wall, and fearless soldiers entered the town single-file, vulnerable to snipers, who fortunately did not materialize. The mandarin from Peking who commanded the fort demonstrated greater bravery than his fleeing subordinates. Cornered, he refused to surrender, so a tired Captain Prynne of the Royal Marines pulled out his revolver and shot the mandarin dead, taking his peacock feather cap as a trophy of war. After a few hours, the fort had been secured. Casualties were atypically large, with the British and the French each losing about two hundred men. Almost two thousand Chinese lay dead, another fifteen hundred having fled. Nine thousand remained and surrendered to General Collineau, kneeling at his feet. Motivated perhaps less by mercy than an inability to guard such a large group of POWs, Collineau freed them on the spot. The Chinese tore off their military insignia and melted back into the civilian population. Hope Grant awarded six Victoria Crosses to celebrate the taking of a Dagu Fort, which had once been a symbol of British military failure and now symbolized a Britannia triumphant.

The fall of the fort had a predictable psychological impact, and within five hours of the surrender, two emissaries from Heng Fu, the Viceroy of Chihli province, turned up at the allied camp to negotiate. They found themselves forced to deal with the irascible Harry Parkes, whose xenophobia was infamous among the Chinese. Heng's spokesmen offered to remove the bamboo booms blocking the Bei He River and allow the allies safe passage to Tianjin, where peace negotiations could resume in earnest.

Earnest being a relative term among the dilatory mandarins, Parkes flew into a rage that may have been more tactical than real, crumpled Feng's letter and threw it in the face of one of the emissaries, a man named Wang, an anglophile who spoke fluent English, which he had learned at the American Mission School at Shanghai, and a previous acquaintance of Parkes. In response to the offer, Parkes screamed that if the other three Dagu Forts did not capitulate within the next two hours, they would suffer the same fate as the fort the allies now held. A European present at the parley commented on Parkes's "harsh and unnecessarily violent demeanour" toward Wang, who after the incident wrote Elgin that violence against a white-flagged emissary "was not customary among European nations" and because of his ambassadorial rank he "ought to be treated with the courtesy common to civilisation." But Parkes's rudeness was more strategic than emotional, and his petty violence had a magical effect on the Chinese's usual evasiveness.

Long before Parkes's two-hour deadline elapsed, white flags popped up on the three remaining forts without a single shot being fired by the allies. Parkes's strategy also benefited from great timing that seemed providential. Shortly after the Chinese surrender, an electrical storm that lasted for days caused the Bei He to overflow and flooded the area around the forts, creating a natural moat and immobilizing the heavy European artillery, all of which would have made a frontal attack on the forts impossible. The Chinese found a face-saving silver lining in the clouds that poured down on them. Providence, not military incompetence and fear, they decided, had caused their rout. Referring to the deluge, a courtier wrote, "You took the forts because the Heavens themselves were against us."

With the causeway to Tianjin now open, on August 23, 1860, Hope Grant and his armada of steam-powered gunships passed unchallenged up to Tianjin, where they enjoyed a bloodless victory because the city had no defenders. The fall of the Dagu Forts and Tianjin at last mobilized the sclerotic Imperial court into action, and a senior mandarin, Guiliang, who had negotiated the Treaty of Tianjin in 1858, got word to Elgin and Gros that the Emperor had given him plenipotentiary powers to make a permanent settlement.

After the Earl and the Baron discussed strategy at their base in Tianjin, they presented new demands harsher than the previous ones. The Chinese would have to make a formal apology for the British slain at the Dagu Forts in 1859, pay double the original reparations of four million taels of silver for expenses incurred by the allied expeditionary forces, and confirm the Treaty of Tianjin, which the Chinese had violated. Tianjin would remain under allied occupation, which would allow the Europeans to control the flow of food from the city to the capital, giving the victors the power to create artificial famine if the Chinese reneged on the new agreement. The Dagu Forts would be held as security until all the other terms were met. The Earl and the Baron also demanded admission to Tongxian, a suburb only fifteen miles away, where the allies planned to bivouac. Their proximity to the capital would further strengthen European leverage on the capital. This demand caused panic in Peking. The last time a foreign army had gotten so close to the seat of power two hundred years earlier, a dynasty had fallen. The Manchus saw their fate in that of the previous Mings.

Finally, the Westerners reiterated their half-century-long obsession, a face-to-face meeting with the Emperor—the kowtow issue wasn't even broached since both sides knew it was dead. On the other hand, the weary allied leaders didn't demand a permanent ambassadorial presence in Peking as they had in the past. Perhaps they feared that this final humiliation would topple the Emperor, and there would be no controlling authority in Peking to comply with the other terms of the treaty. In fact, the mandarins warned Elgin and Gros that this was exactly what would happen.

While Guiliang pondered the demands of the plenipotentiaries, Elgin and Gros massed more and more troops outside Tianjin to pressure him. After their decisive victory at the Dagu Forts and the investment of Tianjin, Gros and Elgin believed that peace would break out at any moment. General de Montauban designed commemorative scarves for the French soldiers to wear in their inevitable parade through the streets of Peking.

Although Guiliang had carte blanche from the Emperor, the mandarin found the Europeans' terms so unacceptable he resorted to the old ruse that he did not have plenipotentiary powers, which contradicted his original position. Elgin recognized the stalling tactic because he had encountered it so often in the past, but now felt the Chinese had out-strategized themselves by this self-defeating gambit. "The blockheads have gone on negotiating with me just long enough to enable [Hope] Grant to bring all his army up to this point. Here we are with our base established in the heart of the country, in a capital climate, with abundance [food] around us, our army in excellent health, and these stupid people give me a snub which obliges me to break with them," Elgin wrote in his diary on September 8, 1860.

The diplomat refused to negotiate any further, and the next day he cajoled Gros, who wanted to remain in the safety of Tianjin, into accompanying him and the troops up the Bei He and on to Peking. The closer the allies got to the sacred city, the more amenable the Chinese court became. Elgin and Gros were flooded with letters from senior courtiers explaining that Guiliang had been "confused." All the terms Guiliang had mistakenly rejected were now acceptable to the Emperor...if only the troops would stop their advance on his capital. The hysteria of these pleas increased as the distance between the two antagonists decreased. Couriers begged the ambassadors to return to Tianjin, whither senior Chinese officials were going now. Elgin was fed up with the Chinese's delays and told them he would not stop until he reached the Peking suburb of Tongxian, just outside the capital. The mandarins made a counteroffer, suggesting Elgin stop at Hesewu, midway between Tianjin and Peking. Hope Grant preferred that option because he was having trouble supplying his troops, and a delay would give them time to refurbish and refresh. But Elgin worried about the grumbling of the men, who blamed him for the current delay. Even so, their complaints did not impress the Earl, who wrote in his diary what he suspected was the real reason for Hope Grant's request to resupply. *"Entre nous,"* he wrote, "the difficulty of getting our army along is incredible; our men are so pampered that they do nothing for themselves and their necessities so great that we are almost immovable." Elgin noted with disgust that the soldiers refused to drink their daily ration of grog unless it was iced.

On September 14, 1860, the Earl sent the interpreter Thomas Wade and Parkes to negotiate with two mandarins, Cai and Muyin, at Tongxian. The sincerity and gravity of the Emperor's intentions were underlined by the fact that Cai, the Prince of Yi, was his cousin, and Muyin was the President of the Board of War. Wade's characterization of the Imperial emissaries hints at the racial divide and contempt that poisoned both military and diplomatic relations between the Europeans and Chinese. Cai, Wade later wrote, was a "tall dignified man with an intelligent countenance, though a somewhat unpleasant eye." Muyin looked "softer and more wily in his manner, but also intelligent." The Chinese continued to remain, in Western eyes, the eternal unknown, the inscrutable automaton with an "unpleasant" (read slanted) eye. After only eight hours of negotiations on September 14, Parkes persuaded Cai and Muyin to accept the allies' terms.

Meanwhile, in Peking, the Emperor vacillated between a fight-or-flight response, although inclined toward the latter. His *generalissimo*, Prince Seng, shared his ruler's inclinations and felt discretion was better than valor. Seng urged the Emperor to go on a hunting expedition near the northern border and far from the capital—hunting in the middle of a crisis that could topple the two hundred–year-old Manchu Dynasty! Seng did not want the Emperor taken hostage, although some courtiers suspected Seng's real motive was to place himself on the Emperor's abandoned throne. The Emperor's concubine-turned-consort, Cixi, however, displayed more courage than her husband and urged him to remain in the capital. His courtiers summoned the courage to rebuke the Emperor with an abruptness and abandonment of protocol that revealed how far respect for the crown had fallen. One advisor scolded the Emperor, "Taking up a post to the north [the hunting trip] would be a deviation from the seat of war, and accordingly that what in name was campaigning was in reality a hunting tour." Another mandarin was even more blunt. "In what light does Your Majesty regard your people? In what light the shrines of your ancestors or the altars of the tutelary gods? Will you cast away the inheritance of your ancestors like a damaged shoe? What would history say of Your Majesty for a thousand generations to come?"

Before the series of military defeats, such bluntness would have sent the courtier into exile or to the headsman's sword. Instead, the Emperor responded with equivocation. His own cowardly suggestion pleased no one. He proposed to march out of the capital at the head of a huge army, make a feint at the European troops, then flee to the safety of his hunting lodge at Rehe in Tartary one hundred miles away near the northern edge of the Great Wall. Rehe held an ironic significance that showed how far the fortunes of the Manchus had fallen. At the same lodge in 1793, Lord Macartney had met the Quianlong Emperor, who had still had the authority and dignity to insist on the kowtow from "tribute-bearing barbarians." Seven decades later, it would be the Emperor who would approach the foreigners with "fear and trembling."

The appeal of courtiers and consort to honor history no doubt shamed and frightened the Xianfeng Emperor. Everyone still remembered the fate of the last Emperor of the previous Ming Dynasty, who two centuries earlier had hanged himself in his palace courtyard upon learning that another band of barbarians were about to descend on Peking. And now the barbarians were at the gates once again. Would Xianfeng accept the same fate?

Chapter 24

A HOSTAGE CRISIS

———•••———

*"You have gained two victories to our one. Twice you have dared
to take the [Dagu] forts. Why does not that content you? I know your
name, and that you instigate all the evil that your people commit.
It is time that foreigners should be taught respect."*

—Prince Seng to his prisoner, Sir Harry Parkes

Terror galvanized the Chinese negotiators at Tongxian into action. After
a single day of haggling with Wade and Parkes, the Imperial emissaries gave the allies everything they had sought since the first war in 1839,
and more. Tongxian was approved as the site for quartering the allied
troops, and Elgin and Gros were granted permission to enter the capital
with two thousand men-at-arms to finalize the Treaty of Tianjin there.
Allied advisors warned the plenipotentiaries that such a small armed escort
would be suicidal and feared a trap followed by slaughter. But by now,
Elgin and Gros felt so assured of success, they considered the two
thousand–man retinue an honor guard rather than bodyguards. The European ambassadors understood psychology, in particular the Chinese's current mind-set, which they believed had by now been so demoralized by the
string of military successes and diplomatic concessions that the Imperial
court was too immobilized by terror to countenance such dangerous
treachery. Even so, despite their lack of bargaining power, the mandarins
continued to balk at the minor concession of Elgin's wish to present a
letter from the Queen to the Emperor.

Harry Parkes returned to Tongxian on September 17, 1860, to finalize
an agreement he had reached four days earlier with Cai and Muyin. Parkes
was accompanied by a bodyguard of twenty-six dragoons and Sikhs, whose
turbans, beards, and reputation for random atrocities terrified the Chinese.

With the savvy of a modern-day publicist, Elgin asked Thomas Bowlby, *The Times of London's* China correspondent, to accompany Parkes to record the agreement for posterity, political capital, and free publicity back home.

But there was no finalization of the terms this day. For reasons unknown, the once pliable Cai and Mu refused Elgin's request to deliver Queen Victoria's letter to the Emperor. Parkes had a change of mind or temperament too and agreed to table the issue for a future date. After an entire day of bickering, Parkes did get the courtiers to agree to let the allied arms bivouac at a camping ground just three miles outside Tongxian called Zhengjiawan. On September 18, 1860, as Parkes rode to Tianjin to confer with Elgin, he noticed Prince Seng's cavalry massing behind rows of corn. The cavalry occupied Zhengjiawan, the site promised the Europeans for lodging their troops.

Parkes suspected a trap was being set for the army before it could decamp at Zhengjiawan. More likely, the cavalry had been put in place to provide a psychological if impotent buffer between the barbarians and the capital. Parkes sent Henry Loch, Lord Elgin's private secretary, post-haste to his boss with the news of the Chinese military maneuvers. Despite the danger, Parkes, accompanied by only two soldiers (he made sure one was a reliably intimidating Sikh), returned to Tongxian to confront the duplicitous Cai and Mu.

As it turned out, Loch's mission to warn Elgin was unnecessary. When Loch met Hope Grant in Tianjin, he learned that the General had already spied the covert military operations of the Chinese cavalry and had ordered his troops to halt their advance on Tongxian and dig in. Evincing incredible courage that bordered on suicidal, Loch then returned to Tongxian to consult with Parkes accompanied by only one bodyguard. Chinese troops began to fire on Loch and his escort, halting their progress. When Loch and Parkes arrived in Tongxian, a mandarin suggested a meeting with Prince Seng himself and offered the two men safe conduct. They agreed, but this time their courage seemed more like folly because when they were admitted to the Prince's presence, he had them immediately arrested. Seng's boldness would turn out to be self- and nation-defeating, a combination of folly, cruelty, and—morality aside—just plain, bad strategy.

At this juncture, the resolute Hope Grant hesitated. Parkes and Loch were hostages in Tianjin, and the general feared an attack would cost the negotiators their lives. But after pressure from the French, Grant gave the order to attack at midday, September 18, 1860. First, however, one last attempt at diplomacy was made. Interpreter Wade with a mounted escort that was more symbolic than effective vis á vis Seng's twenty thousand troops, who had created a three-mile wide human barrier between Tongxian and the allied forces, approached Seng's camp under a white flag of truce and with new demands. If Seng did not free the hostages at once, the allies would march on Peking. It was a sincere but innocuous threat because the Europeans had only thirty-five hundred men to hurl at Seng's twenty thousand.

Blonde, blue-eyed, relentlessly middle-class, Harry Parkes remained fearless as he confronted royalty in the form of the acne-plagued, short, fat Prince Seng. At this surreal juncture, the century-old issue of the kowtow raised its hoary head. Despite his nonexistent bargaining power, Parkes rejected the kowtow, and for his defiance had his head smashed into the marble floor multiple times. Parkes was the last European to kowtow to the Chinese, and it was an involuntary bow. While soldiers kept Parkes pinned to the floor, he had to listen to a paranoid harangue from Seng, who took out all his impotent rage at the powerless envoy. "You have gained two victories to our one. Twice you have dared to take the [Dagu] forts. Why does not that content you? I know your name, and that you instigate all the evil that your people commit. It is time that foreigners should be taught respect."

The intrepid Parkes managed to free his head so he could look up at his captor as he shot back that he had come to Seng under a flag of truce and promise of safe conduct "by express agreement with the Imperial Commissioners," which was now being so violently reneged on. Seng laughed and nodded to a henchman, who slammed Parkes's head back on to the floor. Apparently believing vinegar a more effective douceur than honey, Seng shouted, "Write to your people and tell them to stop the attack." For all his bluster, Seng had been thoroughly discombobulated by the small army of allies near Tongxian. Parkes offered his tormentor no consolation or reprieve and said, "I cannot control or influence military movement in any way. I will not deceive Your Highness."

Suddenly, the sound of allied artillery fire invaded the palace, undercutting Seng's bluster and sending him scurrying to the front. Parkes,

Loch, and their Sikh escorts were dumped in a springless garbage cart that must have seemed like a Jacobin tumbril because of its destination, the Board of Punishments, a place of execution. The captives' agony was increased by the fact that their hands and feet were bound with leather straps, and they couldn't stop themselves from crashing into the sides of the cart. It was a nightmare version of the American ambassador William Reed's recent transportation humiliation.

The treatment of other British, French, and Sikhs snared by Seng's cavalry outside Tongxian had been was much worse than the psychological intimidation and head-banging endured by Parkes. The prisoners' hands were secured with leather straps that were moistened so they would shrink and cut into the victims' wrists. Some of the POWs were sent to the Summer Palace for private inspection and public humiliation by the Emperor, whom Seng hoped would be emboldened by the powerlessness of this handful of his persecutors and remove the aura of invincibility that had enveloped the allies in the Chinese mind because of their quick and easy victories. The prisoners were forced to kneel in the palace courtyard, still bound and without food or water, for three days. Their hands swelled, then became gangrenous. Disease and dehydration led to fatalities, and Elgin's unfortunate publicist, *The Times'* Bowlby, found that he had become part of the story he had been assigned to cover by dying after four days in captivity. (Bowlby was seized while shopping in Tongxian, presuming the same flag of truce that was supposed to protect Parkes would do the same for him. He was tragically optimistic.) Seng was not only a barbarian; he was ignorant of the toxic power of bad press. When it trickled back to London, the British press would eviscerate Seng and the Emperor for killing one of their own.

At the Board of Punishments, Loch and Parkes were put in separate cells. Loch tried to signal his whereabouts to his colleague by singing "God Save the Queen." Loch later wrote a book about his one-week incarceration that displayed a remarkable stoicism. He wrote that the food was awful but not starvation rations. His only fear was that the ropes that bound him would cause an infection and a food trough for the maggots that infested his cell.

Parkes's nightmare worsened with each successive day of imprisonment. Immobilized by heavy shackles, he shared his cell with seventy common

Chinese criminals, soiled with their own feces and near death from a starvation diet that the captured Europeans would share. Loch seemed to be the only one who found their diet adequate.

The weight of a prisoner's chains represented the seriousness of the charge against him. Parkes was labeled a "rebel," and so had the heaviest chains. Thieves and murderers who shared his cell wore less chains because their crimes were considered less serious than Parkes's "treason." Despite the bad company, Parkes was surprised to receive kind and respectful treatment from these common criminals. "Instead of following the example set by the authorities and treating me with abuse and ridicule, they were seldom disrespectful, addressed me by my title, and often avoided putting me to inconvenience when it was in their power to do so," he wrote in a report to Elgin.

Parkes endured a series of interrogations. The first one took place at midnight, and the questions alternated with relatively petty physical abuse, although his examiners also threatened him with torture. At one point, they announced he was about to be beheaded. He knelt before his inquisitors, still burdened with chains. When his tormentors did not find his answers satisfactory, they dragged him around the room by the hair and ears.

On September 22, 1860, Parkes was removed from the cell he had shared with friendly felons and lodged alone in another cell. During his next interrogation, the mandarin who questioned him did not order him to his knees. Parkes suspected some of the Chinese officials feared retribution by the allies for their mistreatment of European prisoners, and had begun to let up the rigors of their captivity. The mandarin soon revealed the reason for Parkes's improved treatment. He asked Parkes to write Elgin a letter seeking better terms. Parkes seized this tiny window of opportunity and agreed, but only if he and Loch were freed from prison.

In preparation for the inevitable final clash, Prince Seng began to dig in. For a change, the Chinese had a lot of firepower—seventy guns in all. Seng's three-mile wide force of cavalry at Zhangjiawan served as an effective roadblock against an allied assault on the capital. Arrayed against Seng's twenty thousand was a one thousand–man force of French and twenty-five hundred British. As ever, the numerical mismatch between the two sides was illusory. The allies had state-of-the art artillery and rifles, and the troops had the benefit of a commander-in-chief who commanded their loyalty. They followed his orders with strict discipline. Seng's cavalry was six times bigger than the allied force of foot soldiers and horsemen, but as usual it was a case of different centuries fighting one another. Chinese strategy focused on the use of bow and arrows by mounted men. The Chinese had only a handful of antiquated firelock muskets against the British modern Enfield rifle. Seng's strategy of encircling the enemy, then going in for the kill was also based on medieval tactics and had the serious flaw that encirclement stretched Seng's lines and made them easier for the enemy to penetrate.

As the Chinese spread out, the allies took advantage of the enemy's weakened position. De Montauban, who had borrowed a squadron of Sikh and Spahi (Arab horsemen) from the British, attacked Seng's left flank, while French infantry assaulted the town of Zhangjiawan. Seng's Mongol horsemen on their miniature ponies were no match in firepower or size for the Sikhs and Spahis and their huge mounts and superior personal weaponry. De Montauban's cavalry began to penetrate the Chinese troops, who fired on them with gingalls and firelock rifles, while the French devastated the enemy with the accuracy of the Armstrong field pieces. The Armstrongs caused panic among the Chinese cavalry, who began to retreat in disorder away from Zhangjiawan and toward the dubious safety of a nearby river. The merciless Sikhs and Spahis chased after the enemy, bayoneting stragglers. Despite the carnage of artillery and bayonet, Seng lost only fifteen hundred men during the battle, but the allies' casualties of thirty-five made the Chinese loss seem huge by comparison and more dramatic than the numbers suggested.

The conscientious Elgin had other things on his mind besides this pivotal allied victory and worried about the inevitable aftermath of such a triumph. In his journal entry for September 17, 1860, he wrote, "I rode out very early this morning, to see my general before he started, and to give him a hint about the looting which has been very bad here. He disapproves of it as much as I do." Elgin overestimated "his" general's sensitivity to the issue, which in fact did not exist, because the following day, Hope Grant allowed his troops to sack Zhangjiawan. The General considered the rapine reparations rather than revenge or thievery, and "reparations" were a great motivator for the troops, a reward for success.

The army's interpreter, Robert Swinhoe, expressed the consensus about plundering shared by everyone except, it seemed, the fastidious Elgin. In his memoirs, Swinhoe wrote with approval, "No steps were taken to prevent looting, as the town was a capture in war, and hence lawful booty." The looters combined wanton destruction with a certain connoisseurship for *objets d'art*, as long as they were also portable. Eyewitness Swinhoe reported, "A rare old house, with its exquisite carving and hangings, and its rooms filled with curiosities too big to carry away, was completely ransacked. Our people were in this case the destroyers."

Tea was also portable; one British officer seized five hundred thousand pounds of tea leaves and sent them for "safekeeping" to Tianjin. Veterans of the frigid Crimean campaign expropriated every fur coat they could lay their hands on, while other allied soldiers traded their loot for cash provided by Chinese pawnbrokers who had no problem dealing with an enemy that was annihilating their town.

The women of Zhangjiawan feared rape despite the track record of the Europeans, who for the most part were more interested in booty than bodies. Soldiers came upon a ghastly scene at one opium den filled with women ranging in age from toddlers to late middle age. Most of the women had committed suicide by overdosing on opium, but heavy users had developed such a tolerance to the drug that their deaths took longer and were still alive when the Europeans found them. Swinhoe recalled, "The more conscious of them, beating their breasts, condemned the opium for its slow work, crying out, 'Let us die; we do not wish to live.'" Their dying wish was refused. A British chaplain sent for an army surgeon who pumped the victims' stomachs with such success that only one of the victims still alive when the troops arrived perished.

The complacent Gros began to share Elgin's angst about the looting. He communicated his concerns to the French Foreign Minister: "*J'ai le coeur serré par les actes de vandalisme que j'ai vu commis par nos soldats, comme par nos alliés, charmés de pouvoir rejeter mutuellement les uns sur les autres les actes abominable dont ils se rendaient coupables.*" (I was heartbroken by the acts of vandalism that I saw committed by our soldiers as well as by those of our allies, each delighted at the chance of heaping upon the other the blame for abominable deeds for which all deserved punishment.)"

Punishment did not deter determined pillagers. On September 21, 1860, after fierce bayonet fighting, the allies took Tongxian in a flanking movement, spearheaded by the French, against Chinese artillery to secure the bridge of Baliqiao, which spanned a canal connecting Tongxian to the capital. The commander of the Chinese, General Bao, sent word to the French that two of their captured colleagues, a French cleric named Abbé Duluc and the British Captain Brabazon of the Royal Artillery, would be executed if the attack continued. With none of Elgin's tender conscience and fretful obsession over the fate of the British hostages Loch and Parkes, de Montauban pressed the attack until the Chinese defenders leapt to their death in the canal (the nonsuicidal were bayoneted by the French). Bao, unlike Heng and Gong previously, made good on his threat, and Father Duluc and Captain Brabazon were murdered and dumped in the canal. The final body count again reflected the Sino-European mismatch: three French dead, two thousand Chinese.

The near bloodless triumph prompted Napoleon III to ennoble de Montauban, who chose his place of victory for his new aristocratic title, Comte de Palikao, joining the list of name-place conquerors from B.C. Rome's Scipio Africanus, Germanicus, to the Duke of Marlborough's palace named after his victory at Blenheim in Belgium. De Montauban found a giant marble tortoise near the bridge and ordered it returned to Paris to symbolize his victory, but the sculpture weighed twenty tons, and, unlike the Parthenon friezes, remained in its native land.

A mile closer to Peking on another bridge over the canal, General Hope Grant did not enjoy his French counterpart's easy victory at Baliqiao. Hope Grant thought a horde of Mongol horsemen in the distance were French soldiers and didn't open fire on the enemy. The Mongols mistook Hope Grant's forbearance for cowardice and charged. As the cavalry drew near, the British realized who they were and at close range blew the Mongols to pieces with field guns, including the deadly accurate Armstrongs.

Tongxian surrendered without a fight, but it still suffered the same fate as Zhangjiawan. Two members of a gang of coolies in the employ of the British were killed by merchants while the coolies tried to plunder a shop. The merchants captured the remainder of the coolies and turned them over to the British, who had the looters flogged—a rare punishment for a common crime in the war. With a newfound conscience after allowing the original sack of Zhangjiawan, General Hope Grant had three rapists—coolies again—flogged with one hundred strokes by a cat-o-nine-tails, then hanged one of them. The viciousness of the coolies could be explained by the fact that they had been recruited from Hong Kong's criminal class, but the disciplined Sikhs behaved even worse and specialized in rape.

The British and French blamed one another for their rampaging soldiers, when in fact both parties were equally guilty, although the British preferred to destroy while the French tended to protect their newly acquired property: vandals vs. connoisseurs. Lord Elgin had a practical reason for opposing looting because it antagonized the locals and made it harder to control them. He laid the blame on the French in his diary: "The French by their exactions and misconduct have already stirred to resistance the peaceful population. They [the French] are cautious enough when armed enemies, even Chinese, are in question, but indisputably valorous against defenceless villages and little-footed women." A Frenchmen said after the plunder of Beitang, "*Quant aux anglais, ce sont nos maîtres: on ne trouve pas un clou où ils ont passé.*" ("As for the English, they are our superiors [when it comes to looting]. You can't find a nail where they have passed.")

Prince Seng panicked after the only two obstacles to the capital, Tongxian and Zhangjiawan, fell. With what was left of his decimated army, he fled the capital, but remained a minor threat to the allies after he made camp outside the northwest corner of the city walls. With the capture of the two bridges across the canal between Tongxian and Peking, the way to the capital now lay open—Peking's only remaining defense its thick walls, sloping, forty feet high and sixty feet thick, bristling with towers that housed defenders armed with antique guns, spears, and bow and arrows. Sikh horsemen reconnoitered, reporting inaccurately that there were no Chinese troops defending the city. The reconnaissance failed to encourage Hope Grant, who feared that his artillery were insufficient to breach the walls of the city, especially if the citizens of Peking put up the same vigorous resistance that had humiliated the allies at Dagu. Despite pressure from both Elgin and Gros, who feared the hostages inside the city would be massacred if they delayed, Hope Grant refused to budge until heavy siege guns were shipped upriver from Tianjin.

Elgin and Gros's fears about the fate of the prisoners were not unfounded. By now, they were dealing with the very top of the Imperial administration in the person of Prince Gong, aged twenty-eight, the Emperor's younger and more capable sibling. Despite their fears, however, the European ambassadors refused to negotiate with Gong until after the prisoners were set free. They allowed Gong the face-saving gesture of blaming the hostage taking on his subordinates, but Gong was not moved and made a counteroffer: withdraw from Peking and the prisoners would be released. Gong also implied that the hostages would be beheaded in public the moment the assault on Peking began.

Chapter 25

"I AM NOT A THIEF"

———

"Don't commit sacrilege! Don't come within the sacred precincts!"

—Imperial Court eunuchs as they tried to
prevent the sacking of the Summer Palace

On October 5 and 6, 1860, the heavy artillery needed to blast a hole in Peking's forbidding walls arrived from Tianjin. By now, the Emperor had fled to Rehe, leaving Prince Gong in charge with orders to dig in and fight. Gong's position was made more equivocal by the fact that large portions of the Emperor's army had run after him to the safety of the far north. On the 5th, Heng told his captives, Parkes and Loch, that what was left of the Imperial Court had decided to reject the allies' demands. The prisoners were told their execution would take place the next morning. Parkes was given a cameo of his wife, which had been taken from him by his captors, and both prisoners received paper to pen their last will and testament. But by now, the captives had become too important a political pawn to be wasted on a retaliatory execution, since their survival might help their captors survive the coming victory of the allies. When in the early morning of October 7, 1860, the prisoners heard the sound of gunfire, they presumed the bombardment of the city had begun, heralding their deaths, but they were mistaken. The British were firing their guns in the air to let the French know their position. The men were spared.

On October 6, 1860, the French and British agreed to march around the city from opposite directions and meet at the Summer Palace just outside the walls. The two armies soon lost contact with each other. Hope Grant felt that the French had purposely severed connections with the

British in order to enjoy the spoils of the Summer Palace alone. And indeed, in the afternoon of the day the two armies separated, the French reached the Summer Palace first, only to learn that its Imperial occupant had fled to Rehe two weeks before with thirteen wives—a fraction of his harem.

Expecting the Emperor's personal guard to defend the Summer Palace to the death, the French were surprised to find that the guards had also fled. But the invaders endured a tragicomic "attack" by the Emperor's only remaining champions, five hundred unarmed eunuchs of the court. The castrated courtiers screamed in shrill falsetto as they charged the French, "Don't commit sacrilege! Don't come within the sacred precincts!" The French remained unmoved by the pitiful state of the unarmed men and shot about twenty of them on the spot. The remainder fled, shouting curses and warnings about divine and earthly retribution.

———·—·———

For the moment, it was fortunate that French "connoisseurs" instead of British vandals had invested the palace, a real-life Xanadu of sybaritic living and priceless artifacts of antiquity. "Summer Palace" was actually a misnomer; a more accurate term would have been Summer Palaces, since the Emperor's suburban getaway was a complex of two hundred main buildings set, jewel-like, in an eighty-square-mile park dotted with vermilion tents, artificial lakes, and gardens that would have made Louis Quatorze's landscape architect weep with envy. The interiors boasted an eclectic historicism, including a Baroque audience chamber designed by Jesuit missionaries in the seventeenth century, and two Baroque palaces with gold roofs also designed by the Jesuit priests.

The current Emperor spent entire days on the lakes staging mock naval battles with miniature boats representing the Chinese and British. Although in reality the British had sea superiority, in these comforting battles the Emperor's fleet always won.

The Summer Palace was not only an architectural jewel and national treasure, it was a storehouse of centuries of tribute the Emperor had received from barbarians, who were now at his gates with the obvious intention of "reclaiming" some of this tribute. The palace libraries contained unique volumes that would be lost to posterity.

De Montauban realized what an historical treasure now lay in his possession, and he tried to preserve the place by telling his senior staff that "he counted on their honor to respect the palace and see that it was respected by others...until the English arrived." But the temptation created by the priceless artifacts, which lay littered across palace floors, proved an irresistible temptation to the French. De Montauban's orders that the treasures of the Summer Palace were to remain untouched broke down within twenty-four hours as the French soldiers could not resist helping themselves to an Ali Baba's worth of lucre and loot. Unfortunately in their haste and greed, the soldiers abandoned their previous conservational ways and destroyed the precious interiors as they ripped jewels and entire marble walls off to make the treasures portable.

De Montauban was condemned by the novelist and political gadfly, Victor Hugo, for destroying a nation's cultural and artistic legacy. Others shared the author's opinion. In 1874, de Montauban found himself before a government committee set up to investigate the looting. The general lied when he told his examiners that French soldiers under his command had not participated in the looting. "I had sentries posted, and directed two officers with two companies of marine infantry to protect the palace from depredation and to allow nothing to be moved until the arrival of the English commanders. Thus there would be no pillage. Nothing had been touched in the Palace when the English arrived."

Hope Grant contradicted de Montauban's testimony with his eyewitness account of the French "depredations" already evident when an advance detachment of King's Dragoons Guards arrived at the Summer Palace at 2 P.M. on October 7, 1860. Years later, Grant testified to the extent of the French avarice. "It was pitiful to see the way in which everything was being robbed. Only one room in the Palace was untouched. General de Montauban informed me he had reserved any valuables it might contain for equal division between the English and French." Another officer present gave a slightly different account of de Montauban's offer, where the Frenchman said to his British counterpart, "See here. I have had a few of the most brilliant things selected, to be divided between the Queen of Great Britain and the Emperor of the French."

Grant's criticism of de Montauban's inability to control his troops turned out to be ironic because the British General also found his men unable to resist the fabled wealth that surrounded them. Despite orders from Grant similar to de Montauban's, the British found the cornucopia irresistible and joined in the melee of acquisition and destruction, a rare break in the usual *esprit de corps* of the British officer class. Indeed, the British officers initiated the destructive aspect of the occupiers by shooting their pistols at two hundred–year-old mirrors. The French had more practical things to do at this opportunity of a lifetime. Jewels lay scattered all over the Imperial residence. One French officer snatched a pearl necklace whose gems were the size of marbles and sold it in Hong Kong for £3,000. De Montauban realized he was fighting against the implacable force of greed and acquisitiveness, so he relented and allowed his men to take home as "souvenirs" a single prize per soldier. But again, these orders were impossible to enforce, and when the French left the palace around 10 P.M. to return to their camp outside the city walls, their pockets bulged with stolen treasure. The lucky winners were an advertisement to their comrades of the riches they could also acquire, and soon the word was out that the Palace was easy pickings.

Although de Montauban had left two companies of marines to prevent further looting, as news about what the marines were protecting spread, a mob of three thousand French soldiers pushed their way through the marine guard and began an orgy of acquisition that lasted twenty-four hours.

When British infantry arrived on October 7, 1860, they saw the French tents piled high with jewels and other plunder, and their occupants casually wearing jewels worth millions of francs. A British chaplain said the tents were "a perfect blaze of silk and embroidery." Discipline deteriorated to such an extent that the next morning at reveille outside the palace, only 10 percent of the British soldiers showed up, because the majority were inside helping themselves to antiquities. Hope Grant conceded defeat—at the hands of his own rampaging men. Swinhoe said, "The General now made no objection to looting...no pass was required, the place was open to the ravages of one and all." The Summer Palace hosted the most luxe gameshow of all time, and every soldier was a lucky winner. The intoxication of instant wealth percolated all the way to the top of the British command. On October 8, 1860, Hope Grant demanded that de Montauban split the gold bars that had been found in the palace with the British troops.

Restoring some discipline, Hope Grant also ordered his men to surrender their prizes, which were sold at public auction. The money did not go to charity. Swinhoe wrote in his journal, "To make matters more equal for those whose duties prevented them from sharing in the work of spoliation, [Hope Grant] issued orders to call in all the loot acquired by the officers, appealing to their honour as officers and gentlemen to restore faithfully all they had taken. This measure, of course, caused great grumbling." An inkling of the huge amount of wealth looted comes from the tale of one British major who turned in £8,000 worth of gold ingots. Technically, these spoils of war belonged to the Queen and the unapproved auction could have destroyed the general's career, but Victoria herself later intervened on his part.

The auction began on October 11, 1860 under the gavels of two noncommissioned officers in the courtyard of the temple requisitioned as British HQ. The auction "catalogue" listed a cornucopia of Chinese art and artifact, sculptures of gold and silver, and thousands of bolts of silk in the Imperial Yellow, a color worn only by the Emperor. The three-day auction netted nearly £100,000, with one-third of the proceeds going to the officers, the other two-third to the NCOs. A private received £17, an officer £50. Most of the non-coms blew their share on grog.

The French let their men keep what they had stolen. It was rumored that Baron Rothschild had an outstanding order with one French officer to buy anything he could at whatever price. The British soldiers also bought looted valuables from the French because the former received additional pay for their onerous duty in China, while the French were cash strapped. "You had only to ask the first French soldier you met if he had anything for sale, and he would soon produce gold watches, strings of jewels, jade ornaments or furs," one British officer wrote. The treasures were priceless, however, and the British auction's proceeds of £100,000 represented only a fraction of the consignment's inestimable worth—not to mention a firesale-priced bonanza for the lucky buyers at the auction. The wealth of the Summer Palace metastasized into a Chinese Parthenon, but instead of ending up in a gallery of the public British Museum, many objects from the palace remain to this day adorning private stately homes of Britain—stolen interior decor. De Montauban tried to mollify the conscience-stricken Hope Grant by offering half of a pair of gold and jade scepters as a gift for Queen Victoria, the other half going to Napoleon III.

The French did not share Hope Grant's hand-wringing, but they did have a transportation problem. Although the allied armies arrived outside Peking with no baggage carts, the French managed to commandeer three hundred local carriages, which left the Summer Palace overflowing with treasures. The plunderers could not believe their good luck. A French officer described this Chinese Xanadu in a letter home to his father, with a rapture that bordered on orgasmic. "*Je prends la plume, mon bon père, mais sais-je que je vais te dire? Je suis ébahi, ahuri, abasourdi de ce qu'j'ai' vu. Les mille et une nuits sont pour moi une chose parfaitement veridique maintenant. J'ai marché pendant presque deux jours sur plus de 30 millions de francs de soieries, de bijous, de porcelaines, bronzes, sculptures, de trésors enfin! Je ne crois pas qu'on ait vu chose pareille depuis le sac de Rom par les barbares.* (I have my pen in hand, dear father, but I don't know what to say. I am astonished, rapturous, swooning from what I have seen. The 1,001 [Arabian] Nights now seem perfectly real to me. For almost the past two days, I have strolled among thirty million francs' worth of silks, jewels, porcelain, bronzes, sculptures, an infinity of treasure! I don't believe that anyone has seen anything like this since the sack of Rome by the barbarians," the officer added with no sense of irony over his and his comrades' barbaric behavior.)

The accumulated wealth became an obsessive topic of conversation among the French and British, much like today's cocktail party chatter over killings made in real estate and, until recently, the dot-com lode. Everyone, it seemed, had a not-so-tall tale about his sudden good fortune that was more truth than exaggeration or fabrication. "Nothing was talked of but curiosities purloined from the Summer Palace, and what they were likely to fetch," Swinhoe recalled. Author Jack Beeching wryly notes, "At this historic juncture the armies of Queen and Emperor [Napoleon] appear to have been thoroughly impregnated with the spirit of Free Trade." Adam Smith's invisible hand allowed the looters to take what they liked in a vicious parody of laissez-faire. Widely divergent political and social philosophies nevertheless united to justify the pillage of the palace.

The newly minted Comte de Palikao (Montauban) knew enough to feed the hand that ennobled him. On his return to Paris, he gave the Empress Eugénie a pearl necklace valued at £72,000 and a diamond necklace worth

£90,000 to an Imperial relative. Hope Grant refused his share of the loot, but made an exception when his men offered him a solid gold water pitcher used in the Emperor's ritual hand-washing, although Hope Grant used the vessel as a wine decanter.

Not everyone was seduced and corrupted by the wealth of China. A French Huguenot army chaplain decried the Emperor's pornography collection, which was snatched up with almost as much eagerness as the baubles and fabrics. A British interpreter salvaged half a dozen wagonloads of books from the Imperial library just before it was torched, and sent the volumes to that repository of foreign plunder, the British Museum.

When Lord Elgin arrived outside the gates of Peking on October 7, 1860, he was horrified not by the looting of the Summer Palace, but by the destruction of *objets d'art* in the process. Growing up the son of a bankrupt peer widely considered the vandal, not conservator, of the Parthenon, Elgin had an aesthetic inferiority complex. Watching the precious stones and sculptures, etc., ripped from their settings must have seemed like déjà vu all over again for the son of the pillager of the Parthenon. Reading the plaintive entry in his diary, "I am not a thief," one cannot help but sense the filial reproach dripping along with the words from Elgin's pen.

Chapter 26

RESCUE AND RETALIATION

"It is no uncommon thing for the Chinese to deal cruelly with their prisoners, or even to take their lives."

—Sir Harry Parkes commiserating
with one of his Chinese jailers

W hile the Europeans gorged on a feast of jewels and textiles, a drama of quite a different sort was going on in another part of Peking. On September 26, 1860, and again on October 8, Heng Chi, an Imperial Commissioner assigned to treat with the invaders, visited Loch and Parkes after trying to negotiate the prisoners' fate with the interpreter Wade, in a bizarre manner straight out of the New Testament. Wade waited for Heng just outside the city walls, but the Chinese soldiers guarding the city refused to let Heng pass through the gates to confer with the interpreter because they feared Heng would defect to Rehe, where most of the Imperial Court now resided with their Emperor two hundred miles away. So Heng had himself lowered, St. Paul-like, in a basket outside the locked city gates. The negotiations proved so fruitless that when Heng returned to his prisoners he neglected to inform them of the meeting. Instead, he nervously engaged in a surreal debate with Loch and Parkes over whether the sun or the Earth was the center of the universe—an unlikely topic, because the Western-educated Heng must have known that Galileo and Copernicus had settled this argument some four hundred years prior.

Despite the strained atmosphere and their brutal confinement, the prisoners almost enjoyed Heng's company. Parkes and the Imperial Commissioner had a long history together, dating back to the days when Heng had been a member of the Cohong in Canton and had been briefly imprisoned under gentler circumstances by Canton's Consul Parkes. Heng now returned the favor by treating the prisoners with respect and blandishments that alternated with threats. Heng claimed that the Emperor had a secret army of hundreds of thousands of men in Mongolia (a bluff). As a former Hong merchant, Heng lamented the disastrous financial consequences of continuing the war. "Suppose all is lost. The dismemberment of the Empire will follow, and all trade will be at an end," the Commissioner told his prisoners. The man who controlled China's army, however, felt foreigners were an impediment not a boon to the Chinese economy, and did not share Heng's concern about trade between Britain and China. Prince Seng had argued to the Emperor, "Though the Imperial Treasury might receive four million taels in Customs duty from foreigners annually, this income was almost completely wiped out by the $21 million indemnity of 1842, the six million taels claimed in 1858 and the extra indemnity of 10 million taels recently demanded."

Heng also delivered a request from Prince Gong that the prisoners write a letter to Elgin urging an end to hostilities. Parkes declined to help the Chinese; the feisty Consul had no intention of becoming a quisling who undercut Elgin's hand. Desperate, Heng made a personal appeal that verged on begging. If he did not succeed in securing a cease-fire, the Emperor, prodded by his stepmother, the concubine of the previous Emperor, planned to order Heng's execution. Having lived daily under threat of death at the hands of Heng's colleagues, however, Parkes remained unmoved, observing simply, "It is no uncommon thing for the Chinese to deal cruelly with their prisoners, or even to take their lives." Then in a bid to secure his own survival, Parkes added a threat to his indifference toward Heng's fate if the commissioner failed to secure a truce. "Although you would do the Allied forces but little injury by killing the few prisoners…you would by such an act bring down on yourselves a terrible vengeance." Still hoping to effect with kindness what bluster had failed to do, Heng promised, "You will be in no danger for the next two or three days."

On September 29, 1860, Loch and Parkes were transferred to the Gao-miao Temple in the north of Peking where their treatment underwent a miraculous 180-degree turn from the past barbarity. The prisoners were wined and dined at a forty-eight-course banquet catered by a restaurant near the temple. The men were too ill to eat, but happily accepted a bath and

new clothes. These minor kindnesses seem to have turned Parkes's belligerence into acquiescence, and he wrote a letter in Chinese to Elgin recom-
mending a halt in the allied advance followed by negotiations. Heng tried
to influence the content of Parkes's letter, but his prisoner refused and wrote
instead, "The Chinese authorities are now treating Loch and myself well.
We are told that His Highness [Gong] is a man of decision and great intelligence, and I trust that under these circumstances, hostilities may be temporarily suspended to give opportunity for negotiation." At the bottom of
the letter, Loch added in Hindustani that he was writing under duress with
the hope that his Chinese captors couldn't decipher the Indian language.

The letter was greeted with joy, not dismay, by Elgin, who feared that
the captives had already been executed. The Chinese allowed the British to
send Loch and Parkes more clothing. One monogrammed handkerchief
sent the prisoners by the British had an embroidered secret message in
Hindustani to further confuse the Chinese. The message promised that the
allies would begin bombarding the city in three days, which the captives
must have found of minimal consolation since their interrogators had told
them the first shell would be their death sentence. The Chinese continued
to play good cop–bad cop with their prisoners. Mixed in with death threats
were weird acts of kindness and generosity. Prince Gong sent the men a
rare and coveted brand of tea that was so popular among the Chinese that
mandarins with no real business with the prisoners would show up in their
quarters at tea time. Loch and Parkes drew a backgammon board on a
wooden plank and passed the time playing and eating candy supplied by
their jailers.

Elgin remained obsessed with the fate of the prisoners—and frustrated.
He was still unwilling to launch an all-out assault for fear that the Chinese
would probably kill them in retaliation for a humiliating defeat. Elgin felt
as trapped as the prisoners, and knew a tactical misstep on his part could
mean the hostages, as he confided to his diary, "would have been lost,
because the Chinese, finding they had a lever with which they could move
us, would have used their advantage unsparingly." Ironically, as a consequence of the looting of the Summer Palace on the 7th, the prisoners' fate
was an even closer-run race than Elgin knew at the time.

On October 8, 1860, orders arrived from Prince Gong to release the
prisoners at once. Heng felt relieved because he knew from his spies at the

court in exile in Rehe that Gong's orders had come while counterorders from the Emperor to execute the prisoners in revenge for the looting of his summer pied-a-terre were en route. Heng's joy over the news stemmed less from humanitarian concerns and more from the real fear that the hostages' death would have resulted in his own (and countless other residents of the capital) when the allies exacted their inevitable revenge, for which they had an impressive track record of lethal efficiency and consistency. This time, unbound and in a comfortable cart with springs, Loch and Parkes were transported to the city limits, where their anxious guards unceremoniously abandoned them twenty days after their capture.

Despite their previous relationship as jailer and hostage, Heng and Parkes had developed a fondness for each other that may in part have been attributed to Stockholm Syndrome, but for whatever reasons, less than two days after his release, Parkes received a letter from Heng begging him to accompany him on an errand of mercy—to the Summer Palace. Heng was anxious over the fate of a close personal friend, Weng Fu, the Governor of the Summer Palace and the man who reluctantly staged sham naval battles on the artificial lakes of the palace for a feckless Emperor who liked to play at but not make war. Parkes agreed to join him on his quest and helped the old mandarin get into the palace grounds. Heng feared his friend had committed suicide after failing to defend the Palace. Sure enough, after a prolonged search, they found Weng face down in one of the lakes on the palace grounds, an apparent suicide by drowning. Abandoning all mandarin propriety and protocol, Heng sat down on the muddy banks of the lake and buried his head in his hands in an attempt to hide his tears, which were betrayed by the convulsive sobs of a child. The irascible Parkes later wrote that this was the first and only time he felt pity for the Chinese.

The release of Loch and Parkes seems to have released all the pent-up frustration and fury of Elgin and Gros to such an extent that they stopped caring about the fate of the other European prisoners, thirty to forty of them, still in Chinese hands. Less than twenty-four hours after Loch and Parkes were released, the allies on October 9, 1860, positioned thirteen field pieces opposite the An Tung Gate, dug trenches, and posted placards threatening bombardment and obliteration of the city if the An Tung Gate was not opened. Making a noisy show of loading the artillery, Elgin gave the Emperor until noon of October 24 to open the gates of the city or he would begin shelling the ancient fortress filled with treasures of immense historical and aesthetic value. Five minutes before noon, the An Tung Gate cracked open a sliver, and after some hesitation and audible squabbling on the other side of the wall, the portal was at last flung wide open. Without firing a shot, Elgin, at the head of five hundred men, marched into the city as conqueror on October 24th.

The return of the remaining prisoners was not so prompt or effective in warding off an attack. The captives dribbled back. Three days after the An Tung Gate opened, a Frenchmen and eight Sikhs were freed. Two days later, two more Sikhs gained their freedom, but both men were at death's door, and one died the following day.

In all, nineteen prisoners were freed; ten others had died after being forced to kneel in the courtyard of the Summer Palace for days without food or water, their hands bound by moistened ropes and leather straps that shrank and caused excruciating pain and hallucinations. A few days after the survivors' release, grislier arrivals turned up at the British and French camps, coffins with the bodies of the victims, including *The Times*'s correspondent, Thomas Bowlby, the victim of a fatal shopping spree behind Chinese lines. The freed Sikhs described their ordeal in detail. They had been bound with ropes or chains for days and exposed to the elements. The victims met an excruciating end, as the gangrene and infections caused by the leather ties and chains spread from their limbs to the rest of their bodies. The dying may have envied the fate of Captain Brabazon and Father Duluc, who were beheaded at Baliqiao. The Sikh and British victims were interred in the Russian cemetery on October 17, 1860, without ceremony. The next day, the French held an elaborate funeral and high mass for their casualties.

The fate of the dead prisoners seems to have pushed Elgin's already febrile and tortured mind over the edge. While he formulated a suitable response—never revenge in his mind—his less-complicated Sikh cavalrymen enacted their own Mosaic eye-for-an-eye revenge. The Indians abducted two Chinese civilians at random and subjected them to the same roped torture of their dead comrades, although the scenario didn't last long enough to reach the stage of flesh-eating maggots. The Sikhs sipped afternoon tea while their prisoners pleaded for mercy. This scones-and-sadism entertainment was stopped by British officers when they came upon the ghastly scene.

Elgin transferred the wrath he felt for his men's torturers to his military commanders, whose delaying tactics he wrongly believed contributed to the victims' death. If only his generals had advanced faster, lives might have been saved. In a letter to Lady Elgin, the Earl shared dangerous feelings with his wife that he would never have told his professional correspondents like the Prime Minister and the Foreign Secretary. "My dearest, we have dreadful news respecting the fate of some of our captured friends. It is an atrocious crime—and not for vengeance but for future security ought to be seriously dealt with. None of this would have happened if we had moved with celerity and not been scared by bugbears. The system on which we have proceeded is so inexplicable that the whole army lays on me the responsibility for the delays though I have been as persistent an advocate of vigour as I was on the former occasion. After the trouble I got into last time by telling the truth [his criticism of Admiral Seymour] I shall keep silent now, but when we meet I shall say a good deal to you which I do not care to write even to you. God bless you."

Elgin plotted a bloodless revenge that would restore British honor through a symbolic as well as concrete act that could be justified by the Earl's tender conscience as a preventive measure and a warning against harming the contingent of Europeans who would soon take up residence in the capital, including Elgin's brother, the new ambassador to China.

While Elgin pondered preemptive retaliation, Gros was more interested in monetary compensation than profitless revenge, and got Elgin to agree to increase China's reparations by five hundred thousand silver taels—three hundred thousand to the British, two hundred thousand to the French.

Elgin and Gros knew that the Chinese treasury was empty, and in a letter to Lord Palmerston, the Earl suggested that for the next four years the allies should siphon off a whopping 40 percent of Chinese customs revenue. Palmerston agreed, but complained, "I wish Elgin had doubled the indemnity, but I suppose he had good grounds for sticking to the sum before demanded." The dovish Gladstone turned into a greedy hawk upon learning of Elgin's windfall and wrote a colleague: "It is with joy that I snatch a moment to tell you Lord John has just brought in to us after the cabinet had ceased to sit a telegram come this day from St. Petersberg. This really seems to be sure; let us thank God for His goodness. We had just before determined to take another million in consequence of the winter occupation. This is gone; and never did I get a million with greater pleasure than I surrender the chance of this one."

Russia's plenipotentiary, Gen. N.P. Ignatieff, also liked the idea of a public and symbolic humiliation, and suggested a Bastille-like destruction of the dead prisoners' place of incarceration, the Board of Punishments, followed by the erection of a monument at the site. At the base of the monument, a description of China's defeat in Chinese, English, French, Mongol, and Manchu would memorialize in bronze and text a nation's loss of face without destroying priceless antiquities and landmark buildings.

By this point, Elgin's neurasthenic agitation would not be satisfied with a symbolic, nonviolent solution to the Chinese atrocities. Without consulting anyone except Hope Grant, who did not offer an opinion, the Earl decided the most symbolic act, which would cost the Chinese face but no lives, would be to burn to the ground the Summer Palace, one of several places where the prisoners had been tortured.

Baron Gros noted in his diary at this time that Elgin had become impossibly irritable, a defining symptom of depression. While Elgin was depressed to the point of vandalism, the connoisseur and conservator in Gros, who was interested in saving the Summer Palace not as a repository of history but as a capital opportunity for more looting, expressed horror at Elgin's atavistic impulse. Gros deemed the plan "a useless sort of vengeance, which alas would not put right any one of the cruel misfortunes we deplore." One of Gros's subordinates called the plan "*C'est detruire pour le plaisir de detruire* (It is destruction for the pleasure of destruction.)" In a letter to de Montauban, Gros decided to contrast French forbearance with British barbarism. "*Soyez persuadé qu'aux yeux de l'Europe, comme parmi les populations de la Chine, le beau rôle sera pour nous dans cette affair.* (Realize that in the eyes of Europe as well as the Chinese, we will play the role of magnanimous victor.)" Gros's sincerity was undercut when he suggested that instead of the suburban Summer Palace, the allies might torch the Imperial Palace inside the city, a much greater historical and cultural loss.

Elgin explained in copious correspondence with Lady Elgin, Palmerston, Gros, Hope Grant, and the alter ego of his diary that burning the Emperor's home would punish him and spare the Chinese people, conveniently ignoring Ignatieff's alternate of a literally monumental humiliation, which would have punished everyone and destroyed nothing, except perhaps the sensitivities of aesthetes who loathe publicly commissioned art.

The foundation of Elgin's argument rested on an apparent ignorance of the mandarin court or perhaps a convenient ignoring of it. The debauched and ailing ruler was not personally responsible for the horrific end of the allied prisoners. Almost since his accession at age twenty in 1851, the Xianfeng Emperor had lived in sybaritic luxury, drug addiction and indifference in his suburban retreat, while his mandarins ran a bureaucracy of Rube Goldbergian complexity. Xianfeng's hegira from Peking to Rehe only created geographical distance from the locus of power; his self-indulgence and absorption had created a practical distance between the symbolic head and actual executors of power.

Elgin wanted more than Ignatieff's semiotic punishment, and his superiors supported his revenge masquerading as justifiable retribution. The Prime Minister shared his elation over Elgin's plan with the Secretary of State for War and said, "I am heartily glad. It [is] absolutely necessary." Jack Beeching has brilliantly described the Earl's casuistry and the psychodynamics of his actions: "Elgin's decision to burn the Summer Palace at least meant that flesh-and-blood injuries done to people he knew intimately would for once be revenged, not as in war, upon other people—on helpless Chinese—but on inanimate objects, on redundant and expensive things. He had suffered all his life from his father's costly obsession with works of art; now works of art would bear the brunt of his revenge." The son became a strange mutation of the father. Where the seventh Earl sought to preserve (and profit), the eighth chose destruction and the condemnation he well knew would follow him into posterity.

Elgin had more pressing problems than the most appropriate way to humiliate the Emperor of China. He also faced a deadline imposed by Hope Grant, who warned him that a treaty had to be concluded before Peking's harsh winter set in so the allies could return to their secure base at Tianjin. Wintering in the capital, Hope Grant informed Elgin, was not feasible because their supply lines were overextended and could easily be severed by Chinese guerillas. De Montauban seconded his British counterpart's advice. Seng's cavalry also continued to pose a threat. The Mongol horsemen had been routed, but remained intact. There weren't enough allied forces to blockade the city and cut off supplies; Peking could be tortured with starvation, but not into submission. Military advisors informed Elgin and Gros that if the Europeans were expelled from the city, their artillery would almost certainly be unable to blow a hole in the forty-feet-high, sixty-feet-thick walls that had protected the city from enemy incursions for the past two centuries.

By now, the Emperor at Rehe had ceased all correspondence, which had never been voluminous, with his mandarins in Peking. Seng fell into a paralyzing torpor—perhaps caused by the humiliating defeat of troops under his command—but instead of committing ritual suicide as so many of his peers would have done, he retreated into inaction. The lot of saving as much as he could of his brother's capital and China's honor fell on Prince Gong.

Elgin juggled his limited options. He rejected Gros's suggestion to torch the Winter Palace, the Emperor's primary residence, because his agreement with Prince Gong to open the city gates included a promise not to destroy the capital. (The Summer Palace was just outside the city gates, and Elgin was engaging in hair-splitting casuistry again.) Gong's offer to turn over the jailers who had tortured and killed the allied POWs was also rejected by Elgin, who feared Gong would surrender low-level guards instead of the higher-ups responsible, whose number may have included Gong himself.

The Summer Palace remained an irresistible target, the site of the European prisoners' abominable treatment and the Emperor's private getaway, his Petit Trianon, a refuge from the rigorous court protocol and machinations of the Chinese Versailles, the Winter Palace in Peking. On October 18, 1860, D-Day (for destruction) arrived and the burning of the Summer Palace began.

Back in England, news of the conflagration was greeted with euphoria by everyone except Radical MPs and, curiously, by two other individuals on the opposite end of the political spectrum. Prince Albert, who vacillated between a nostalgia for the eighteenth century's *ancien régime* and the liberalizing trends of the nineteenth, received the news from China with distress rather than the jingoist joy that suffused the rest of the country because he feared that the Emperor's humiliation and demonstrated powerlessness would topple the Manchus and bring in the enemies of private property and privilege, the Taiping rebels. His reactionary wife had a different reason for her fear and loathing of the bonfire in Peking.

Queen Victoria was horrified by Lord Elgin's revenge. Burning a royal residence seemed more Jacobin to her than putting an anti-capitalist God-
Worshipper on a faraway throne.

An obscene act of cultural vandalism that would make Elgin a national
hero in Britain for a generation then be conveniently ignored or glossed
over by future historians, the burning of the Summer Palace still has the
power to shock a century and a half later when the event is brought to the
attention of Western readers. It has never stopped rankling the Chinese
since Imperial days, through the Nationalist regime and the People's
Republic today, where the ruins have not been restored as a reminder and
reproach of European aggression. Regardless of the political bent of whatever government happens to be in power, a national humiliation remained
and remains a national humiliation.

Chapter 27

THE *DIKTAT*
OF PEKING

———·•·———

"Keep perfectly still!"

—Lord Elgin's orders to Chinese negotiators
while a group photo was taken

On October 23, 1860, the Chinese Imperial Treasury paid in full the increased indemnity of 500,000 taels to the British and French. On October 24, 1860, Elgin met with Prince Gong at the Board of Ceremonies to sign the Convention of Peking. By now, Elgin had become a student of court protocol and used his knowledge to humiliate Gong and the mandarins by arriving at the Board in a chair carried by eight porters. According to tradition, the Emperor alone had the right to that many porters. After more than a century of refusing to accept the British sovereign as the Emperor's equal, China now had to accept a mere emissary of the British queen on the same footing. It horrified and humiliated the Chinese, which is exactly what Elgin intended.

The Earl also used a show of force that was part intimidation and part survival tactic. He had learned through the Protestant Chinese community that he was a target for assassination, so Elgin showed up with a personal retinue of five hundred troops, and lined the route of his triumphal tour of Peking en route to the Board of Ceremonies with two thousand more soldiers. Lt. Col. Wolseley did a sweep of the Board after hearing that the meeting place was booby trapped with mines, but found nothing there. And for even more control and intimidation, Elgin mounted a huge artillery piece on the An Tung Gate, aimed at the city to ensure good behavior on the part of the population and encourage the courtiers to sign the Convention of Peking.

Prince Gong arrived at the Board in a sedan chair borne by the number of porters prescribed for his rank—six—and immediately recognized the insult to his absent brother caused by the Earl's larger entourage. Elgin was not a gracious conqueror and kept Gong waiting for more than two hours. When they at last met, Elgin gave the Prince a "a proud contemptuous look, which must have made the blood run cold in poor Kung's [Gong's] veins," observed General Hope Grant, who described the Prince as "a delicate, gentleman-like looking man."

The signing took on the flavor of a comic opera. Elgin startled the mandarins when he barked at them, "Keep perfectly still," while the Italian photographer, a Signor Beato, photographed the scene to preserve the Chinese disgrace for posterity. Bad lighting, however, doomed Signor Beato's efforts, and no photographic evidence of the signing was made available to the British press for a visual record of China's complete defeat by their European conquerors.

Again, the Chinese were given a document to sign, not a treaty to negotiate, when Elgin presented the treaty to Gong for his signature. The Convention included an apology for the Emperor's aggression, the British ambassador was granted year-round residency, and $10 million in reparations were to be paid to Britain. Another port city was added to the list opened to trade, and the area across from the island of Hong Kong on the mainland was ceded to the British.

After the signing, despite his ritual degradation, Gong played gracious host and invited Elgin to a banquet in his honor. Elgin declined, citing his fear that the Chinese would poison him.

The French version of the above took place on October 25, 1860, and Baron Gros was graciousness itself. After signing the treaty, the Baron gave Gong a rare collection of French coins and autographed photos of Napoleon III and the Empress Eugenie. The diplomat also apologized to the prince for the burning of the Summer Palace, even though his men had participated in its looting and razing. Gros insensitively compared the loss of the treasure house to the clothing he lost when his ship sank en route to China. One wonders if Gong felt any consolation from such an uneven comparison of tragedies. Unlike Elgin, Gros accepted Gong's offer to dine after the treaty had been signed, and no one was poisoned.

The overwrought Lord Elgin spent the entire month of December, 1860 recuperating in Shanghai, reading Victorian romance novels and Darwin's recent bestseller, *On the Origin of the Species*, which he found "audacious." In mid January, 1861, the Earl left the country for good, but two days before his departure, he annexed Kowloon almost as an afterthought, but in accordance with secret orders from London.

Elgin returned to England a hero and received the ultimate plum job from the Foreign Office, the Viceroyalty of India, a position recently vacated by his good friend, Lord Canning—and one guaranteed to make its holder immensely rich. The new Viceroy enjoyed the lucrative post for only twenty months, however, dying of an aneurysm in November, 1864 in Calcutta, the same city where Canton's Viceroy Ye had perished, adding a symbolic symmetry to the two adversaries' lives.

Xianfeng died prematurely at thirty, only a year after the signing of the Convention of Peking, which had humiliated him so much that he remained secluded and anesthetized by opium and wine in his harem at Rehe. The Emperor never returned to the capital and refused to meet foreign ambassadors or even his courtiers, so deep was his sense of shame.

The fierce Mongol warrior and commander-in-chief of the Chinese forces, Prince Seng, continued to suffer military setbacks and humiliations. To put down a violent tax-revolt in Shandong province, Seng led an impressive force of twenty-three thousand infantry and cavalry against the rebels, but he was so short of artillery he begged the European occupiers to return some of the guns he had surrendered. His pleas were ignored, and the Prince failed to suppress the rebellion. He was reduced to the ranks on a salary of $7.50 per day.

As usual, Queen Victoria played a symbolic role in the subjugation of the Chinese. After centuries of receiving tribute from barbarians with condescension and contempt, the Emperor found himself paying tribute to the British sovereign with an involuntary "gift" of a small lap dog that had been bred to resemble the Chinese heraldic lion. The dog's "Pekinese" breed was named after its city of origin. The bedraggled creature had been found wandering around the ruins of the Summer Palace, where a captain in the Wiltshire regiment rescued it and presented the dog to his sovereign. With no irony and with the supreme self-confidence of the Imperialist Regnant, the Queen named her new pet "Lootie." During an audience with General Hope Grant at Buckingham Palace, Victoria also received the jade-and-gold scepter looted from Lootie's home, and three gigantic enameled bowls from the Summer Palace. To the victors belonged both the spoils and the dogs of war.

EPILOGUE

———•———

*"The Chinese merchant supplies your country with his goodly tea
and silk, confering thereby a benefit upon her; but the English
merchant empoisons China with pestilent opium...The wealth
and generosity of England are spoken by all. How is it then,
she can hesitate to remove an acknowledged evil?"*

—A letter from China's Foreign Office to Parliament, 1869

The Opium Wars had been fought, in large measure, over the trade in
opium and British manufactures, and Britain's success in the conflicts
paid off dramatically. Four years after the second war ended, Britain sold
China seven-eighths of all the conquered nation's imports, more than
£100,000 annually. Opium importation increased from fifty-eight thousand chests in 1859 to 105,000 chests in 1879. Manchester textiles, which
the Chinese had rejected as inferior to China's indigenous production, also
found a more favorable market, quadrupling from 113 million yards in
1856 to 448 million yards a quarter-century later.

Although the Treaty of Tianjin had provided de facto legalization of
opium by setting the amount at which the Chinese could tax it, the Imperial court continued to fight importation of the drug by raising the levy on
it in the hope that more expensive opium would also be less popular
opium. When the Chinese tried to increase the tax from thirty to fifty taels
per chest, the European importers in China saw their profits in danger of
being wiped out and appealed to Lord Granville, President of the Privy
Government in Lord Palmerston's administration. The Liberal government
quashed the tax increase.

In 1870, Sir Wilfred Lawson introduced a motion in the House of
Commons condemning the opium trade, but by now, the percentage of
the Exchequer's income from the business had ballooned from a pre-war

one-eighteenth to one seventh There was simply too much money to be earned from the drug, and Lawson's motion was defeated by a vote of 151 to 47. Wealth from the trade had so corrupted the nation that during the debate over Lawson's motion, William Gladstone, who thirty years earlier had condemned the pernicious effects of the trade with an eloquence that almost toppled the government, now embraced the trade and the revenue it brought to Britain and India in an influential speech he gave in the lower House.

The Chinese government continued to implore Britain to stop importing opium from China. In 1869, the MP Sir Rutherford Alcock received a desperate and despairing letter from Zongli Yamen, the Chinese Foreign Office that said, "The Chinese merchant supplies your country with his goodly tea and silk, confering thereby a benefit upon her; but the English merchant empoisons China with pestilent opium. Such conduct is unrighteous. Who can justify it? The wealth and generosity of England are spoken by all. How is it then, she can hesitate to remove an acknowledged evil?" Better, the Chinese suggested that the British substitute cotton and cereal cultivation in India for opium.

The demoralized Chinese eventually accepted the dubious wisdom of the slogan "If you can't beat 'em, join 'em." In 1871, Sir Rutherford Alcock, who was morally appalled by the traffic, predicted in the House of Commons that eventually British imports would be displaced by local production in China: "There is a very large and increasing cultivation of the poppy in China; the Chinese Government are seriously contemplating—if they cannot come to any terms or arrangement with the British government—the cultivation without stint in China, and producing opium at a much cheaper rate."

Alcock's warning came too late. Although after 1868 homegrown opium was considered inferior to imported supplies, by the 1880s imports had declined (before eventually levelling off until about 1905). Abandoning his moral repugnance, Alcock suggested flooding China with Indian opium, which would make the price plummet and put indigenous growers out of business. This was robber-baron economics applied to nascent agrobusiness.

Despite calls for prohibition in Britain and China, inside and outside of government, opium consumption skyrocketed during the rest of the century. In 1888, *The Times of London* certainly overestimated that 70 percent of adult males in China partook, but the growth of consumption—and addiction—was alarmingly clear. Two years later, exhausted by a century of feckless protest, the Chinese government dropped all attempts at prohibition and punishment. The teenaged Guangxu Emperor, who was controlled by his great-aunt, the Dowager Empress Cixi, revoked all laws against cultivation and legalized the trade. But poison, whether home-grown or imported, is still poison, and in 1906 the Chinese government reversed course and forbade the sale of the drug. The Imperial edict, however, had a curious sunset clause that showed how deeply the drug had embedded itself in China. Addiction reached the very top of society. Users over sixty were exempted for one specific reason: the Dowager Empress Cixi was herself an opium addict.

At the Chinese government's request and with pressure from Britain's Society for the Suppression of the Opium Trade, the British government ordered its colony of Hong Kong to cease trading in domestic opium as well. As Martin Booth brilliantly capsulated the history of the drug and the devastation it caused in his 1996 book *Opium*, the Hong Kong agreement "officially ended the terrible trade by which Britain had earned vast revenues—not to mention acquiring what was to become her most successful, lucrative and thriving colony [Hong Kong]—*by poisoning a substantial portion of the Chinese population.*"

The Xianfeng Emperor and his concubine-turned-Dowager Empress Cixi were not the only Imperial victims of opium. Like a rock thrown into a scum-coated pond, the ripples from the devastation caused by opium continued well into the next century, climaxing with the sad fate of China's last Empress and the ruthless and effective suppression of cultivation, trade, and consumption by Mao. Zero tolerance does work, but only under a totalitarian regime.

Wan Jung, the second wife of the last Emperor, Puyi, began smoking opium at age nineteen, eventually consuming two ounces a day, enough to kill a neophyte. After her husband collaborated with the Japanese invaders by becoming the puppet ruler of Manchuria (renamed Manchuko by the occupiers), the Japanese encouraged her addiction by supplying her with the drug while at the same time publicizing her habituation in Japan to demonstrate the moral and physical inferiority of the conquered Chinese.

Wanjung's next handlers were not so accommodating. In 1946, the Imperial couple were seized and imprisoned separately by Mao. The Communists cut off her supply of opium, and Wanjung went through withdrawal and a descent into hell. Wanjung's last days were chronicled by her companion, Hiro Saga, a member of Japan's royal family.

Wanjung became a grotesque tourist attraction and object lesson in the evils of opium addiction. Soldiers and civilians gathered outside her cell door, giggling and gossiping about the prisoner's pathetic condition. Wanjung pleaded, then screamed for opium and made such a racket other prisoners petitioned for her execution. She sank into a feverish delusion that she had returned to the Winter Palace and ordered nonexistent servants to wait on her and fetch her opium pipe. The delirium turned into merciful unconsciousness, during which she soiled herself with feces, urine, and vomit. Her guards refused to enter her cell because of the stench, and the once pampered mistress of the Forbidden City died of malnutrition and dehydration. Her final days were so ghastly that director Bernardo Bertolucci left them out of his 1987 film, *The Last Emperor*, which otherwise dissected her life in detail, including her leather and foot fetishes. Wanjung's grotesque death may have symbolized Imperial decadence, but was apparently too distasteful even for the Marxist inclinations of the Italian director.

Opium cultivation and use thrived in Ch'iang Kai-shek's China during the 1920s and 1930s. Chiang used the revenue from opium taxes to bankroll his regime and army. By the time of the Japanese invasion of China in 1937, forty million Chinese, 10 percent of the population, were addicted to the drug. British-controlled Hong Kong had an even bigger problem, with an estimated 30 percent of the colony's population dependent on opium. The Japanese occupiers encouraged opium consumption but for political rather than fiscal reasons: an intoxicated population was also a docile.

Within a year of the Communist takeover in 1949, Mao's government proscribed all narcotics, and their cultivation, use, and sale. And Mao put muscle into the prohibition. Dealers were summarily executed. The lucky ones were sent to the China's gulag for "re-education," which included starvation. Users were treated more humanely and detoxed in hospitals, anticipating the United States's recent implementation of rehab instead of prison time. But recidivists were not forgiven and were either executed or sent to labor camps, often a slower form of execution. In 1960, the regime declared with some justification that opium addiction had ended in China. Ten years later, only one hundred tons of opium were produced, enough for medicinal but not recreational use.

After 150 years of struggle and devastation, the Chinese people were at last freed from the *fleurs du mal* in exchange for their political and personal freedoms. More than half a century of legislation by both the British and Chinese had failed, while Mao's totalitarian efficiency succeeded in half a generation. Ironically, Mao was essentially enforcing the policy and plan that had first been tried by Commissioner Lin and his master, the Daoguang Emperor—the plan that had precipitated the First Opium War.

The Great Helmsman just said no.

ILLUSTRATIONS
AND MAPS

The Qianlong Emperor is carried to the embassy with Lord Macartney.
(The British Museum)

The city of Canton. (The British Museum)

Commissioner Lin
(F. Lewis, Publishers)

Charles Napier
(Radio Times Hulton Picture Library)

William Jardine
(National Portrait Gallery London)

James Matheson
(National Portrait Gallery London)

Howqua
(The Tate Gallery)

The Nemesis *attacking several Chinese junk ships.*
(National Maritime Museum)

Sir Henry Pottinger
(Bettmann Archive/BBC Hulton)

The Andromache *and the* Imogene *take fire at the Bogue Forts.*
(National Maritime Museum)

Lord Palmerston
(National Portrait Gallery London)

Lord Elgin
(National Galleries of Scotland)

British and Chinese ambassadors sign the Treaty of Tianjin.
(The Illustrated London News)

Prince Gong
(National Army Museum)

The Hall of the Peaceful Seas at Yuan Ming Yuan, the Summer Palace.
(Houghton Library)

The burnt ruins of the Summer Palace.
(Thomas Childe, Ruins of the Yuan Ming Yuan (c. 1875), Bibliothèque Nationale, Paris).

Lord Elgin enters Peking after the burning of the Summer Palace in 1860.
(Hong Kong City Museum)

The China seacoast.

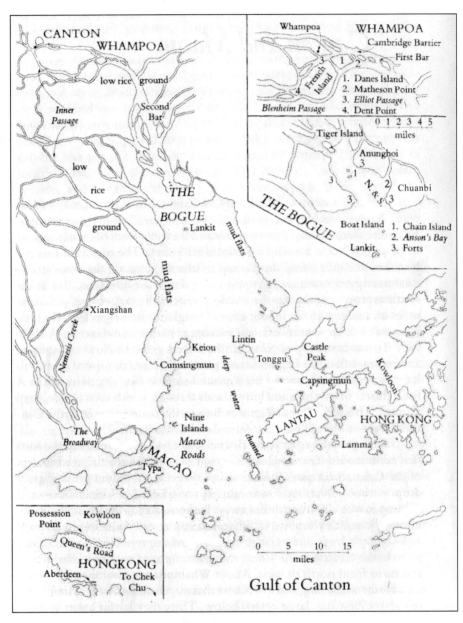

The Gulf of Canton.

NOTES

CHAPTER 1

4   "The Summer Palace was": Jack Beeching, *The Chinese Opium Wars* (New York: Harcourt Brace Jovanovich, 1975), pg 315.

5   "Chinese fairyland": Beeching, pg 314.

6   Swinhoe account: Robert Swinhoe, *Narrative of the North China Campaign of 1860.* As quoted in Beeching, pg 319.

7   "white and green jade": Beeching, pg 320.

7   "Plundering and devastating": Beeching, pg 318.

7   "I would like a great many things": Beeching, pg 318.

8   "struck by its simple beauty": Beeching, pg 326.

8   "The world around": Lt. Col. G.J. Wolseley, *Aktion, Narrative of the War with China in 1860.* As quoted in Douglas Hurd, *The Arrow War* (New York: Macmillan, 1967) pg 236.

8   "The sun shining": Robert Swinhoe, *Narrative of the North China Campaign of 1860.* As quoted in Beeching, pg 326.

10   "That no individual": Henry Broughman Loch, *Personal Narrative of Occurences during Lord Elgin's Second Embassy to China in 1860*, 1900.

11   "indicated that part": Beeching, pg 329.

11   Elgin's speech to the Royal Academy: Beeching, pg 329–30.

CHAPTER 2

13   "I set no value": Jack Beeching, *The Chinese Opium Wars* (New York: Harcourt Brace Jovanovich, 1975), pg 13.

19   "an old, crazy, first-rate man-of-war": Ann Paludan, *Chronicle of the Chinese Emperors* (New York: Thames and Hudson, 1998), pg. 203.

19   "Our ways": Beeching, pg 17.

19   "In his reception": Paludan, pg. 196.

20   "not a necessity": Beeching, pg 24.

21   "Foreigners obviously": Beeching, pg 25.

26   "British Authority" establishment: E.J. Eitel, *The History of Hong Kong*.

27   "It is not desirable": Beeching, pg 45.

27   "the Barbarian Eye": Beeching, pg 46.

28   "It is plain": Beeching, pg 47.

29   "Three of our frigates": Beeching, pg 48.

29–30 Napier quotes: Beeching, pg 49–50.

30   Lu K'un quotes: Beeching, pg 50.

31   "like fireworks": Beeching, pg 51.

32   "very serious offense": Beeching, pg 53.

32   "Attempt to force": Beeching, pg 54.

33   "The smoke of opium": Hsin-pao Chang, *Commisioner Lin and the Opium War*. As quoted in Beeching, pg 66 and Peter Fay, *The Opium War 1840–1842* (Chapel Hill, NC: University of North Carolina Press, 1975) pg. 118.

34   "To arouse reflection": Beeching, pg 71.

CHAPTER 3

39–40 Lin's letter to Queen Victoria: Peter Fay, *The Opium War 1840–1842* (Chapel Hill, NC: University of North Carolina Press, 1975) pg. 143.

40   "neither head nor tail of": Jack Beeching, *The Chinese Opium Wars* (New York: Harcourt Brace Jovanovich, 1975), pg 76.

42   "a mere fraction": Fay, pg. 77.

44–45 Merchants and the CoHong: Fay, pg. 145.

46   "exhibition of humbug": Matheson to Jardine, 1 May 1839, James Matheson Private Letter Books, vol. 4, . As quoted in Fay, pg. 146.

47   "I have no doubt": *Correspondence Relating to China*, 1840, 36 (223), 349. Parliamentary Papers. As quoted in Fay, pg. 147.

48   "British man-o-war": Fay, pg. 148.

48   William C. Hunter, "Journal of Occurrences at Canton during the Cessation of Trade, 1839." As quoted in Fay, pg. 149.

48   "act accordingly": *Correspondence Relating to China*, 1840, 36 (223), 367. Parliamentary Papers. As quoted in Fay, pg. 149.

50   Elliot's decree: *Correspondence Relating to China*, 1840, 36 (223), 370. Parliamentary Papers. As quoted in Fay, pg. 153.

51   "The money of the British government": *Select Committee on the Trade with the Chine'* 1840, 36 (223), 374, Parliamentary Papers. As quoted in Fay, pg. 154.

52   "as usual": Fay, pg. 156.

56   "Judged by their manners": P.C. Kuo, *A Critical Study of the First Anglo-Chinese War*, pg. 247. As quoted in Fay, pg. 161.

CHAPTER 4

56   "full of fright": Elma Loines, *The China Trade Post-Bag*, pg. 71. As quoted in Peter Fay, *The Opium War 1840–1842* (Chapel Hill, NC: University of North Carolina Press, 1975), pg. 164.

57   "left to suffer death": *Correspondence Relating to China*, 1840, 36 (223), 392. Parliamentary Papers. As quoted in Fay, pg. 163.

58   "I tore it up": *Correspondence Relating to China*, 1840, 36 (223), 390. Parliamentary Papers. As quoted in Fay, pg. 163.

58   Matheson to Jamsetjee, April 3, 1839, James Matheson Private Letter Books, vol. 4. As quoted in Fay, pg. 163.

58   "I strongly recommend": Matheson to Henderson, May 29, 1839, James Matheson Private Letter Books, vol. 4. As quoted in Fay, pg. 164.

58   "full of fright": Elma Loines, *The China Trade Post-Bag*, pg. 71. As quoted in Fay, pg. 164.

59   "applaud the firmness": Williams to Anderson, May 17, 1839, South China 1838–44, American Board of Commissioners for Foreign Missions papers. As quoted in Fay, pg. 166.

64   Arthur Waley, *The Opium War through Chinese Eyes* (Stanford, CA: Stanford University Press, 1958) pp. 64–65.

65   "tightly encased": Jack Beeching, *The Chinese Opium Wars* (New York: Harcourt Brace Jovanovich, 1975), pg 90.

66   "violent and vexatious": Beeching, pg 91.

67   Lin poem: Beeching, pg 92.

69   "murderous barbarian": Beeching, pg 102.

CHAPTER 5

71   "Her Majesty's government": Peter Fay, *The Opium War 1840–1842* (Chapel Hill, NC: University of North Carolina Press, 1975), pg. 194.

71   "nearly nine years": John Trotter, May 2, 1839, Bengal Proceedings, P/107/39, India Office Library. As quoted in Fay, pg. 185.

71   "care two pence": Bethune to Maitland, May 28, 1839, Foreign Office series, 17/35. As quoted in Fay, pg. 185.

72   "find it expedient": Matheson to J.A. Smith, May 6, 1839 (enclosing Matheson to Jardine, May 1), James Matheson Private Letter Books, vol. 4. As quoted in Fay, pg. 191.

72   "quite irrelevant": *Select Committee on the Trade with China*, 1840, 7 (359), 124, Parliamentary Papers. As quoted in Fay, pg. 191.

73   Matheson letter: Matheson to J.A. Smith, Sept. 24, 1839, James Matheson Private Letter Books, vol. 4. As quoted in Fay, pg. 191.

73   "anti-slavery agitators": Fay, pg. 192.

74   "It appears to me": Elliot to Palmerston, April 3, 1839, Foreign Office series, 17/31. As quoted in Fay, pg. 193.

74   "No man entertained": Jack Beeching, *The Chinese Opium Wars* (New York: Harcourt Brace Jovanovich, 1975), pg 105.

74   "China problem": Fay, pg. 193.

75   "Her Majesty's government": Fay, pg. 194.

CHAPTER 6

77   Gladstone's counter: Jack Beeching, *The Chinese Opium Wars* (New York: Harcourt Brace Jovanovich, 1975), 110.

77   Forbes to A. Heard, Jan. 21, 1940, BM-8, Heard. As quoted in Peter Fay, *The Opium War 1840–1842* (Chapel Hill, NC: University of North Carolina Press, 1975) pg. 200.

78   "I beg to declare": Beeching, pg 109.

78–79 Gladstone's counter: Beeching, 110.

79   Palmerston's rebuttal: Beeching, 111.

80   "a war more unjust": Beeching, 110.

CHAPTER 7

85   "weaned of his hostility": April 18, 1840, James Matheson Private Letter Books, vol. 5. As quoted in Peter Fay, *The Opium War 1840–1842* (Chapel Hill, NC: University of North Carolina Press, 1975) pg. 209.

85   "their strengths and their weaknesses": Arthur Waley, *The Opium War through Chinese Eyes* (Stanford, CA: Stanford University Press, 1958) pp. 96.

88   "weaned of his hostility": Fay, pg. 209.

91   "Still I must fight": *The Chinese Repository*, 9:223. As quoted in Fay, pg. 222.

92   "crashing of timber": Jack Beeching, *The Chinese Opium Wars* (New York: Harcourt Brace Jovanovich, 1975), pg 115.

92   "first European banner": Lord Robert Jocelyn, *Six Months with the Chinese Expedition,* pg. 54. As quoted in Fay, pg. 223.

93   "killed in cold blood": Thom to Matheson, July 15, 1840, Jardine Matheson papers. As quoted in Fay, pg. 225.

94   "subtle, lying, and thievish.": *The Chinese Repository*, 9:231. As quoted in Fay, pg. 22

95   "playing at war": Beeching, 117.

CHAPTER 8

97   "utmost dread": Elliot to Palmerston, Sept. 21, 1840, Foreign Office series 17/39. As quoted in Peter Fay, *The Opium War 1840–1842* (Chapel Hill, NC: University of North Carolina Press, 1975), pg. 235.

97   Yukien's letter: P.C. Kuo, *A Critical Study of the First Anglo-Chinese War*, pg. 261. As quoted in Fay, pg. 230.

100   "Great moral changes": *Correspondence Relating to China.* 1840, 36 (223), 387 and 385, Parliamentary Papers. As quoted in Fay, pg. 234.

101   "utmost dread": Elliot to Palmerston, Sept. 21, 1840, Foreign Office series 17/39. As quoted in Fay, pg. 235.

CHAPTER 9

103   Matheson letter: Matheson to Jamsetjee, August 4, 1840, James Matheson Private Letter Books, vol. 5. As quoted in Peter Fay, *The Opium War 1840–1842* (Chapel Hill, NC: University of North Carolina Press, 1975) pg. 239.

104   "you are living victims": *The Chinese Repository*, 9:324, 416. As quoted in Fay, pg. 240.

105   "nine-tenths if not every one": *The Chinese Repository*, 9:321. As quoted in Fay, pg. 241.

106   Baldus letter: Fay, pg. 241.

CHAPTER 10

109   "scarcely a yard": *The Chinese Repository*, 10: 191–204. As quoted in Peter Fay, *The Opium War 1840–1842* (Chapel Hill, NC: University of North Carolina Press, 1975), pg. 256.

110   "Even the natives": Thom to Matheson, July 15, 1840, Jardine Matheson papers. As quoted in Fay, pg. 253.

111   Ann Noble's account of capture: *The Chinese Repository*, 10: 191–204. As quoted in Fay, pg. 256.

CHAPTER 11

114, 116   "Externally…Internally": The smoke of opium": Hsin-pao Chang, *Commisioner Lin and the Opium War*, pg. 212; *The Chinese Repository*, 9:413. As quoted in Peter Fay, *The Opium War 1840–1842* (Chapel Hill, NC: University of North Carolina Press, 1975) pg. 268.

116   "The more they get": Fay, pp. 269–70.

116   Arthur Waley, *The Opium War through Chinese Eyes* (Stanford, CA: Stanford University Press, 1958), pg. 120.

117   "far short of the demands": Elliot to Auckland, Dec. 10, 1840, Foreign Office series 17/39. As quoted in Fay, pg. 270.

118   "large forces collected here": Elliot to Palmerston, Jan. 5, 1841, China miscellany, vol. 4, India Office Library. As quoted in Fay, pg. 271.

118   "frightful scene of slaughter": Jack Beeching, *The Chinese Opium Wars* (New York: Harcourt Brace Jovanovich, 1975), pg 125.

119   "slaughter of fugitives": Robert S. Rait, *The Life and Campaigns of Hugh, First Viscount Gough,* 1:230–31. As quoted in Fay, pg. 274.

120   "without further bloodshed": Beeching, pg. 125.

121   "our naval power": Beeching, pg. 127.

121   "admission of opium": Beeching, pg. 127.

122   "no objection": Jan 22, 1841, James Matheson Private Letter Books, vol. 4. As quoted in Fay, pg. 276.

122   "more than six blows": Beeching, pg. 128.

123   Belcher report: *The Chinese Repositroy,* 12:493. As quoted in Fay, pp. 278–79.

123   Ryan report: Ryan to Thomasen, Feb. 27, 1841, Jardine Matheson papers. As quoted in Fay, pg. 280.

124   "Our regular troops": Arthur Waley, *The Opium War through Chinese Eyes* (Stanford, CA: Stanford University Press, 1958) pg. 143.

CHAPTER 12

125   "Exterminate the rebels!": Jack Beeching, *The Chinese Opium Wars* (New York: Harcourt Brace Jovanovich, 1975), 129.

126   "If trade were the solution": Earl Swisher, *China's Management of the American Barbarians,* pp. 69. As quoted in Peter Fay, *The Opium War 1840–1842* (Chapel Hill, NC: University of North Carolina Press, 1975) pg. 286.

127   "Exterminate the rebels!": Beeching, 129.

127   "their protecting joss": Captain Sir Edward Belcher, *Narrative of a Voyage around the World,* pg. 214. As quoted in Fay, pg. 295.

129   "a shame to speak": *The Chinese Repository,* 10:530. As quoted in Fay, pg. 300.

130   Elliot letter: Elliot to Aberdeen, Jan. 25, 1842, Foreign Office series 17/61. As quoted in Fay, pg. 296.

CHAPTER 13

133   "not only prison guards": Jack Beeching, *The Chinese Opium Wars* (New York: Harcourt Brace Jovanovich, 1975), 138.

133   "Throughout the whole course": Palmerston to Elliot, Apr. 21, 1841, Foreign Office series 17/45. As quoted in Peter Fay, *The Opium War 1840–1842* (Chapel Hill, NC: University of North Carolina Press, 1975) pg. 309.

133   Elliot pamphlet: Beeching, pg 130.

134   "might have been got": A. C. Benson and Viscount Esher, eds., *Letters of Queen Victoria* (London, 1907), 1:329. As quoted in Fay, pg. 311.

134   "allow no consideration:": Beeching, pg. 133.

136   "rushed out to drive back": Beeching, pg. 135.

136   "similar acts of atrocity": Parker to Auckland, sept. 25, 1841, *United Service Journal,* 1842, pt. 1, pp. 428–29. As quoted in Fay, pg. 314.

136–37   "Under no circumstances": Beeching, pg. 137.

137 "Everyone on Formosa": Beeching, 138.

138 "with considerable satisfaction": Beeching, 140.

139 "The worst proposal": Beeching, 140.

CHAPTER 14

143, 145 Cao's account: Jack Beeching, *The Chinese Opium Wars* (New York: Harcourt Brace Jovanovich, 1975), pg 148–49.

146 "Nobler and better fate": Beeching, pg. 151.

146 "a very excited state": Beeching, pg. 151.

147 "opium is on sale": Beeching, 152.

147 "a region like a throat": S. Y. Teng, *Chang Hsi and the Treat of Nanking, 1842*, pg, 32. As quoted in Peter Fay, *The Opium War 1840–1842* (Chapel Hill, NC: University of North Carolina Press, 1975) pg. 355.

CHAPTER 15

149 "strongly impress": Jack Beeching, *The Chinese Opium Wars* (New York: Harcourt Brace Jovanovich, 1975), pg. 156.

150 "soothing the barbarians": Beeching, pg 150.

150–51 Zheng Xi's speech: S. Y. Teng, *Chang Hsi and the Treat of Nanking, 1842*, pg, 38–41. As quoted in Peter Fay, *The Opium War 1840–1842* (Chapel Hill, NC: University of North Carolina Press, 1975) pg. 359.

152 "If your people": Granville G. Loch, *The Closing of the Campaign in China*, pg. 172–73. As quoted in Fay, pg. 361.

153 Palmerston's opium dilemma: Beeching, pg. 156.

153 "Our nations have been united": Beeching, pp. 156–57.

154 "procure the drug": Beeching, pg. 157.

154 "shall never forget": Beeching, 155.

156 *Illustrated London News* quote: Fay, pg. 366.

156 "the British opium smuggler": Beeching, pg. 158.

156–58 Pottinger's opium restrictions: Beeching, pg. 159.

158 "did stop the traffic": Beeching, pg. 161.

158 "utterly inconsistent": Beeching, pg. 161.

159 "I am in dread": Beeching, pg. 164.

159 "some moral compensation": Beeching, pg. 160.

CHAPTER 16

163, 164 "iniquities scarcely exceed": Jack Beeching, *The Chinese Opium Wars* (New York: Harcourt Brace Jovanovich, 1975), pg 175.

165 "irregular and fradulent": Beeching, pg. 176.

CHAPTER 17

167–173 Description of Taiping Rebellion: Jonathan D. Spence, *God's Chinese Son* (New York: W.W. Norton & Co., 1996).

CHAPTER 18

175 "The English barbarians": Jack Beeching, *The Chinese Opium Wars* (New York: Harcourt Brace Jovanovich, 1975), pg. 219.

176 "dressed and spoke like a Chinese": Beeching, pg 212.

177 "gross insult": Beeching, 215.

177–78   "I hasten therefore": Douglas Hurd, *The Arrow War* (New York: Macmillan, 1967) pg 17.
178   "carry the city": Beeching, pg. 215.
179   "if any lawless characters": Hurd, pg. 30.
179   "Hereafter, Chinese officers": Beeching, pg. 217.
180   "loss of four or five": Beeching, pg. 218.
180   "Should Yeh": Beeching, pg. 218.
180   "The English barbarians": Beeching, pg. 219.
181   "lives and property": Beeching, pg. 221.
181   "Preserve quiet minds": Beeching, pg. 221.
182   "In the administration": Hurd, pg. 33.
182–83   "Their weight": Beeching, pg. 221.
183   "I have exhausted": Hurd, pg. 33.
184   "I beg to apologize": Hurd, pg. 36.
185   Ye's response to the poisoning: Beeching, pg. 234.
185   Bowring to Canning: Hurd, pg. 37.
186   "I am an advocate": Hurd, pg. 54 and Beeching, pg. 226.
186–87   Earl of Derby's speech: Hurd, pg. 54.
187   "A report judiciously": Hurd, pg. 55 and Beeching, pg. 226.
187   "A sad result": Beeching, pg. 227.
188   "I fear that": Hurd, pg. 58 and Beeching, pg. 227.
188   "disregarded the instructions": Beeching, pg. 228.
189   "so venerable an empire": Hurd, pg. 62.
189   "most valuable trade": Beeching, pg. 230.
189   "No Reform!": Beeching, pg. 231.
189   "this very flag": Beeching, pg. 229–30.
190   "The existing restrictions": Beeching, pg. 231.
190   Gladstone and Victoria quotes: Beeching, pg. 232.
190   "no change": Beeching, 232
190   "an insolent barbarian": Beeching, 235.
190   "one of the most savage": Hurd, pg. 68.
191   "The real object": Beeching, 235.
192   Victoria to King of Belgium: Hurd,

CHAPTER 19
193   "an *idée fixe*": Jack Beeching, *The Chinese Opium Wars* (New York: Harcourt Brace Jovanovich, 1975), pg. 241.
193   Lord Elgin/Countes of Elgin exchange: Douglas Hurd, *The Arrow War* (New York: Macmillan, 1967).
196   "If you send me the troops": Hurd, pg. 97.
196   Elgin's description of opium den: Beeching, pg 240.
197   "an *idée fixe*": Beeching, pg. 241.
197   Elgin on Seymour: Beeching, pg. 241.
197   "A great success": Hurd, pg. 100.
198   Bowring to Elgin: Hurd, pg. 101.
198   "Can I do anything": Beeching, pg. 241.
199   "I have seldom": Beeching, pg. 244.
199   "among inferior races": Hurd, pg. 108.
199   "stamping his foot": Beeching, 244.

200	"dodged and insinuated": Beeching, pg. 224.
200	Elgin's diary entry: Hurd, pg. 113.
202	"Commerce has presented itself": Hurd, pg. 117.
202	"mild proposals": Hurd, pg. 117.
203	"Yeh was fat": Hurd, pg. 119.
204	"great city doomed": Beeching, pg. 248.
206	"honest Jack": Hurd, pg. 124.
206	"word call 'loot'": Beeching, pg. 250.
207	"heap of blazing ruins": Beeching, pg. 250.
207	"no human power": Beeching, pg. 250.
208	"clever but exceedingly overbearing": Hurd, pg. 126.
208	"If Pih-kwei": Beeching, pg. 251.
208	"the presence of Yeh": Beeching, pg. 252.
209	"perfect driveller": Beeching, pg. 256.
210	"only Chinese lives": Hurd, pg. 147.

CHAPTER 20

211	"Twenty-four determined men": Jack Beeching, *The Chinese Opium Wars* (New York: Harcourt Brace Jovanovich, 1975), pg. 260.
212	"without plan of resource": Beeching, pg 260.
212	"Twenty-four determined men": Beeching, pg. 260.
213	"giving me latitude": Beeching, pg. 260.
213	Clarendon to Elgin: Douglas Hurd, *The Arrow War* (New York: Macmillan, 1967) pg 143.
214	"Through the night watches": Hurd, pp. 149–50.
215	"complete military command": Beeching, pg. 260.
216	"made up my mind": Beeching, pg. 261.
217	Elgin quotes: Hurd, pg. 157.
218	Gros quotes: Beeching, pg. 262.
219	Elgin quotes: Beeching, pg. 262.
220	"not a curse": Beeching, pg. 263.
221	"a difficult point": Hurd, pg. 159.
223	"It will be for your Excellency": Hurd, pg. 175.
223	"Most honest men": Hurd, pg. 176.
224	*"Je suis heureux"*: Hurd, pg. 161.
224	"Hostilities with the Empire of China": Hurd, pg. 161.
224	"manly and consistent": Hurd, pg. 177.
224–25	Engels quote: Hurd, pg. 177.
225	Elgin quotes: Hurd, pg. 162.

CHAPTER 21

227	"teach such a lesson": Jack Beeching, *The Chinese Opium Wars* (New York: Harcourt Brace Jovanovich, 1975), pg. 272.
227	"Go forth": Beeching, pg 265.
228	"humbly submit it": Douglas Hurd, *The Arrow War* (New York: Macmillan, 1967) pg. 166.
229	"a rat trap": Hurd, pg. 166.
231	"While the barbarians": Beeching, pg. 268.
232	"Blood is thicker": Beeching, pg. 270.

233   "Had the opposition": Beeching, pg. 271.
233–34 Seng on the Dagu battle: Beeching, pp. 271–72.
234   "in some way": Beeching, pg. 272.
234–35 "teach such a lesson": Beeching, pg. 272.
235   "Dearest, you see": Hurd, pg. 179.
236   Wood and kowtow: Beeching, pg. 276.
236   "I would enter": Hurd, pg. 186.
237   "The Chinese Government": Hurd, pg. 186.
238   "very unpleasant news": Hurd, pg. 190.
238   *Times/Telegraph* quotes: Hurd, pg. 190.
239   Elgin to Wood: Beeching, pg. 273.
240   "cheeky in the extreme": Beeching, pg. 278.

CHAPTER 22
241   "the greatest fool": Douglas Hurd, *The Arrow War* (New York: Macmillan, 1967), pg. 208.
241   "Nothing more vicious": Jack Beeching, *The Chinese Opium Wars* (New York: Harcourt Brace Jovanovich, 1975), pg 271.
241   "blow up their forts": Beeching, pg. 271.
241   "The Chinese government": Beeching, pg. 278.
242   "carry destruction": Beeching, pg. 278.
242   Ellenborough quotes: Beeching, pg. 278.
244   "Can I do anything": Hurd, pg. 205.
244   "Going to sea?": Hurd, pg. 205.
245   "Our object": Beeching, pg. 279.
246   "Lawless and cruel": Beeching, pg. 282.
247   "great simplicity": Hurd, pg. 206.
247   "a gentlemanlike person": Hurd, pg. 207.
248   "the greatest fool": Hurd, pg. 208.
249   Elgin quotes: Hurd, pg. 208.

CHAPTER 23
251   "Here we are": Douglas Hurd, *The Arrow War* (New York: Macmillan, 1967), pg. 217.
251   "atrocious villains": Jack Beeching, *The Chinese Opium Wars* (New York: Harcourt Brace Jovanovich, 1975), pg 286.
253   "bore unflinchingly": Beeching, pg. 289.
253   "so pluckily": Beeching, pg. 289.
253   The *Times* poem: Hurd, pg. 212–13.
254   "I shall nevertheless": Beeching, pg. 291.
256   Accounts of Parkes's outburst: Beeching, pg. 293.
257–58 Elgin's diary entry: Hurd, pg. 217.
258   Wade quotes: Hurd, pg. 218.
259   "a post to the north": Hurd, pg, 219.
259   "In what light": Hurd, pg. 219.

CHAPTER 24
261, 263 "gained two victories": Jack Beeching, *The Chinese Opium Wars* (New York: Harcourt Brace Jovanovich, 1975), pg 301.

263   Seng/Parkes exchange: Beeching, pg. 301.
265   "Instead of following": Beeching, pg. 302.
266   "rode out very early": Beeching, pg. 305.
267   "no steps": Beeching, pg. 305.
267   "A rare old house": Beeching, pg. 305.
267   "more conscious of them": Beeching, pg. 305.
267–68 *"J'ai le coeur"*: Douglas Hurd, *The Arrow War* (New York: Macmillan, 1967) pg. 222 and Beeching, pg. 305.
269   "by their exactions": Beeching, pg. 306.
269   *Quant aux anglais"*: Beeching, pg. 306.

CHAPTER 25

271–72 "Don't commit sacrilege!": Jack Beeching, *The Chinese Opium Wars* (New York: Harcourt Brace Jovanovich, 1975), pg 314.
271   "I am not a thief": Beeching, pg. 318.
273   "he counted on their honor": Beeching, pg. 314.
273   "sentries posted": Beeching, pg. 316.
273   "It was pitiful": Beeching, pg. 316.
273   "See here.": Beeching, pg. 316.
274   "perfect blaze": Beeching, pg. 318.
274   "made no objection": Beeching, pg. 318.
275   "make matters more equal": Beeching, pg. 319.
275   "had only to ask": Beeching, pg. 320.
276   *"Je prends la"*: Douglas Hurd, *The Arrow War* (New York: Macmillan, 1967) pg. 222 and Beeching, pg. 228.
276   "Nothing was talked of": Beeching, pg. 320.
276   "At this historic juncture": Beeching, pg. 320.
277   "I am not a thief": Beeching, pg. 318.

CHAPTER 26

279   "no uncommon thing": Jack Beeching, *The Chinese Opium Wars* (New York: Harcourt Brace Jovanovich, 1975), pg. 308.
280   "Suppose all is lost.": Beeching, pg 307.
280   "the Imperial Treasury": Beeching, pg. 307.
280   Parkes quotes: Beeching, pg. 308.
280   "be in no danger": Beeching, pg. 308.
281   "The Chinese authorities"; Beeching, pg. 308.
281   "would have been lost": Beeching, pg. 303.
284   Elgin's letter: Douglas Hurd, *The Arrow War* (New York: Macmillan, 1967) pg. 222 and Beeching, pg. 235.
284   "I wish Elgin had doubled": Beeching, pg. 324 and Hurd, pg. 240.
284–85 "It is with joy": Hurd, pg. 240.
285   Gros on Elgin: Hurd, pg. 236.
285   *"C'est detruire"*: Beeching, pg. 324.
286   "I am heartily glad": Beeching, pg. 324.
286   "Elgin's decision": Beeching, pg. 324.

CHAPTER 27

289   "Keep perfectly still": Beeching, pg. 327.

290   Grant's observations: Beeching, pg 327.
290   "Keep perfectly still": Beeching, pg. 327.
291   "audacious": Beeching, pg. 329.

EPILOGUE

293–94   "The Chinese merchant": Martin Booth, *Opium: A History* (New York: St. Martin's Press, 1998).
295   "officially ended": Booth.

SHORT
BIBLIOGRAPHY

Annals and Memoirs of the Court of Peking, 1914.
Beeching, Jack, *The Chinese Opium War*, 1976.
Bingham, J. Elliot, *Narrative of the Expedition to China, 1842.*
Bonner-Smith, D., and Lumby, E.W.R., *The Second China War 1856–1860*, 1954.
Booth, Martin, *Opium: A History*, 1996.
Bowring, Sir John, *Autobiographical Recollections*, 1877.
Checkland, S.G., *The Gladstones*, 1971.
Cooke, G.W., *China*, 1859.
Dermigny, Louis, *La Chine et L'Occident: Le Commerce a Canton au XVIIIe Siecle, 1719–1833.*
Eitel, *The History of Hong Kong.*
Elliot, Sir George, *Memoir of Admiral the Honourable Sir George Elliot*, 1863.
Downing, C. Toogood, *The Fan-Qui in China*, 1838.
Ebrey, Patricia Buckley, *The Cambridge Illustrated History of China*, 1996.
Fairbank, John King, *China: A New History*, 1992.
Fay, Peter Ward, *The Opium War, 1840–1842*, 1975.
Gutzlaff, Charles, *China Opened*, 1838.
Hsu, Immanuel C.Y., "The Secret Mission of the Lord Amherst on the China Coast, 1832," *Harvard Journal of Asiatic Studies*, 1954.
Hummel, Arthur W., *Eminent Chinese of the Ch'ing Period (1644–1912)*, 1943.
Hunter, William C., *An American in Canton (1825–44)*, 1994.
Hurd, Douglas, *The Arrow War*, 1967.
Inglis, Brian, *The Opium War*, 1976.
Kahn, Harold, *Monarchy in the Emperor's Eyes: Image and Reality in the Ch-ien-lung Reign*, 1971.
Keswick, Marie (editor), *The Thistle and the Jade*, 1982.
La Motte, Ellen Newbold, *The Ethics of Opium*, 1924.
Loch, Granville G., *The Closing Events of the Campaign in China*, 1843.
Loch, Henry Brougham, *Personal Narrative of Occurrences during Lord Elgin's Second Embassy to China in 1860*, 1900.
Lucy, Armand, *Lettres intimes sur la Campagne de Chine en 1860*, 1861.

Michael Franz and Chang, Chung-li, *The Taiping Rebellion*, 1966.

Michie, Alexander, *The Englishman in China*, 1900.

Morison, J.L., *The Eighth Earl of Elgin*, London, 1928.

Morse, H.B., *The International Relations of the Chinese Empire*, 1910.

Oliphant, Laurence, *Narrative of the Earl of Elgin's Mission to China and Japan*, 1860.

Osborn, Sherard, *The Past and Future of British Relations in China*, 1860.

Ouchterlony, John, *The Chinese War: An Account of All the Operations of the British Forces from the Commencement to the Treaty of Nanking*, 1844.

Paludan, Ann, *Chronicles of the Chinese Emperors*, 1998.

Rait, Robert S., *The Life and Campaigns of Hugh, First Viscount Gough*, 1903

Rowntree, Joshua, *The Opium Habit in the East*, 1895.

Slade, John, *Narrative of the Late Proceedings and Events in China*, 1840.

Spence, Jonathan D., *God's Chinese Son*, 1996.

Spence, Jonathan D., *The Search for Modern China*, 1990.

Steuart, James, *Jardine, Matheson and Co.*, 1934.

Stevens, G.B. and Markwick, W.F., *Life of Reverend Peter Parker*, 1896.

Swinhoe, Robert, *Narrative of the North China Campaign of 1860*, 1861.

Swisher, E., *China's Management of the American Barbarians (1841–1861)*, 1951.

Teng, S.Y. *Chang Hsi and the Treaty of Nanking*, 1944.

Teng, S.Y., *The Taiping Rebellion and the Western Powers*, 1971.

Thelwall, A.S., *The Iniquities of the Opium Trade with China*, 1839.

Walrond, Theodore, *Letters and Journals of James, Eighth Earl of Elgin*, London, 1872.

Wolseley, G.J., *Narrative of the War with China in 1860*, 1862.

Wu, Wen-Tsao, *The Chinese Opium Question in British Opinion and Action*, 1928.

Wylie, Alexander, *Memorials of Protestant Missionaries to the Chinese*, 1867.

ABOUT THE
AUTHORS

———•—•———

Historian and educator W. Travis Hanes III is an internationally recognized expert on nineteenth-century Britain and holds a doctorate in British Imperial History from the University of Texas at Austin, where he received the prestigious Lathrop Prize for best doctoral dissertation. Dr. Hanes brings his formidable knowledge of British colonialism to the subject of the Opium Wars.

Dr. Hanes has also written two books on the twilight of the British Empire in Africa and its aftereffects, *Imperial Diplomacy in the Era of Decolonization: The Sudan in Anglo-Egyptian Relations, 1945–1956* and the upcoming *Imperialism or Expatriate Nationalism?: The Sudan Political Service and the Making of the Modern Sudan.*

Dr. Hanes also contributed to two popular textbooks, *World History, Continuity and Change* and *World History: People and Nations.*

A respected academic, Dr. Hanes has served on the faculty of the University of North Carolina at Wilmington, Southwestern University, and Southwest Texas State University. Most recently, he has been a contributing author to the *Oxford History of the British Empire* and the *Oxford History of the Twentieth Century* and *Railway Imperialism.*

———•—•———

Nationally known author and syndicated columnist Frank Sanello has written fifteen books on history and film, including *The Knights Templar: God's Warriors, the Devil's Banker* and *Reel vs. Real: Separating Fact from Fiction in Historical Films*. He is currently writing *Faith and Finance in the Renaissance: The Rise and Ruin of the Fugger Empire*, about the influential banking family who were the German equivalent of their contemporaries, the Medici.

Sanello's articles have appeared in the *Washington Post*, the *Los Angeles Times*, the *Chicago Tribune*, the *Boston Globe*, and the *New York Times Syndicate*.

Sanello was formerly the film critic for the *Los Angeles Daily News* and a business reporter for UPI.

The author graduated with honors from the University of Chicago and holds a master's degree from UCLA. Sanello also has a purple belt in Tae Kwon Do and volunteers as a martial arts instructor at AIDS Project Los Angeles.

Sanello lives in Los Angeles with three cats.

INDEX